IN HIS GRIP

...a Walk through Breast Cancer

by
AMY K. HAUSER
&
TOM HAUSER

Edited by Marge Thompson
&
Frankie M. Leisering

WESTBOW
PRESS
A DIVISION OF THOMAS NELSON

WestBow Press books may be ordered through booksellers or by contacting:
WestBow Press
A Division of Thomas Nelson
1663 Liberty Drive
Bloomington, IN 47403
www.westbowpress.com
1-(866) 928-1240

Because of the dynamic nature of the Internet, any web addresses or links contained in this book may have changed since publication and may no longer be valid. The views expressed in this work are solely those of the author and do not necessarily reflect the views of the publisher, and the publisher hereby disclaims any responsibility for them.

Any people depicted in stock imagery provided by Thinkstock are models, and such images are being used for illustrative purposes only.
Certain stock imagery © Thinkstock.

Unless otherwise noted, all author's Scripture taken from the HOLY BIBLE, NEW INTERNATIONAL VERSION. Copyright 1973, 1978, 1984 by International Bible Society. Used by permission of Zondervan. All rights reserved.

TNIV - Scripture taken from the Holy Bible, Today's New International Version™ TNIV ® Copyright © 2001, 2005 by International Bible Society®. All rights reserved worldwide.

NKJV - Scripture taken from the New King James Version®. Copyright © 1982 by Thomas Nelson, Inc. Used by permission. All rights reserved.

NASB - Scripture taken from the NEW AMERICAN STANDARD BIBLE®, Copyright © 1960, 1962,1963,1968,1971,1972,1973,1975,1977,1995 by The Lockman Foundation. Used by permission.

NLT - Scripture taken from the Holy Bible, New Living Translation, copyright © 1996, 2004, 2007 by Tyndale House Foundation. Used by permission of Tyndale House Publishers, Inc., Carol Stream, Illinois 60188. All rights reserved.

WEB – Public domain

Scripture quotes from guest comments are from their own various translations.

IMPORTANT NOTICE
Any mention of medical treatments, medicine, supplements, vitamins, minerals, treatments, health, nutritional supplements and adjustments, et al, are only a part of the memoir and strictly the author's own perspective. They are not meant as medical advice or to take the place of treatment from medical professionals. Readers are strongly advised to consult with qualified medical professionals on all medical issues.

ISBN: 978-1-4497-6435-7 (e)
ISBN: 978-1-4497-6436-4 (sc)
ISBN: 978-1-4497-6437-1 (hc)

Library of Congress Control Number: 2012915614

Printed in the United States of America

WestBow Press rev. date: 9/10/2012

⟨⟩ DEDICATION ⟨⟩

After moving to Texas, I remember secretly wishing there was a way to combine all the things I loved about our many years in Iowa with the exciting newness of what our family was drawn to in Texas and 'having the best of both worlds.' That dream was to have family and friends from all over in one place...on this side of heaven, if only for a short while.

Oh how our Father gives good gifts in the most creative ways.

This book is dedicated to the family of God who all came together in such miraculous ways, to love, lift, serve, and encourage our family during this unexpected and difficult journey. It has been put together in part because of ALL of you. Each group of people in our lives showed not only our family, but each other, just what community is supposed to be, especially Christian community.

So many of you encouraged us from afar and didn't let go of us just because of the time and the miles that work to separate us. Through technology, we were able to keep an ongoing connection. Through the Counselor's promptings, He taught us all what pleases Him greatly when we lay down our own desires. When we share our hearts and lend a hand, the outcome can be so beautiful!

Because of the commitment from so many to come alongside of our family, we had the strength to keep "looking up" and remain in His grip throughout the journey and beyond.

Make new friends, but keep the old. One is silver and the other gold.

Hide me now
Under Your Wing.
Cover me within Your Mighty Hand.

When the oceans rise and thunders roar,
I will soar with You ABOVE the storm.
Father, You are King over the flood.
I will be still and know You are God.

Find rest my soul,
In Christ alone.
Know HIS pow'r -
In quietness and trust.

When the oceans rise and thunders roar.
I will soar with You ABOVE the storm.
Father, You are King over the flood.
I will be still, and KNOW You are God.

Lyrics from the song, "Still" by Rueben Morgan. These words were included in a prayer email sent by family members, Aunt Elsie and her daughter Sue, as one of many that were offered up during the knot-tying process while making a prayer blanket on my behalf. My sweet sister, Deb Theriault of Granger, Indiana, organized this gift.

CONTENTS

~ FOREWORD ~

My wife, Karin, first met Amy while attending a ladies' bible study; it was through this and a large group "dinner for the husbands" that the four of us first met. From that encounter, Amy and Tom were simply some cheerful faces who said 'hi' at church every Sunday. As our family was about to head off on a summer vacation driving down the west coast from Seattle to Carmel, Karin asked me if I remembered Amy from her bible study, telling me that she had just been diagnosed with breast cancer. We talked about it a little and then headed off on our vacation. Little did I know how this would change my life, not to mention Amy's.

A couple of days into the vacation Karin showed me a blog that Amy had started and I read it that night, and the next day, and the next day... something just grabbed my attention. I signed up to get the blog myself and would look forward every day for the next one. I had never dealt well with things like cancer and had only experienced the negative; people feeling down and sometimes hopeless, me feeling sorry for them and ultimately for myself. Yet here was someone who was taking positives from the experience, who truly believed God was taking care of her.

This was a new experience for me. Driving down the west coast provided a lot of time for Karin and me to talk and to start corresponding with Amy and Tom via text and email. We were trying our best to encourage her and express our support. During these three weeks this gradually started to change for me; no longer did I feel like I was the one doing the encouraging, but rather that God was speaking to me through Amy. I was starting to ask myself questions and not liking some of the answers very much. We all really connected during this time and felt like good friends by the time we got back.

The day we got back to Houston the four of us went out for dinner. This was the day Amy shaved off her hair and made her first public appearance. Our hearts just melted that night, and for me, I was never to be the same again! The power of Amy and Tom's faith and absolute trust in God was just so powerful that it made me realize how "weak" my relationship with Him was. Amy's "story" changed my life and compelled me to recommit myself to God and to make many significant changes in my life.

Amy and Tom have become the dearest of friends, and perhaps the circumstances of how we became friends in a time of need for us all will mean that we will always have a very special bond. I know the priorities in my life have changed forever.

Amy's story is a most inspiring one to read for anyone going through life's struggles - one that will give encouragement whatever one may be dealing with. First and foremost, this is an account of a "cancer journey;" a journal revealing an absolute faith that God is willing to walk the journey alongside of you, all the way! If you are reading this and you are someone setting out on, or already in the middle of, a similar journey, this is an important read for you! Amy's story will certainly not hide any of the rough times; but it will tell you about many positive aspects as well, and how faith is the only way to make the trip. This book is not just for cancer sufferers, but also for anyone experiencing life's many trials, whatever they may be.

Amy's raw and emotive style tells it just like it is. You will feel the emotion; shed some tears and certainly draw many smiles. There is little more powerful than hearing this story told literally, while experiencing each and every aspect of the journey along with her. The power is in hearing God's story, as told through Amy, and that's just what this is.

You will be encouraged that it's okay to have roller coaster emotions, to feel anger, to experience joy, to feel spiritually low and equally high; that it's okay to ask "why me?" Amy is one amazing lady who turned what could have been a very negative experience - focusing on feeling sorry for herself - to one that focuses on making an impact on others. For example - Amy refused to wear a wig once she lost her hair so she would not miss opportunities to testify to others who would otherwise not have approached her.

Perhaps most compelling is how many people have told Amy that while they should have been supporting her in keeping a positive attitude, she was in fact being the inspiration for them. I know! I was one of those people! I pray for them every day and I know that they do the same for me. It is this, together with God, that will keep us all positive and moving forward, whatever the challenges of life that are thrown our way.

For whatever reasons you chose to read this book, I hope and pray that you put your trust in the Lord that it reveals and allow Him to guide you through turbulent times. May you come out the other side with a new, positive and wonderful future in front of you.

May God Bless you.
Barry Wood - Honored friend & partner in Christ

Acknowledgements

Amy and Tom would like to thank the countless people who made this book possible. We apologize if any individual or group is overlooked, it is strictly unintentional (chemo brain!). You are all loved and cherished more than you can ever imagine.

To everyone who prayed for us – we felt each and every prayer and its uplifting, healing power. Also for every card, letter, email, text, visit, gift bag, note, etc., et al. The little things can mean so much.

To the army (God's army) who marched in to help our family through this trying time, led by the intrepid Ladies of the Loft, and the all around invaluable Kristie. From all y'all - meals, taxiing, taking the kids overnight (and to Orlando!), calls, cards, notes, cookies and treats – we are overwhelmed and sustained by His hands and feet around us.

To everyone who posted a note on Amy's Caring Bridge site. All the encouraging words and great insights were hugely sustaining during the worst of the cancer battle. Lee, Kristie, Russell, Ronda – you consistently made everyone laugh, and reflect – thank you!

To our editor, Marge Thompson. For working through the various styles, moods and Amyisms and getting them all into a form of English that conveys the message without destroying the feeling. Also for her insights into the flow of the book as it reflected the flow of the journey. We are indebted to her patience, wisdom and speedy turnaround of material.

To Frankie Leisering for her "last read," reviews and invaluable insight. Frankie, you were a gift just when we needed it most to pull it all together. We could not have "finished the race" without you.

And especially from Tom: To the guys [and y'all know who you are] that gave me the quick emails, calls or texts of affirmation when I needed them most. Sorry some of you have had to watch my back for 30+ years, some for less, and some are new brothers in Texas. You are what it is all about. Thanks from the bottom of my heart.

For CaringBridge.org that allowed us to keep in daily touch with our friends and family. For providing the physical vehicle that God would use to spread His story. We encourage all who go through life's medical trials to use this wonderful resource.

To all those who have encouraged us to go forward with this book; believing that it would encourage others.

To Phil Callaway for suggesting the self-publishing route.

To Paul Kurtz, Jennifer Sims and Barry Wood (our *Made For More ministries* board) for their encouragement, support, prayers and constructive feedback through the process.

To Brian Wood for his invaluable insight, constructive review and flying half way around the world to help (and see his grandbaby!). Thanks Barry for arranging and getting Brian to Houston.

To Andrew Brockenbush of Creative Consulting for his invaluable expertise in helping us get M4M going – logo design, website creation and overall creativity.

To our families for their support.

To Barb Murphy, Amy's mom, for all her prayers that never ceased even though living across the country. For her encouragement not only to our family but others through her heartfelt, biblically referenced reminders of God's provision through her guestbook comments. For sister Debbie's daily calls and prayers that made it seem as if she were here. To both for journeying to Texas to help out.

To Ross and Sara, for being troupers and rising to the occasion time and time again when mom and dad were busy, tired, sick or simply not always fully engaged. We love you more than we can ever express. You are both gifts from God and great kids. We are so very proud of you, even when you "kinda tick us off!"

INTRODUCTION
(Amy)

As I finally begin to write with the intention of piecing together a compilation of several years' happenings that make up my story, I am overwhelmed with just where to start. It has taken the past several months to get to the point where I actually sat down and allowed the Holy Spirit to work this out. Despite all that I have worked through and learned about pushing fear out of the picture, it still creeps in. I ask myself if there is enough relevance here to expect anyone to take the time to read it. I certainly don't have a star-studded bio that would entice a reader with its validity and credibility. Because it is a telling of how God scripted me into HIS story, the validity and credibility belong to HIM.

I am a 40-something mother of two growing kids, a pretty much stay-at-home mom with a college degree that has been sitting on a shelf for more than a decade. Instead of building a career, I am building a family and myself. Most of the time I work on whatever is right in front of me and redefining myself as the years pass by. It's a good life, for the most part, but it is not a whole lot different than that of any other middle class woman... or at least not in ways I care to share with just anyone...at least not yet.

As these and many other like thoughts worked their way into my being, they kept me from taking a stab at writing with a purpose. Yet, in many ways, I have been continuously reminded that I have something far greater than MY story, MY bio, or MY belief to tell. It is a story that I am now convinced will be worth someone's precious time to read, because I have living proof of God's power at work in the lives of yet another one of His children. This is HIS story, not mine.

Over the past several years, God has taught me how we can uniquely hear His voice through encountering the inevitable high peaks and low valleys we all face. Now He has asked me to share a glimpse of His heart and His deep desire to connect with His children through the love of others. I will not write for me, but for Him. With that, I can take on this task.

Introduction
(Tom)

Before I say anything else, it is only fair that I warn the reader that my sense of humor is not, shall we say…mainstream. If you come across something in my posts that makes you say, "huh?" please keep reading. It may come to you later, it may not. Such is the bear that we each must cross. I'm just sayin'…

─────

This book was not easy to write nor comfortable to share. Since well before the cancer, we have had a concern that we would be perceived in an improper light, especially as we began making serious efforts to put our lives on a better path.

We are to be like the moon, shining no light of our own, only reflecting a greater light. Yet even if only reflected, there is a very real danger that light will expose flaws…or make us look better than we deserve to be viewed. While battling our self-centered tendencies, we truly only want to pass on the lessons and blessings, to help others and let God have all the credit. We are trying very hard to walk this walk with honesty and transparency - about both our flaws and mistakes (many, and some were/are colossal) and His power to change any life.

As we re-read the postings and guestbook entries, our fears increased. Have we revealed too much of our dark sides? Are we getting credit that is not our due? This walking in the light business might be more than we bargained for. There are two very dangerous giants that lurk here and we want to bring them down to size, both in our own lives and so the reader will clearly see the purpose of our writing and the true power in our lives.

David picked five stones when he took on Goliath. I admire both his total faith in God and his preparedness by not taking just one stone. I bring up David for another reason: Amy's and my life have many parallels to his. Let me quickly clarify that neither of us is on the level of King David: his faith, accomplishments or relationship with God. However, like David, we both have major mistakes and sins in our lives. Also like David, we have kept returning to God and asking for His help and forgiveness.

Our two giants have gradually been reduced in size, but unlike Goliath, still have the ability to cause serious damage. These two related giants employ nearly opposite approaches, but I am certain they are in cahoots and play off each other like good cop, bad cop. Their tactics are very subtle, crafty and devious.

Giant #1 is a two-headed monster and plays right into the mentality of today's world. He is Pride and The Appearance of Pride. "Look at what I/we have done, what we have gone through, I, I, I, we, we, we." The world only sees a carefully selected, very small portion of each of our lives (unless we are Charlie Sheen or Britney Spears). We carefully control what is seen and the world often carefully selects what it wants to see.

The first head is kept under control (I wish I could lop it off like David did with Goliath; it would be worth the mess) by God repeatedly reminding us that we are *all* His children, no better, no worse, no favorites. He quickly and lovingly brings us down to size whenever and however necessary. By the way – *lovingly* does not always equate to *gently*. There have been some very hard landings and we both (Amy and I) have the bruises to prove it. One good thing about God's school of hard knocks is that it effectively takes both the allure and temptation of pride and puffed-upness down a few notches.

The second head is more bothersome than the first because it often leads to God getting a bad rap due to our faults. Even as we are trying our best to make this story about others and about Him, it is our face that people see first and, sadly, often only see. It is God's job to work on others' hearts, but it is ours to present ourselves in as genuine and humble a manner as possible. We pray that others see Who this is all about, but if they choose to think it is about us, or that we are trying to make this about us, that has to be between them and God. I am not trying to be egotistical, aloof, uncaring or avoiding of responsibility, but I/we can only be responsible for what we can control. The rest is God's domain. That, by the way, is another very hard lesson to learn.

Giant #2 often steps in as we are resisting the upward pull of giant #1 and tries to take our own momentum and yank us down into the pits. His name is Unworthy. If his two-headed partner is unsuccessful, or sometimes even wildly successful, Unworthy steps in and attacks, like a bad TV wrestling tag team. Unworthy is dead-weight gravity on the soul: constant and unrelentingly pulling downward. It whispers every failure, every mistake, every sin. "You are not worthy. Look at all the terrible things you have done. Hide your past in a deep hole. If anyone finds out the real you and all you have done, it will be a disaster. God doesn't forgive what *you* have done and neither will anyone else." He taunts us like Goliath taunted the Israelites. Like the Israelites, we listen to him and cower in our tents. Unworthy has a great deal of material to use on us; he even stoops so low as to enlist others to remind us of our past. They may be right about our past, but they are wrong about the future and His forgiveness.

Throughout the Bible, God specializes in using the unlikely; so we take comfort in being in the good company of other screw-ups, misfits and unlikelies. It is said that He doesn't call the equipped; He equips the called. Looking back over the last several years, He must have really been equipping us! During this entire time, He has continually crossed our paths with others who were going through similar life struggles. James 1:2-6 has finally shifted from near lunacy to perfect sense – troubles *will* come our way and we should use them to grow in our faith, ask for wisdom and trust in Him alone. 1 Peter 4:10 then kicks in and we are to use our gifts well to serve others. There is seldom any one better equipped to help with a struggle than one who has been down that same road.

If there are too many *I*'s or *we*'s or too much praise or credit to Amy or us, especially in the guestbook notes (BTW - they fed our souls when we needed it most), please smite whichever monster is behind it and focus on God who is above it all. Whether effectively done or poorly done by us, this is about Him, what He has done and guiding as many others as we can, for as long as we can, to a similar point, hopefully with less earthly strife, struggle and pain. Whatever the route, the goal is for all to truly find Him by whatever road.

The David and Goliath lesson came full circle recently as Pastor Rob pointed out an interesting characteristic about giants from 1 Samuel

17: When facing them, there is always a large crowd of related mini-giants ominously standing right behind your giant. Yet when your giant hits the ground, all those other mini-giants usually turn tail and run. Brothers and sisters who were cowering with you suddenly become emboldened and rush forward.

The point of this, and maybe of the whole book and the rest of our lives? Alone we are not equipped to face our giants, but with God's help we *must* face them. It will free us and encourage others that they too can conquer their own giants. David was just an inexperienced kid, but he knew where his strength came from. He didn't even fit into proper armor. We are very similar to David. He chose to go into battle armed with only a staff, a sling and five stones *and* in the name of God. We choose to share openly and honestly *and* in the name of God, and for His glory alone. God can slay any giant and use anyone to do it.

⤙ Background ⤚

As I work on this writing during the fall of 2011, several dates stick out in my mind. September 21, 2011 marked one year since the final chemotherapy session. October 20 marked one year since my bilateral mastectomy and November 24 was one year since the reconstruction surgeries. A lot has happened in one year. So much good has come from something so many see as something bad. From where I stand, I wouldn't trade my experience, starting with that phone call in May of 2010, revealing that I had breast cancer, for whatever would have happened if the news had been that my cancer screenings had come back clear.

Without that call, I know I would not have had the drive to live life from a new perspective - seeing each day as an opportunity rather than a hassle or a burden, and focusing on the blessings rather than on what is lacking. Now I know that I am the sum of all my experiences. What I choose to do with them...now that is up to me.

With much support and encouragement from my family and friends, today I am living cancer free, regaining my strength and stamina, and striving toward the balanced life God intends. As I pieced together the journal and guestbook entries compiled throughout my illness, it became clear to me that my entire experience had SO MUCH to do with the support we received in such abundance from others. Our site received over 18,000 visits in the process of others following this journey with us, and we believe a prayer accompanied every one of them.

While re-reading the journal and guestbook, I sensed that the best way to share what God can and did do through my cancer is to share the bulk of my and Tom's journal entries just as they were written. I have added reflections in ***bold italics***; otherwise everything is from either the journal entries or a tiny portion of selected guestbook entries (from over 800 - all feeding my need for earthly support).

Other than some general editing to make it easier for the reader, the journal entries remain faithful to the originals - full of "Amyisms" as we have now dubbed them. Structure, syntax and grammar were not the priority – feelings and faith were. Some days were good; others dark - the impacts of cancer, medications (chemo brain!) and stress, and the counterbalancing impact of friends and the Lord, are all starkly visible.

My hope in sharing them is to show how God works in the midst of struggles. I pray that this writing will lend helpful insight to anyone who may read it, and that it will be a source of encouragement along whatever path his or her life may be exploring.

Re-reading the guestbook, it is no small wonder that I was able to remain strong during the battle! When others reach out and take the time and energy to serve another in need, the possibilities are endless! For me, this is the point of this whole story. When we choose to take the risk of opening up our lives, allowing others to look in, God is present and His power is boundless. Becoming vulnerable to perceived risk allows us to learn community, however it might look. When our hearts are real and have no selfish intentions, beautiful things happen.

The guestbook entries that are included are only a very small sampling of those actually posted. While there were so many to choose from, all of which impacted our family each and every day, for the space allotted we could choose only a few. I trust that those I have shared will be effective in providing hope and encouragement **to others** who may be facing similar circumstances. As this book goes to press, I pray that these encouragements will serve as reminders to us all, to keep our Hope in Him and our focus on the blessings that come to us through others.

This book is a foretaste into what God can do in the lives of His children (just maybe into what He is yearning to do in your life!) when we allow Him to take messy situations and expose them to His guiding, gentle hands, leading us to a new place that is peaceful and secure. It is a story of how, though we may feel that our lives are just too messy (the cancer was just the icing on an already messy cake) to let others in on it, we learn that very often others have similar struggles and longings. They also yearn to be vulnerable enough to share and grow together, as we do. Doing life alone is not in God's plan. Says so in the bible; I'm pretty sure.

I pray that these words will be a blessing to each of you in some way.

1

"Wait One Year"

OUR FIRST FALL IN TEXAS - 2009. Houston already felt like home, we were settling in, and I distinctly recall two conversations, one that led to a dark place and one that led to the light. The amazing thing is, one directly led to the other.

The first one, the dark one, was with my husband Tom and it led me to wonder if we should finally just go our own ways. I remember the deep sadness over the once again rehashing of our extreme differences in personality and understanding of one another, even after close to 20 years of marriage. The frustration and dissatisfaction was aging both of us and we mutually verbalized that we were not sure it was worth the drain to keep up any longer. As I took a walk, sadness and despair beyond anything I had experienced since our near split five years earlier was settling into my being. Maybe this is what we had to do. I knew God had gotten us through so much pain and had taught us so much about each other, about His love and grace and plans for our family, but once again, we were at the end of our ropes, yet for different reasons than before. We were just plain tired. I suppose we had not yet truly realized the need to fully cast our hurts on Jesus, to give him real control of every aspect of our relationship and of our lives.

Searching for satisfaction through expectations cast onto another person was still inside of me somewhere. It wasn't until recently that God has shown me that He is the only one that can carry the load of my heart's deepest needs and desires. To place that on another human

1

only sets us up for disappointments that rear their ugly heads at times when we least expect it. I hadn't yet realized that I had not surrendered our marriage to God at the level that was going to be required.

I collapsed down on a park bench on that crisp fall day. I remember every detail. I was so tired, so alone and once again, felt like a complete failure as a wife and mother. After all we had been through, after God had picked us up and placed us in Houston where we felt so at home, were we going to give up now? Why were both our hearts feeling so fed up? I could not do "this" any longer; nor could Tom. It seemed as though it was time to move on. It would be easier to do so in a new town; less explaining to do, fewer expectations on us as a family. Maybe this was going to be okay. My heart said otherwise. After all we had been through and so much we had faced together, we did not come this far in our marriage to let go now.

I closed my eyes and prayed. After a few minutes of pouring out the details that God already knew, I clearly heard Him (almost audibly) say, "WAIT ONE YEAR." My eyes must have shot open as that phrase echoed in my ears. I heard it again faintly over and over again after the initial booming, almost as if to solidify what words had been so clearly uttered. Honestly, I was thinking, "Of all things I had hoped God might clearly say to me, why this?" It was not exactly the "revelation" that I hoped for or was expecting!

I was processing what I heard and questioning why on earth had that come to mind? Almost simultaneously, I felt a peace that transcended all understanding come over me. Suddenly I had forgotten all the selfishness I was focusing on that had been hardening my heart. I continued to pray and ask for direction for what we were to do next.

Something amazing happened between my Father and me on that fall afternoon. I think it had to do with gaining a new level of trust - maybe because I had never before totally trusted His devotion to me, my marriage or my life. If I was capable of breaking sacred trusts, maybe I didn't really know what trust was. I know that I did; but the lines had been blurred and the redefining had not yet been fully restored. As I was beginning to learn, God was going to do the defining.

Thinking back on the feeling of total peace I encountered on that park bench, I am reminded of similar feelings while growing up which derived from conversations with my mother. There were times filled with devastating heartaches for this very social young girl, and talking and crying with my mom for hours seemed to help. The weight of the world would be lifted just from being in her presence and hearing her soothing and familiar voice.

Over time, the relationship with my Lord has gradually filled that child-like need for comfort that could once be filled only by my mother's tender embrace. I felt safe and knew I could trust her, regardless of my own ability and understanding of the world around me. For a child, that was all I needed to know. As a grown child of God, it is still all I really need to know about my heavenly Father. I believe the transition from leaning on earthly parents to leaning on God the Father is His plan for each of us. On this particular day, He was waiting for me to tune into Him and listen for His comforting voice. I still didn't have all the answers just as I didn't after leaving my mother's arms, but the knowledge that someone was on my side and there for me provided me the strength and courage to keep going forward.

I am letting God define what trust needs to look like for me - letting go of my own wounds as well as the guilt of pain I brought to others, and starting fresh. His Word says it is never too late to learn and grow. The choice is ours to make.

I have to trust that God's knowledge surpasses my understanding. In HIS time, He will make my/our path straight. (Paraphrasing Proverbs 3:5-6)

He knew I would need Tom and his strength and unwavering ways to lean on, grow and learn from in the months and years ahead. God knew that He would turn a dark situation into something that would glorify Him. That choice to trust in Him and take Him at His Word was a priceless gift. A gift that keeps on giving.

2

The Lump

It was early May 2010 and another school year was about to come to a close. It had been a big year for us as our family had just moved to the Houston area the previous summer. We were transplants a long way from our Iowa roots, with big hopes and a bright future ahead. It had been a good school year for both our kids. Ross was finishing up eighth grade at a large middle school in The Woodlands and Sara was finishing fourth grade. Both had made several friends, yet since we had prayerfully made the commitment to send them both to a private Christian school in Conroe for the upcoming school year, the stress level of newness was still high. As a mother, I was stressing about yet another change and praying for peace to fill their hearts as we would be heading into yet another summer that lacked the feeling of being settled. There were so many details to be ironed out. That's what we moms do...think about what is next and how to keep the path as clear of debris as we humanly can. Or think we can.

Tom and I both love adventures and that is exactly what we saw in this move to Texas. Just the year prior our Heavenly Father had prepared our hearts to say goodbye to so many special friends in Iowa and we felt an unusual peace about the change to the unknown. Tom had made a total career change, answering an ever-stronger tug to transition from the corporate finance world to work in a ministry related field. Was the call to a ministry or to Houston? I'm not sure we really knew or still know for certain. What we did know is our family was beginning to settle in, the connections were happening and our hearts on the whole were feeling content.

The year had been filled with blessings all around, as we quickly became involved in a church that was vibrant and full of wonderful families. The membership was large and allowed us to quickly find our niche. Both kids loved the programs and we felt blessed beyond words as the struggles of change were quickly minimized. We breezed through that first year and were now hitting new milestones. Another grade completed successfully. Only one week until summer vacation. It was that week that I found the first of two lumps.

I was taking a shower when I felt something that seemed as large as a walnut under my right arm. This was new. It was obviously a lump. How could I have not found this earlier? I had Tom feel it. It was time to call the doctor.

I had been to the doctor's office two days prior for my annual wellness exam. How was this missed? Enough with the questions! Just get it checked out. My doctor had gone on medical leave the day before so now I would meet with the Physician's Assistant.

A diagnostic mammogram immediately followed. After the mammography report is reviewed, a radiology physician does an ultrasound of the breast and lump in question. No big deal...that's what I told myself. Surely this is just an infection in the lymph gland...or was it? When you get this sort of alarm signal and life is crazy-busy, you just fit it in and do what you are told to do. That's what I did, so when the mammogram did not show any real signs of trouble, I was slightly relieved. The ultrasound, however, quickly told a different story.

The doctor's face showed immediate concern. Little did I realize the new reality I was about to come in to. While she never said it was certain that I had cancer, she was preparing me for the chance that the biopsies would not be clear. The cells looked suspicious and the cell activity was rapid. The right breast had a sizable area of cell division as well. I was somewhat in denial. In fact, I didn't even have Tom come with me to the biopsy as my world was on cruise control. I was not prepared. I didn't have time for cancer to even enter the picture. I would be fine.

The drive home from North Houston was a blur. I probably should not admit that for the safety of drivers on the road, but wow! What was going to happen now? I am a person who likes to plan and micromanage my world. What was I to do with this news? Or was it news? Maybe I was just borrowing trouble. The tears started to flow and it was getting hard to see. My first concern...is anybody watching me bawl like a baby as I drive north on I-45 right near my exit? I couldn't reach Tom; so I called my one and only sister, who is also my dearest friend. She just listened. What do you say? Tom was not home and I needed her. She always has been just what I need. Unfortunately, she was far away in Indiana.

I gathered up my fears and held it together.

The waiting game was in full swing and would be for five days. Five long days of talking to mom, Tom and my sister and a few new close friends. I don't really remember those days very well. What I do remember, though, are the feelings I had inside. I was preparing myself just a little bit each day for what was going to be cancer.

It was a dark unknown place, yet not as terrifying as I might have thought. I didn't know then, and am just starting to realize now, that my Shepherd was leading me right from the start of this journey. He was preparing me for what lay ahead. This time He was not asking me to grow spiritually with emotional struggles, nor relational, nor parenting challenges like in the past. He was taking me by the hand and clearly leading me into a different battleground, yet letting me know He was going to see me through and guide me to the other side. I had no idea what lay ahead or if He was even really in front of me. I was only aware of a challenge and I was feeling equipped.

When that fifth day finally rolled around I was not anxious. I simply waited for the call. It was the PA from my doctor's office, whom I hardly knew at the time. She told me I had breast cancer in my right breast and it had spread to my lymph nodes, one for certain and likely more. I needed to see a breast surgeon the next day.

The call was not a shock. Nothing like I imagined a call like that would be. I was alone when I got the call. I hung up the phone, sat on the bench in the kitchen and didn't cry. I was preparing for battle. There was a strange sense of relief. I now knew what was waging war inside of me and it was time to fight. So often the unknown is far worse than the reality of what we are actually facing.

I talked to Tom, mom and Deb. I know it was harder for them to hear than for me to say. The next discussion was going to be the hardest. How do you tell your children that you have cancer? Once that word is uttered, the rest of the conversation becomes blotted out so easily, especially for young minds. The news was received better than I anticipated and I knew that the way Tom and I reacted going forward would have a huge impact on Ross and Sara.

Our lives kicked into overdrive and the summer of 2010 would not be one like the Hauser family had ever experienced before - uncharted waters for us, but not for Jesus.

3

To Journal, Reluctantly

$\mathcal{M}$Y WALK THROUGH BREAST CANCER was not to be alone. God placed before me a gift - a gift that at first, I had absolutely NO interest in. It all started with the gentle nudge from Tom to document medical updates and information online, in order to keep friends and family in the loop. Because I was self-conscious about my life-long inability to properly start and stop paragraph formations, among other things, I was not keen on the idea.

I prayed about journaling and decided I would do this for the sake of information and sanity, thus not having to retell my medical history to every well-intentioned person with whom I wanted to keep in touch. God knew just what I needed and provided beyond what I ever would have imagined.

In no time, this journaling experiment became an outlet for my emotions and daily toils. A means of connecting my former life and my current one. A bridge across the miles and across town. From one heart to another. So begins the story that continues to unfold today.

~ 4 ~

Sharing the Journey

JUNE 1, 2010 AND TOM'S first posting simply read, "Romans 12:12." I may have looked it up at the time, but didn't recall. As I now look it up, it says, *"Be joyful in hope, patient in affliction, faithful in prayer."* This brings a smile to my face as I think back over the past 18 months. Boy, I wish I had looked this one up earlier. Funny thing is, this is exactly what we did. Tom lived it out in knowledge; I just followed his lead I suppose.

After Tom's first reference to scripture in that original post, he went on to explain:

Tom: Amy has stage II Invasive Ductal Carcinoma (IDC) - breast cancer. Stage II means it has moved from its original spot; in this case from breast tissue to a sentinel auxiliary lymph node. This means that there is a chance that the cancer has spread to other parts of the body. At this point CT and MRI scans are taking place to insure that the other organs are free of cancer clusters. We will keep you posted on those results.

Here's how it all happened:
- May 3 - annual exam. Clean bill of health, but need to schedule annual mammogram.
- May 6/7 - found lump under arm while showering – Day 1 of the journey.
- May 13 - "get in here right away" appointment. Results in "get a mammogram right away" appointment.

- May 19 - Mammogram/ultrasound. Doctor is "very concerned" about lump and surrounding tissue.
- May 24 - Biopsy and further ultrasound
- May 27 - Biopsy results in - the node and tissue both show the IDC.
- May 28 - met with surgeon and oncologist to determine next steps:
  - More tests to determine if there are any measurable traces elsewhere in the body.
  - Determine if Amy is triple negative - meaning that different new hormone/chemotherapy treatments will not be effective. The first two will definitely not be effective according to the initial biopsy. The third will be determined by an HER2 test. If the HER2 test comes back positive, there is a newer, very effective drug that will be added to the chemo mix.
  - Schedule chemo education June 4.
  - Install a port near left collarbone for chemo infusions on June 8 and first chemo set for morning of June 9.

Houston has one of the nation's best cancer centers at MD Anderson. With great medical resources and many new friends with MD Anderson ties, we are confident in how this area chooses to do chemotherapy first, then surgery. This is different than many areas but MD Anderson paves the way for all of this area's cancer treatments; and they feel this is the best way to kill free floating cells in the body, shrink the tumors and nodes, and then have options for less invasive surgery if lumpectomy is an option at the end of chemotherapy. Amy's type is a common breast cancer so we are comfortable with the plans of our team at this point in time. We welcome other schools of thought or suggestions if you feel so inclined.

Phil 4:13 – *"I can do all this through Him who gives me strength."* (TNIV)

We told a few friends about the lump but didn't want to get too worked up until the results were in. Since then we have tried to let many know and the outpouring has been incredible. We are truly blessed with such caring and giving friends and family. It is living proof of Christ's hands and feet working in our lives.

Mark 9:23 – *"If you can?" said Jesus. "Everything is possible for one who believes."* (TNIV)

I will take a liberty by answering the big question: "How is Amy doing?" The short answer is...amazingly well! Don't get me wrong, we are both very scared and there are moments of blackest despair, deep anguish, anger and bewilderment. Through all of life's journey, God prepares us for moments such as these, and we have had quite a lot of preparation over the last few years! It has all culminated in an overall peace that the situation is in hands greater than ours. We can only accept the grace and support of our friends and look to whatever happens as "fitting into His best" for a greater plan than just our little corner of the world.

James 1:2 – *"Consider it pure joy, my brothers and sisters, <u>when</u>ever you face trials of many kinds."* (TNIV, underline mine)

That said, I pledge to keep you updated and Amy will most likely be doing most of the talking worth listening to from here on out.

Please keep us all in your prayers - Amy for strength, peace and healing; the kids for peace and understanding, and me for strength and wisdom to help guide and support the family through it all.

Amy is physically fine right now. Until the chemo starts, the only impact is a small scar from the biopsy.

We ran off to Port Aransas for the Memorial Day weekend to get away and enjoy one of our favorite family things - the beach. It was a wonderful getaway.

5

This is Amy

$\mathcal{N}$OW AT DAY 28, WEDNESDAY, JUNE 2, 2010 10:41 PM

Amy: First official entry. This is Amy.

Well, we are getting our schedule jam packed with appointments, procedures and treatments. Not like it wasn't full enough. I think the hardest part of all this is the lousy timing. Tomorrow is the last day of school for Ross and Sara. I am so sad that I am not emotionally there for the parties and ceremonies. I am physically there but a bit out of it. My mind is trying to wrap itself around all of this - dealing with coordinating schedules with so many well-meaning friends, and trying to learn about what kind of a journey we have ahead of us. Anyway, I am really tired and some things yet to do tonight. I will try and write a bit each day as we get the kinks straightened out for this battle ahead. Remember though that God is good...ALL the time!

In His grip,

Amy

Looking back on this first entry, I am glad to see that I chose to believe I was "In His grip" right from the start. I recall having seen this phrase many years ago. It struck me when I saw it, but I never felt inclined to use it personally for some reason. I suppose it seemed almost as if one had to be invited into a special club to be worthy of such a precursor to one's signature. I can't really explain it. When I started this blog, I was so self-conscious of my writing, even with my "news." I should have known it was going to be a blessing for me when I automatically and almost unknowingly signed off for the first time, "IN HIS GRIP."

Guestbook Note
Pray this twice daily (Ephesians 6:10-18) in a quiet place. Print it out and place it where you can see it on a regular basis. Know that Good is always under attack by evil, however through God and Jesus you WILL be healed!

Try not to worry about anything else except you and your family. Focus. All the other things, camps, etc. will work out. God wants you to concentrate on You. You must find peace.

I love you and I AM covering you in Prayer.

Day 29, THURSDAY, JUNE 3, 2010 9:20 AM

Amy: I just heard from Dr. S. (surgeon and breast specialist) and they read my CT scans before they actually got to the oncologist who will officially read them, BUT THE DOCTOR SAYS THE REST OF MY ORGANS LOOK CLEAN AND FREE OF CANCER!! Praise God. This is huge!!

Last day of school for the kids. Off to the gym then to Sara's school party. Ross is having friends over then Sara wants to go to her riding lesson anyway. Hot day at the barn! God is good...ALL the time!

Guestbook Note
When you sign off, In His Grip, I know that you are in the best hands, the only hands you need to be!

Guestbook Note
From my mother, Barb - To my precious daughter and her dear, dear family...my heart aches for you and yet I celebrate your faith and strength. I find strength in God's amazing grace and His obvious plan for all of us.

As I shared with you late last week after receiving the news no mother ever wants to hear, the Lord gave me the words of John 11:4..."This sickness will not end in death. No, it is for God's glory so that God's Son may be glorified through it." Already I see His hand guiding and causing so many to give Him that glory that He so deserves. We all must stay in His grip and hold on...it may be a bumpy ride but He will never let us go!!

Day 30, FRIDAY, JUNE 4, 2010 10:51 PM

Amy: Just getting home from a crazy long day but a good one for the most part. Tom and I just got home from a treat night with Rick and Vanessa at the Astros vs. Cubs game. Astros won and we had awesome seats. 14th row behind the dugout/home plate. Nice.

Ross is at a party at the Loft (youth ministry building of our church) and Sara is at a sleepover. Quiet at 10:30 on a Friday night!

The earlier part of the day consisted of surgery prep work for Tuesday's surgical procedure of installing my chemotherapy port. This is the internal "cork" that will allow treatments to flow more easily in and out of my body rather than having to always get fresh veins from my arm. Saves veins from collapsing. The port will be installed on the right side of the upper chest. From 9-11am we did paperwork, blood work and EKG work up. After this I ran kids for a while, took them to Landry's for lunch then back to the hospital for chemo training for Tom and I. Wow. Will be doing chemo once every 3 weeks. I will write those details tomorrow as I have had several people ask me what I am getting and how much and so on. Not sure why y'all wanna know that stuff but anyway...I will give it to you doctor wanna-be's if you feel the need...

No real other news to report, other than it is AMAZING to me how many wonderful people I get to talk to during all these appointments. I would normally not be really talkative but God has given me such a good attitude right now and people want to know all about me and this journey, and I am LOVING telling them. God just wants me to make him famous. It is so cool to get to do it, if you just listen to Him and let him do HIS THING!!!

14

Have a great night and weekend because GOD IS GOOD...ALL THE TIME!

In His tender grip,

> **Guestbook Note**
> Isn't it amazing how God can open a crack of opportunity and let the light of His majestic presence shine in during the otherwise dark and scary moments of our lives? Keep listening for His still "small voice."

> **Guestbook Note**
> You ARE making Him Famous!

Day 31, SATURDAY, JUNE 5, 2010 5:38 PM

Amy: What a great Saturday. Sun is pounding down (as it does almost every day in Houston) at a balmy 96 degrees. One good thing about losing your hair in the summer time...no more bad hair days with the humidity in Houston. My fellow Iowans, I just want you to know that you do not KNOW what humidity is until you live in the stinking jungle. It gives humidity a whole new meaning. I never had a green thumb before now though. Everything grows like crazy here and everything has blossoms too! Who knew?

Anyway, started this morning out with an MRI scan that actually has to be rescheduled until Monday for various reasons I will not get into. After that, a wonderful new friend, Kristie, and her family brought an awesome lunch over and all of us hung out and went over plans for meal schedules and shuttle service/appointment coverage for our family's upcoming ordeal. I cannot tell you what a blessing she has been, along with so many other wonderful women from this group I joined at our church, The Woodlands United Methodist Church and the Loft Church (one and the same...kind of like MDRC and The Bridge in Iowa).

Anyway, back in September I decided that in order to really meet some women quickly I had better join a bible study or something; yet our church had so many to choose from it was a bit overwhelming... but I saw a flier for this group called 'Ladies of the Loft' and I checked it out. We started with about 18 women and we meet once a week for 90 minutes, discussing various women's studies of all styles (like Discerning the Voice of God...my favorite!) and it was amazing. By the end of this school year, we had over 50 women join us and we have had so much fun. We have had social gatherings with and without spouses, which has helped us get close very quickly. God has so blessed this group and given it unbelievable leadership. I don't exactly know how I would be handling all this change without them. They are stepping up to the challenge of embracing our family during this chapter in our lives and I cannot thank them enough. It's funny because so many of us were sad that we would not be meeting regularly over the summer but now we get to keep on working as TEAM LOL! Anyway, God started laying the groundwork for this challenge long before I knew what I was up against! This is only one example, and believe me that I could go on and on but I won't, or at least not just yet because I don't want you to stop reading my journal. :)

Looking back, it was clear that God put the Ladies of the Loft in my life long before I ever knew how much I would need them. As time passes I realize that each person had a role to play in our lives. Some will remain for a lifetime while some were there for a season of serving. Learning to see the whole package, for the true gift that it is, has been beautiful. Not always easy, because life never remains the same for very long, but beautiful just the same.

Okay...now here is next week's schedule for those that are like my mother (she is known as "Doctor Barb" in our family) and need to know the details, here you go:

MON: MRI and Echocardiogram

TUES: Port surgery

WED: 1st chemotherapy treatment. Each will take 3.5 hours. They are using Taxotere, Adriamycin and Cytoxan (TAC) at this point. When the tests reveal if I am HER2 positive or negative, they will decide if I will also get Herceptin.

I will do the chemo treatments once every three weeks for 6 treatments total (18 weeks in all). I will go in on a Tuesday for blood work, Wednesday for the chemo for 3 or 4 hours and Thursdays for injections and IV fluids for a couple of hours. I then see the oncologist one week later for follow up on how the chemo is working, if it is shrinking the tumors, etc. Any adjustments will then be made accordingly. If Herceptin is an option (which we hope it is) that chemo is given for one year. Good news is that Herceptin will NOT make my hair fall out so my hair will be able to grow back after the 18 weeks of TAC is up.

Hope this gives you an idea of what is happening here. As for the kids next week, Ross has a trip to Dallas (Six Flags, etc.) for 3 days and Sara starts church day camp for incoming 5th graders to the Planet 56 youth group. Perfect timing. My dear friend Rhonda will be taking Sara to camp with her daughter, Mia, so this is perfect. Of course Tom will be hanging with me during most of this week. His work is being flexible with his time and they are such a supportive group. We have gotten to know many of his colleagues and I cannot tell you how wonderful each and every one of them and their families have been. Can you tell we really like Houston? PLEASE don't get me wrong, Iowa friends and family...we miss you more than you know but there is something to be said about a new adventure. Never underestimate the gift in change. Enjoy the weekend.

IT'S NICE TO BE IMPORTANT BUT IT'S MORE IMPORTANT TO BE NICE!

In His grip,
Amy

So much cancer jargon started to flow so easily, so quickly. For those of you that have never really had to experience all this, let me clear up a few things for breast cancer patients and a little for cancer patients in general. First of all, not all chemotherapies are the same. They target different kinds of cancers and serve multiple functions. A chemotherapy cocktail will only work on the specific cancers it is designed to battle. Not all breast cancer patients will receive the same treatments that I had. TAC is very common for my type, but it is not a blanket treatment therapy. Not all chemotherapy treatments make your hair fall out. Not all treatments are through an IV, although TAC is. When I mentioned fluids and injections, fluids are often times given the day after treatments to provide nourishment through saline, vitamins and minerals; just a boost to keep you healthy. The injection is administered to help reduce the risk of infection and boost neutrophils (a type of blood cell needed to fight infection).

Looking back, I realize how much there was to learn about breast cancer and what was involved. I think I had an image in my head of what cancer patients go through. Much of which was inaccurate. When in doubt, ask, ask and ask again!

Guestbook Note
It is so good to hear that you have found a church family as well, one that will care for you as only the church family can do.

Guestbook Note
This is Barb, Amy's mom, writing not only to Amy and her family, but to the wonderful, faithful people who are surrounding them with love and caring. I've always known how our Lord's grace is abounding but I am simply blown away. I know He gives the grace and the call, but if faithful people don't answer, not much happens.

Day 32, SUNDAY, JUNE 6, 2010 5:46 PM

Amy: Went to see the Astros again today! Beat the Cubs AGAIN... and yes, I am sorry to say to those that are wondering via my emails...I have turned into an Astros fan. I know we lived in Chicago for 6 years but I have to follow the team that is in my town. I know that means I was never TRULY a Cubs fan. We took the kids today because our new friends Jerry and Nell, another AWESOME Woodlands family, gave us fabulous seats. They go to the same church AND get this, Jerry is from DES MOINES! They have been in Houston for 20 years and Jerry actually used to work for the Astros. He graduated from Hoover High School just down the road from my old school! Small world. Anyway. That's it for today. Just love all the notes, you all are so kind. Amazing what a little cancer causes people to say about you...Love, Amy

Day 33, MONDAY, JUNE 7, 2010 10:17 PM

Amy: Hey all. My tired side has officially arrived and chemo doesn't even start for two days. What a long day it's been at the hospital. They messed up my MRI appointment again. I am so aggravated that I don't even want to get into it. Let's just say I have been stuck more times than a pincushion. I am now welcoming my port surgery tomorrow so I can stop getting poked in every vein imaginable.

The fact that today was the first official day of summer for Sara and I couldn't be with her was on my mind. All the cancer books are getting the best of me and all the waiting and poking REALLY made me miss familiar hospitals, doctors and mostly PEOPLE. I am just emotionally drained today. Not to mention really hungry. So for all you who thought I was so strong…today I am not. I could use your extra prayers for support. A good night's sleep will do wonders on me (just ask Tom, I am like Jekyll and Hyde sometimes, always have been!) OH WAIT…I have to be in Houston at 5:30 a.m.! Forget the good night's sleep.

God is good ALL the time though. Sometimes you just have to read, pray and think yourself into that good place. Try it; I think you just might like it.

Oh and thank you all for your great notes on my guestbook. These mean so much to me and my family! It's sort of like getting a card in the mail. I love you all so much.

In His grip…even when you don't exactly feel it.

Amy

As I reflect on "think yourself into that good place," I have to smile. That is exactly what I had to do most days, regardless of the situation at hand. It could be cancer, death, relational issues, finances, or anything. It feels really strange at first, but self-talk, whether positive or negative, is extremely powerful! I started small, and now looking back, it is a habit that has changed my life. At first it was not biblically driven, but then I began to find verses that resonated in my heart, I memorized them and now they are part of me. The second half of my life will be better than the first!

Guestbook Note
I really like this line, *Amy:* "In His grip…even when you don't exactly feel it…" It's easy to feel His grip when things are good. But it takes faith to feel that way when you have a day like today.

Guestbook Note
The type of Mom who is concerned about being there for the kids' first day of summer is the type of Mom who has raised a couple of strong, faith-filled, caring young people … don't act too surprised at their level of maturity and thoughtfulness in the coming weeks. You raised them that way. Now they'll have a platform to showcase what they can do for you.

Day 34, TUESDAY, JUNE 8, 2010 8:56 AM

Tom: Good morning, this is Tom at the hospital. Amy is in surgery to have her port installed. The day started at 4:45 a.m., fortunately we live only about 15 minutes from the hospital. Since napping is not working, I will try an update…

Ross is in Dallas with his youth group; they went to a Rangers game, Six Flags, a water park and game place – all in one overnight! Sara spent the night with friends and has her church camp each day this week. We won't see either until this evening.

Tomorrow starts chemo – every three weeks for six sessions. Spirits are still good, but we've really leaned on God and friends these last couple of days. I think the reality of the surgery and the start of chemo has started to sink in for both of us. We are glad that it has started and we can be moving forward.

The outpouring of support has been absolutely overwhelming. We both so look forward to reading the guestbook and hearing from old and new friends from places near and far. The humor is very sustaining!

I will get an update out after surgery and recovery. Please keep us in your prayers as you are in ours.

It didn't take long to see that Tom was being carried and equipped to handle the huge task at hand as husband and father, to name just a few of the many roles that a caretaker must shoulder. God was that equipper, no doubt. We may have had our struggles; both as a couple and as parents, but what once seemed to be more than we wanted to bear quickly became bearable.

When faced with cancer, the acceptance that we were not perfect, but that we were a family and it was time to pull together, really came to the surface. God was hard at work and we were finally ready to follow his promptings. Trusting the Father and accepting that He would work both on us and in us to stick together as a family, through thick and thin, was not easy. It has worked better than any therapy ever could have though!

Perspective was the only thing that had really changed. It was all that really needed to change, now that I look back; learning to focus on what is going well, rather than what is not.

Day 34, TUESDAY, JUNE 8, 2010 9:47 AM

Tom: Amy just got out of surgery and all went well. Dr. S. said she did great. The incision is off to the side where the shirt and/or straps will hide it. The actual port is more toward the collarbone and the tube is connected up near the base of the neck. The port bump will be visible because, as the Dr. says, she is so thin!

Since chemo starts tomorrow, they left a needle in so that she does not have to get poked tomorrow. Since everything is under the skin and the incision is glued up, Amy can get in the water right away after the chemo tomorrow – very important for her!!!

I will get to see her in a few minutes – don't know if she will feel like updating today or not – she really likes to keep it up to date and loves reading the guestbook. Thanks again to all for the concern, support and prayers.

t

When you stop long enough to think back over a period of time (easier to do after an illness, I realize) sometimes you can get a closer look at the loving character traits of our God. When I see all He has done in my life and in our marriage over the last few years, I am in awe of His desire to bless our lives and have us know Him better. As we seek Him more and more we begin to understand what obedience to His voice looks like in our individual lives.

Tom and I struggled for years. We still struggle, but not in the same ways as before. What we once thought was almost hopeless, when we genuinely sought to trust God with everything, became loaded with hope! I realize it is not as easy as it sounds in a sentence or two!

I have been blessed, even though I really don't deserve all that I have.

That, my friends, is God's graceful love; it can take a long time to learn to accept it. I think I am finally getting there...

Guestbook Note
Angels exist, but sometimes they don't have wings...we call them "friends."
Praying always and standing in the gap for you.

Day 34, TUESDAY, JUNE 8, 2010 10:31 PM

Amy: Trying to get things done and running around crazy tonight. I finally got on here to look at the guestbook and I LOVE THESE NOTES! They totally make my day. The only problem is that I SO want to get on and reply to each and every one of you; no lie. I love you all. I just would never get anything done if I did. I knew I thrived on relationships but this is really feeding my soul. Thank you.

I am thrilled that the port deal went so smoothly today. I thought general anesthesia would wipe me out but it really didn't. No pain either. Took a hit of morphine just for kicks before I left the hospital (figured I was paying for it anyway) and that is all I have had all day so that is good news.

Chemo tomorrow but God has taken away the anxiety totally. Thanks for your prayers...see, they work! Rest in the Lord. As the sticker on my mirror used to say to me every morning when I was a little girl..."Nothing will happen to me today that you and I cannot handle together, Lord!" Yee Haw.

"LIFE IS WHAT HAPPENS WHEN YOU ARE MAKING OTHER PLANS" -- the late Art Linkletter

(Once things slow down I will be writing much more about what that means to me...bet you can't wait for more long entries! Tough. You are my captive audience and I think it's funny!)

Gently in His grip,
Amy

6

God Got There Before All of Us

$\mathcal{D}$AY 35, WEDNESDAY, JUNE 9, 2010 1:30 PM

Tom: This be Tom. 1:30 p.m. and the chemo is about done. 5 IV's – Two for anti-nausea and the three actual chemo's. The nurse is great and Amy had an 8:30 welcoming committee of cheerleaders from her Ladies of the Loft (LOL) group. Then lots of sitting and reading emails and journal updates. We may drive out to Porter and see how the camp is going afterwards – a four-day camp for foster kids and it runs through Thursday. We love being out there and we can take Tess (our Golden Retriever) and let her run.

One small area of concern. The recent MRI showed some other questionable areas on the right breast, so an ultrasound is scheduled for Monday the 14th. Also possible biopsy. With all of the types of tests – mammograms, MRI, CAT scans, PET scans (maybe, if insurance allows), airport scan, ultrasound - we hope they catch everything.

Please keep lifting the support team up in prayer for strength too, and Ross and Sara.

Over and out,

t

Guestbook Note

So the battle is on as God, your body, prayers, family, friends and your wonderful spirit begin their chemo-aided conquest over the handful of rebel cells causing all this commotion. Looks like a landslide victory for the good guys on this one.

Guestbook Note

Loved having Sara over to play in the clay today! She is so sweet and helpful. I was working on a banner and she did a lot of tedious knot tying. She also made 2 pots. One on the wheel (I see potential there) and a hand-built coil vase. She'll have to come back once they're fired to glaze them. Soooo neat that you had LOL there to cheer you on today! You're on my mind and in my prayers.

Guestbook Note

Yesterday morning, Rhonda, Julie and I got to the clinic WAY before Amy (which as some of you may know is not hard). While we were waiting, I marched myself back to meet her chemo nurse. She patiently listened while I explained to her how very special and precious Amy is to all of us. She promised me she would care for Amy like the treasure she is. She came out later where we were waiting with our signs and asked, "She is coming, right?" As though any of us can predict Amy. Amy did show up and, oh, yes, God was there, too. He got there before all of us.

Day 36, THURSDAY, JUNE 10, 2010 8:24 AM

Amy: Was a bit too tired to journal last night after my first chemo round, a visit to the foster kids camp at Porter then home cleaning up the place then off to Wal-Mart. I think I over did it just a smidge. Didn't feel too bad other than a queasy stomach but crackers took care of that straight away. Was super tired at 10 p.m. but really did not sleep for more than 15 minutes at a time all night. I had steroids given via IV and have been taking steroid pills for 2 days so I am sure that is why. I go in today for a white blood cell boosting injection then 2 hours of saline/fluids to flush out some of the junk. That should make me feel pretty good, or so I have heard.

Busy day today with a few meetings but will have to pace myself. Should be interesting to see how this all plays out. The kids are so helpful right now and I am loving that. I am pleased to see how they rise to the occasion so nicely.

Last night while I was laying awake so much of the time, so many bible verses would come to my mind in their entirety. It was really amazing to me how much scripture has been ingrained in my heart and mind over the past few years. This was such a comfort. God works in every nook and cranny of your existence when you just tell Him what you need Him to do. All you have to do is trust that He will do what He says He will. And He always will...if it aligns with HIS WILL. That can be the tough part. Always a work in progress. Always.

In His grip, regardless,
Amy

Learning to listen to my body and actually pace myself was not easy. Slowing down in this "multitasking on steroids culture" that we live in makes it almost impossible not to get caught up in trying to be everything to everyone. If I were to grade my success at this, I would give myself a 'C.' Managing stress is crucial to feeling well and staying well during cancer treatments. I found myself wanting to prove to the world that I could still do everything, but the fact is, I could not. On days I tried to "do it all", my family would pay the price. Exhaustion beyond anything I had ever experienced would hit, along with scattered thoughts and shortening tempers. In hindsight, it wasn't a bit worth it.

I know women going through similar battles that continue to do EVERYTHING just as they had before, mainly because they fear their spouse and children will not be able to cope. It is almost a guilt response that we harbor inside. I say; "Let them rise to the occasion just like you are!" Beautiful things can happen when we dig deep and ALLOW our loved ones to do the same in order to see just what we are all made of. Sometimes it is painful, but this is where beautiful things can happen. Don't take on what isn't yours, you may be depriving others of an opportunity to learn and grow. God has plans for everyone involved, not just you.

Guestbook Note

This is a post for Amy's friends and family far away: This morning when I first saw Amy, she was barefoot and bath-robed and beautiful. At lunch, it was Siren Amy. She was in high heels and this flitty, flirty little sundress, laughing like she didn't have a care in the world. Every now and then when she moved, the edge of the port bandage would peak out, which was actually hysterical, like some kind of "what's wrong with this picture."

Guestbook Note

You sound very positive, as usual. I laid awake all last night too, in my house not far from yours. Funny - I worried about unknowns, like my elderly father's health and my kid's safe return from Austin, road trip to camp....blablabla, nothing real heavy like you are going through. I did not have those bible verses so easily in my mind and wish I did. I need to read God's word and use it in my life everyday, like you do. It is so inspiring to see how God's word eases your burdens and gives you such strength. Setting a goal for myself this summer to read His word more and use it in my life more. Thanks for your inspiration.

Day 37, FRIDAY, JUNE 11, 2010 3:24 PM

Amy: It is almost 3:30 p.m. on Friday and I am still in my pj's. Needless to say, today is a rough day. I have slept most of it away. I just got up to have a banana and I had oatmeal around 10 a.m. Very tender stomach and just wiped out feeling has settled in. I pray that tomorrow is not this rough. As soon as I sign off I am going into my email folder that is packed with verses and upbeat notes from so many of you. Many wrote prayers for me and I intend to read them asap! Signing off for now. Enjoy the day for me...k?

In His grip,
Amy

Before I had my own battle of cancer to deal with, I was never very good about sending notes of encouragement to others when they were in a season of struggle. Since I had no personal experience with what they may have been going through, whether an illness or a loss, I thought my words might make them sad or could be seen as insignificant. Oh what even the shortest text or note means! It was like a moment back in time with each person; a reminder that others are thinking of you. To you it may seem so small or that your words may be lacking depth…that is not what a human being in need expects. When you are facing the dragon, love is all you need. Hey, someone should write a song about that.

Day 38, SATURDAY, JUNE 12, 2010 1:48 PM

Amy: Another rough day in the neighborhood. I've decided I would rather not go through all this after all. Not sure who I talk to in order to back out. God is still holding me just fine but I prefer he just put me down for now and let me get back to normal.

Have a new friend from our church that emails me so many tips on how to get through this rough patch after chemo. Bless her heart. Sue just went through this last summer so it is pretty clear in her memory bank. I am so grateful.

I do not make a good patient. I am a bit of a wimp. Tom and Ross just left for the store and Sara is with a friend today. Tess will hardly leave my side. What a faithful friend she is. Golden Retrievers are known for that anyway, but wow. Time for another nap. Enjoy the weekend. Have not been out since Thursday night but I hear it was a real humdinger around here this weekend. Guess I will stay put.

In His grip,

Amy

> **Guestbook Note**
> Again, I am so grateful for the faithful "soldiers" standing with you in your new home. They are a blessing to all of your family who are so far away.

> **Guestbook Note**
> Amy I promise you this is the worst of it. You will feel

so much better next week! You are normally such an energetic person and I know it is so frustrating to feel bad. Yes, you make a rotten patient, but NO, you are not a wimp! You're a rockstar! Rest when you need to, and don't feel guilty about it. In a few days you will be a different person! I am thinking of you and praying for you constantly!!

Day 39, SUNDAY, JUNE 13, 2010 12:27 AM

Tom : Spousal unit here. Ross is at a friend's for the night – some friend, the kid pushed me into the pool last weekend! But I have time, experience and treachery on my side. Sara and I watched old home movies tonight and laughed at her first try at riding a scooter and her brother's antics – seems like a long time ago and they have grown up entirely too fast. Ross and his friends would be mortified to see themselves at seven!

Amy turned in early - very exhausted and not feeling too well. It is after 11 and Sara is fast asleep, the dishwasher is unloaded and reloaded, the clothes are almost all washed and put away, the pool acidified and my car safely back in the garage; thanks to the kindness of our neighbor, Jerry, a fellow Iowan and all around good guy (albeit Hawkeye). Our guess is the alternator gave up the ghost.

Since you didn't sign on for my ramblings, here is the latest from deep in the heart o' Texas:

The effects of the chemo, surgery, steroids (no major league career now), meds and general weight of the situation really started to hit Amy late Thursday. She has most of the expected symptoms – flu like aches, lack of energy, little appetite, nausea (morning-sickness like) and no interest in much at all, not even watching a little television. She pretty much feels crappy. She has eaten a little – an Immunizer smoothie from the Smoothie King (made with blueberry substituted for strawberry to cut down on the acid), some sugar snap peas – raw, a baked potato, some crackers, and homemade soup that was thoughtfully provided by a fellow breast cancer survivor who simply stepped forward after first meeting her today!

Amy has not felt like getting out of bed much and even a brief time talking to friends in the kitchen wore her out. We are going to have to learn to conserve the energy that we have during the post chemo week. According to several veterans of similar campaigns, the crappies could last from Thursday/Friday to the following Wednesday after treatment; then pretty clear sailing for the next two weeks. This is tough news for our heroine as she was really hoping that she would only have the Saturday-Sunday impact and a minimal one at that. Always the optimist, hoping for the best during the worst (she married me remember)…

Tomorrow was to be her introduction Sunday working at our church, The Woodlands United Methodist Church (TWUMC), more specifically at the Loft. The Loft is the more informal branch/service of the TWUMC; somewhat akin to The Bridge at Meredith Drive, our church in Des Moines. She was to address the junior highers in the morning and wanted to do so before the Sinead O'Connor look sets in. Next Sunday should still work to accomplish both.

As Amy said, she makes a lousy patient, but she is really soldiering through. She has a tough side and a strong spirit and had high hopes that this would not hit so hard, especially the first cycle. We are praying that this was the worst, both the days and the cycle, but we will take one day and one cycle at a time. God only rolls out what we need to see, as we need to see it. I guess He knows from experience that we would manage to botch it up any other way. The ancient Israelites, who got to see mega-miracles first hand, kept falling down; but we have the advantage of His Son in us, helping us avoid some of the falls and when we do fall, helping us get back up. As my good friend Russell often says, we are very fortunate that God does not give us what we deserve!

Back to the patient – seems to be sleeping somewhat soundly, hopefully a full night's equivalent. Maybe the clean sheets will help! Tess is finally allowed on the bed, the fulfillment of both her and Amy's dreams. She rarely leaves Amy's side, but still gets so excited when someone stops by. There aren't enough (or long enough) walks to ever wear her out, and she had gotten even less walking lately. Tonight she is at her more usual overnight spot, on Sara's bed, to keep from waking up Amy in the night.

We continue to be in awe at the outpouring of prayers, cards, emails, notes, and sincere offers of help and food. The freezer has about a dozen serving size soups ready to go, a pot of chicken enchilada soup, dessert, barbecue, salad and others that I can't remember, all having been delivered right to our door. I am coming to realize that there is a large and very tight sisterhood of survivors out there who quickly rally around each other with support (mental, spiritual, emotional and physical), and borne from front line experience, lend advice, love, and genuine concern. I am thinking that this experience could serve the country well! The US of A could do a lot worse than having these kinds of qualifications for those in office...

As a guy observing from the periphery of the sisterhood, I offer my sincere thanks, deepest appreciation, admiration and love to all – you are remarkable. To all the others who are helping sustain us, new and old, for whatever other reason God called you to us, my very same thanks, appreciation and love. Maybe this is a foretaste of what heaven will be like – the unquestioning relationships and constant and indefatigable outpouring of love.

Good night: actually now morning.

t

I can't help but be in awe of my guy here! He seemed really strong, and he was. While Tom is not the average guy, and can take on most chores and motherly responsibilities as well as most any real mom I know, I do know that support for the husband is crucial. It is hard enough for the patient to accept help, but a guy...come on! Reaching out to the kids is a given, but the guy can get left behind. Tom is blessed with many friends that have rallied from near and far. It does take a conscious effort to remember the caretakers and not just focus on the patient. I'm just sayin!

Day 39, SUNDAY, JUNE 13, 2010 9:11 AM

Tom: Spousal unit again – Sunday morning. The patient is feeling a little better. Not quite as achy, not quite as nauseous, but still very little energy. Actually got some rest last night with a little help from modern science...

Bright, sunny day and the kids and I will all meet up at church to celebrate our gifts and ask for continued healing, strength and peace.

Day 39, SUNDAY, JUNE 13, 2010 2:19 PM

Amy: Wow. So many notes! I love hearing from you all. It is strange though how I couldn't read them yesterday. When you feel so ill, it's all you can do to just have your eyes open and stare at a wall. Very hard to explain the feeling. It's different than the flu, different than having been in a car wreck or injured...just painful and exhausting beyond words. Anyway, I am showered, fed and up for a while. Sue, a new friend from the Loft (also a nurse and 1 year breast cancer survivor) has been such a blessing to me. Yesterday she came over with tons of small containers of homemade organic soups. Very tasty and extremely healthy. She told the family they are only for me when I need to take care and eat well. So my freezer is full for when my tummy needs light, healthy and soothing food. Sue has also been emailing me daily with simple things to do to keep my spirits up and strength up. She is another angel from The Woodlands, TX.

As I am typing this, Kristie just showed up with a juicer bullet or something? She got this for Sara and is giving her a lesson on how to be the smoothie queen for our house. She and Sara are bonding well. Ross is with Michael...a neat friend from church who had him over last night and they are still together. Sara starts riding camp tomorrow. A friend from soccer that also rides weekly will be getting her to and from camp each day as they go right by. Networking is flowing well so far. Well, I need to go taste this smoothie but I have something very important to post later. I will be back.

That juicer bullet is used constantly to this day. Healthier eating habits have made their way into our lives. I was almost obsessive about it at first but eventually let it take a more natural course. I realized that forcing my family to start eating healthy foods, cutting out all the "bad," AND insisting that we all make the changes NOW would only cause them to be resentful and sneaky. While it is a natural reaction for someone with cancer cells wreaking havoc on their body, not everyone else sees the urgency quite the same as you do!

We are still not the poster family of an organic, chemical free lifestyle, but we are certainly far better than we were before the cancer diagnosis. Not only are we eating better but living more chemical free as a whole:

household, yard, skin care and more. Gradually, awareness and change is becoming a part of our lifestyle. Not allowing ourselves to be overly swayed by public opinion, but bringing EVERY NEED before God brings balance...eventually.

Coping with stressors, finding and offering forgiveness, and embracing joy are the keys. God designed our bodies to function and serve us well. Just becoming aware of all that we do that gets in the way of His good intentions for our body is a good start to letting them function as they should, but true "inner health" is first and foremost.

Guestbook Note

Jake came in the other day and said how much he missed having Ross around to run with. It really made me think how much I missed having you around for a cold drink and to talk through our troubles of the day. I guess they don't seem so big. I wish I could be there to hold your hand and talk through our new troubles. You are in my prayers and thoughts always. Let's just count the days until we can be together to have that drink and talk through our new troubles. We miss you guys!

Day 39, SUNDAY, JUNE 13, 2010 11:09 PM

Tom: Tom here – We had a bit of a turn for the worse tonight. Amy may have overdone it by being up and about for an hour earlier tonight (amazingly while Ross and I were at the gym, go figure!) or it may be the natural flow of the process, but either way Amy suddenly felt really lousy about 7:30. Very achy, her shoulder on the port side being especially bad. Only a couple of bites of supper and smells are starting to cause nausea – kind of like when she was expecting. Loud noises and anything but very gentle contact cause pain and discomfort. Tylenol PM about two hours ago so far has not had much effect – still awake. The best news is that she has kept what little she has eaten down.

I seem to be the bearer of the bad news. When Amy is feeling good, she updates, but I know that there are many of you who check regularly and want all of the latest. Thanks for your dedication and concern and the related help and prayer.

Amy mentioned in her last entry this afternoon that she had important news to share. While she still wants to more fully fill everyone in, for now we want to ask for the combined prayer firepower behind us to comfort another…One of Amy's oldest, closest and best friends – we are talking from grade school to this very moment, with no breaks – has had a personal tragedy, actually a series. She lost her mom 10+ years ago after prolonged illness. Her only sibling (sister) died suddenly from a blood clot 9 months ago and her dad had a sudden heart attack last week. Although he was up, and we all hoped on the mend, we got word that he passed away sometime yesterday or this morning. Please reach out to Krista with the same fervent prayers as for Amy. Also her husband, Jim, and kids, Abbie, Olivia and Jack. Amy so wants to get on the next plane to be with Krista and it breaks her heart that she cannot.

Sara starts horse camp in the morning. She has been riding for about 2 years now – western in Iowa and English (similar but the horses talk funny and ride on the wrong side) in Texas – go figure! She is a very accomplished horsewoman and it tickles me to see her stand her ground with some very large horses. As usual, there is no doubt who is in charge!

Ross has an open day – something fairly rare. I am preparing for the barrage of "what can I do to earn my 15 points questions." By an almost inconceivable alignment of the cosmos, two of the most important things that he has ever wanted in his entire life have somehow merged. At least my car may be cleaner for a while and I don't have to pay out allowance until the fall!

For those of you who supported his Iowa fundraising for the People to People trip that was delayed so that it could take place this summer with a Texas group, he is planning to shift that support (which was firmly and totally put in a bank account under my lock and key!) to another mission trip, whenever we get through this medical trial. When the new mission trip gets finalized, Ross will be writing each of his original supporters with more details and asking for your clearance to shift the support to the new trip.

Wow, I get kind of windy at night. Must be good therapy. One last piece of good news; we now have a Magic Bullet smoothie machine thanks to Kristie. She has fully trained Sara as our key operator. It is a slick little one-serving blender-like machine that makes it easy to make a treat and easy to clean up. Sara has several recipes to make for Amy, and the rest of us might be able to sneak in a malt or two as well.

Good night to all.

Guestbook Note

Thought of you this morning at church when one of my favorite songs was played. It reminds us that he never lets go, no matter what the storm may be, how high or how low. While simple, it can hit home for all of us.

Guestbook Note

Remember...the hands that fashioned the universe are strong enough to heal you -- and gentle enough to hold you during these difficult times...praying that you find rest and healing in the arms of God.

7

Starting to Feel Better

DAY 40, MONDAY, JUNE 14, 2010 8:08 AM

Tom: Tom here - The patient is up and about! Kristie is taking Sara to horse camp and Amy is riding along (in the car, not on the horse) – this is a good sign! Amy is still not feeling very well – same symptoms and very low energy, but definitely is more aware of pacing herself today and going forward.

Sara and Ross have been big helps and are also learning some good life lessons about taking the good with the bad and serving others. They both have such big hearts. Sara pitches in, especially in the kitchen where she loves to experiment and I am sure we will be fully supplied with smoothies for many years. Ross continues to make us so very proud as a steady stream of compliments come in from parents who observe him serving at church and camps. He has a real heart for others and relates naturally to the younger kids – never too cool to be with them or help them find a good hiding spot during a spirited game of hide and seek at Rebel Base (the youth area of the Loft Church – an awesome facility). He has volunteered, on his own, to work several younger kids' events; even spending a week as a cabin counselor for some of the foster kids.

Despite her worries, Amy is still looking radiant. I have always told her that she has a wonderful natural look and not to worry about all that time and effort (and $) in front of the mirror. Despite all of the inner pain and distress, when she manages a smile she still looks more lovely to mc than on our wedding day. I am just praying that she will feel more like smiling as the worst of the first cycle gets past.

We are blessed in many ways and want to thank our family and friends, old and new, met and not-yet-met, for all of the support and prayers.

As time continues to pass, I can see the fruits of what this experience has done for our kids; gaining the independence and ability to see beyond themselves more than they might have if they had not experienced the need to put someone before themselves much of the time. As a parent, we want to protect our children and shield them from pain. This is natural and what we ought to do. Growth DOES come through trials though. It isn't easy, but I have to say it is worth it in the long run.

When I look in the mirror now, I see many more lines than I feel I should at 44. They are the price I think I have to pay for all this body has endured over the last 18 months or so. War wounds, maybe. Not exactly what a woman wants to have. This is still an adjustment for me to work through. Wisdom and knowledge are good, visible signs of growing wisdom are not an easy pill to swallow!

Guestbook Note

Hang in there woman! You are a warrior! Don't overdo it, if you can help it. It is completely OK if you do not check off a thing on your "to do" list. Just tuck that list away, and let God wrap you up in a blanket of peace.

Ross and Sara,
You guys ROCK! What a testimony it is to see how you rise to the occasion. Give your parents a big hug for leading by example, and give yourselves a big high five for becoming such great role models for others. Lean on the Lord...He has got your back!

Day 40, MONDAY, JUNE 14, 2010 1:46 PM

Amy: I just read Tom's entries. Wow. He writes a bunch. I don't think I need to say much as you probably know more than you care to anyway. Just a note to say I am feeling much better today but the energy level is rock bottom. Less aches in the bones and joints, which is great. Lying in bed before my ride comes to take me to another ultrasound and possible biopsy or two. That is my day.

Sorry I didn't get back to my posting yesterday but that is just the way the day went. Tom did a nice job for me, of touching on what was on my heart. I just wanted to let Krista know how much she was being carried in prayer. She has had a doozy of a year. Can't even imagine the feeling when all of your immediate family has gone before you and you are only 42. She has an amazing husband and family and Jim's family is this great big loving Italian family that has soaked her up from the day they met her 20 years ago; so God had a plan all along...imagine that.

I also have been writing a bunch with another family dear to us. Joe and Carole were our neighbors on Diamond Lake north of Chicago (back in the days when we were first married and up until Ross was three). They were the most AWESOME family fill-in, as we were away from our own. Huge Italian meals, music all the time as they were both professional musicians, great talks, tons of laughs and just everything we needed at that time in our lives. Anyway, Joe was diagnosed 14 mos. ago with a rare form of cancer. He has been treated fairly successfully with chemo this past year and that was a miracle in and of itself. Carole wrote today that the family is there with them now and hospice is also coming into the home. My heart aches for Carole and the kids and now grandkids. More prayers than you can count are prayed for you Carole!

Anyway. Just wanted to add those. As you can see I don't like to proofread my entries. Sorry if my writing is lousy but I AM WHAT I AM! Blessings to everyone! May tomorrow be a super day. I have visitors (My LOL leaders and of course friends!) coming at lunch.

In His grip,
Amy

As I write this, another close family friend is under hospice care. Life keeps moving at an unstoppable pace. Memories last a lifetime. Trying to cling to earthly things only caused me a deep sense of despair. As I learn to focus on the blessings and on scripture that reminds us of God's constant and unchanging ways since the beginning of time, I find comfort and the ability to focus on what is to come from a more eternal perspective. No one we have crossed paths with here on earth, nor those lives that have impacted us at one time or another, will be wasted. God will use all these things for good. Life here on earth is just a foretaste of our heavenly lives. I get pumped when I think about it. I cannot begin to fathom it, but I love thinking of it!

Guestbook Note
Dear Sweet Amy, As far as your "I am what I am" that's exactly why we love you.

Day 41, TUESDAY, JUNE 15, 2010 1:55 PM

Amy: Yesterday was my appointment with radiology and the doctor did another ultrasound based on the fact that an MRI showed a few questionable spots in my right breast. This is the same side as the other tumors. Anyway, she did NOT see anything out of the ordinary with her 3rd ultrasound! That is great. Problem is that she says JUST TO BE SURE...we need to do another MRI and biopsy those pinpointed areas of question. That will be this Friday noon. More toxic lemonade to bind up the ol' system and more laying on a board with two strategically cut out circles, while laying as still as one is humanly capable as my arms are contorted behind my back. Oh how vanity has been tossed out the window for now!

On a lighter note, I just want to thank everyone who has sent cards, gifts and more gifts to us. I am simply BLOWN AWAY. I cannot soak this in, really. It is too much attention and I don't like so much focus on me. If it weren't for the cancer, I'd have to make you take it all back but I won't! Your love is great. Tom would take some chocolate chip cookies though...

Anyway. Having a great day for the most part, really! Sore a bit, like post flu energy level but nothing I can't handle. Went to Beck's Prime for a salad with three TO DIE FOR friends. They simply made my day. Home resting with Sara and Ross now and Sara is sitting here chomping at the bit waiting to help me open a huge basket full of individual gifts from gals in the LOL group. One sent me a cool t shirt that says, "I've got CHEMO BRAIN...WHAT'S YOUR EXCUSE?" HILARIOUS!!

Signing off for now.

Look for the blessings in every day you have been given.

In His grip,

Amy

I remember this day well. I remember the joy. I was fed both literally and figuratively by my friends that day. As time has passed and so much good has come from the valley of the shadow, I cannot express enough what God can do with our junk. I realize now just how much junk I had. Cancer was just a visible piece. Most of us have hidden junk all around. What if we "fed" each other in the midst of all our battles? Imagine what a world this would be? The light would be shining in all of those scary places. Even if we put ourselves in the valley, we need to have help walking out sometimes. Beautiful things can and DO happen when we come together and shine truth on Satan's lies – I have witnessed it firsthand and it is an awesome sight.

Day 42, WEDNESDAY, JUNE 16, 2010 6:13 PM

Amy: Hey all, just a quick note as I am trying to do 46 things at once and slow down a touch all at once...

First off, I added a new photo for some of you that might be interested in seeing it. My mom, sister Deb and her family made me a chemo blanket that is simply beautiful. The best part is that the knots were tied as prayers were being said on my behalf. So many of my mom and sister's friends sent prayers to be read as knots were being tied for me! It was made in Indiana when my mom was there a few weeks ago. So much love, faith and friendship all tied up into one HUGE BLESSING! Thank you from the bottom of my heart. I simply love this. The tears were a flowin' when I read the note explaining all who had contributed time and thoughts. I just miss you sissy and ma, so much today.

On a different note, Tom and I met with the oncologist today. Found out I am TRIPLE NEGATIVE after all. This means I am not a candidate for the Herceptin chemo drug that we were hoping I was going to be able to use.

The treatment will continue to be TAC chemo. I will go for another ultrasound around July 12 to see if the tumor and lymph node are shrinking, the same or ... growing. I didn't realize that was a possibility but I guess it does happen sometimes. Anyway, pray that it is SHRINKING and the chemo plan is working as it should. In the meantime...ROCK ON!

Gotta check the meat on the grill.

IN HIS GRIP, and He is SO GOOD ALL THE TIME!!

Amy

Triple Negative. Another one of those labels that we (breast cancer survivors) are all familiar with. In the breast cancer arena, this is not a label anyone wants. This is the group with the highest rate of recurrence within the shortest amount of time. To this day, it is still the little demon that creeps into my thoughts when I least expect it. Labels often become self-fulfilling, labels like: "foster kid," "wild mustang," "has cancer" and now, "triple negative." It is another negative label and I do not intend to wear it on my shirt or in my heart, even if it is on my medical record.

When labels are attached, a crushing of the spirit begins. What label are you carrying?

Guestbook Note

Today's devotional email that I received was titled "Hope for the Tired". Just had to share since I immediately thought of you...

"The Lord will guide you always; he will satisfy your needs in a sun-scorched land and will strengthen your frame." Isaiah 58:1. God will replenish His exhausted children, too. When you give Him control, He promises to meet your heart's sun-scorched needs and give you hope-filled strength for the healing process.

Guestbook Note

We are praying for you both @ the Loft. Even though you guys have not been in town all that long you have formed a connection with many - a great testimony to you both. Pastor A.

Day 44, FRIDAY, JUNE 18, 2010 8:44 PM

Amy: I have not felt much like writing lately but will do a brief entry. Just busy with life I guess!

Feeling pretty good these past few days. Energy is great starting out in the morning but fades pretty quickly. Try and get things done in the morning and TRYING to slow down by mid-day.

Today I had the MRI guided biopsy. Caught some flak since I went alone but it is 5 minutes from my house and I knew I would be waiting and just hanging around a bunch. The people, once again, were SO NICE and SO CARING! I think the biopsy was harder on those ladies and the Doctor doing it than it actually was on me. They ended up only doing a biopsy on one area rather than two, as one area of concern was actually gone. Yeah! Ended up with a huge hematoma in that area though, and trouble with bleeding but all is well now! Should get results Wednesday...means probably Thursday. Off to bed soon.

Ross hung out with friends today, Sara had her last day of riding camp then went to a friends. Tonight, Sara and Tom had a father/daughter dance at the BIG church in one of the dance type halls. They had a great time. I will post a photo later. Astros vs. Rangers tomorrow night! An early Father's Day outing for us! Should be fun. Game is in Houston, not Dallas!

I seem to be losing my funny. My back hurts a bunch these days. Hope to get my mojo back soon. Bummer. God IS good...all the time. No trout about it! {family fishing trip joke}

In His grip,
Amy

I caught flak for going to an appointment alone, and this was not the only time. People want to support and help so much, and that is great. I just remember having the need to feel independent too. It is important to maintain control of certain elements of your circumstances. There is not a more crucial time to be you than when you are trying to be as strong physically and mentally as you can in order to heal.

The attention can be overwhelming. Take time to draw any necessary boundaries for your sake and for the sake of others! Frustration and resentment can build and that is not good for anyone!

Guestbook Note

Amy, hold tight to His "grip," there is healing in those hands and my prayers continue that he release that healing in and through you. Don't forget to praise Him for His faithfulness and remember ... He'll NEVER let you down and He'll NEVER let you go!

Day 45, SATURDAY, JUNE 19, 2010 11:11 PM

Amy: Several notes posted today and you know what...it is like fuel to the soul. Strange really, but it is!! There is something about just KNOWING that people all over the country (and Costa Rica, Ruth Ann!) are thinking of you. Just seeing your names can light up my day, as if you were all right here! Sometimes just a sentence or a funny comment or the strangest thing can encourage me more than you know. Thank you from the bottom of my heart. This journaling site has been such a gift in this new diagnosis and walk with cancer.

It is getting really late and I do have to talk in the morning during the 9:30 and 11:00 a.m. youth ministry services so I have to hurry... but I AM FEELING FABULOUS today! I think this is the first day I can say I feel 100% back to the old Amy. It just is a bummer that it has taken 10 days to get there and then on the 28th I have my next chemo treatment. Well, we will make the most of the really good days, that is for sure. We had a great time at the Astros vs. Rangers game. It was SO HOT in there tonight though. Roof was closed but it felt like the air was barely on. 'Stros lost 5-1. They lost last night, too. Boo.

A verse for you to meet you where you are. It has been floating in my brain and being for several days now.

"COME TO ME, ALL YOU WHO ARE WEARY AND BURDENED, AND I WILL GIVE YOU REST. TAKE MY YOKE UPON YOU AND LEARN FROM ME, FOR I AM GENTLE AND HUMBLE IN HEART, AND YOU WILL FIND REST FOR YOUR SOULS. FOR MY YOKE IS EASY AND MY BURDEN IS LIGHT" - Matthew 11: 28-30

Signing off,
Amy

I wasn't very good about memorizing scripture during my illness. However, as things were seemingly returning to normal and the regular flow of written words of encouragement were starting to fade, I sensed God telling me to read His daily notes of encouragement and prayers. It was that first summer, one year out from my diagnosis that I started to keep a journal of verses I sensed God wanted me to memorize. While there are only a handful that I know like the back of my hand, the one above became one of my favorites and I still recite it on nights that my heart may be aching. It helps soothe me into sound slumber.

Guestbook Note
Hang tough! I hate when His plan doesn't match up with mine, but ya gotta trust and ya gotta hold on to Him tight.

8

Father's Day and "Normal" Life

Day 46, SUNDAY, JUNE 20, 2010 7:26 PM

Amy: Another great day in the neighborhood! And I still have hair to boot! I wake up every morning and ever so gently give my hair a tug. If it stays where it's supposed to, I say a profound "THANK YOU GOD!" to myself and get up. I am not looking forward to the day that I am not so lucky. I'll be sure to post a picture when my red hair turns to skin. I will ask all our fellow skinheads to do the same so I have some company! Not sure if you can post pics for me or not but you can try!

The talk at church this morning went really well, or so I hear. The first group at 9:30 was a little shorter than the second and I think the second was best. That's the way that kind of thing usually goes anyway. Ross was there and seemed to be good with it all. That is the most important opinion to me in such a setting!

We took Tom to Rudy's BBQ for lunch. Tons of testosterone in that place. It is such a guys place to eat. Ross and Tom LOVE it there. Sara and I tolerate it. This is what I think the guys in there are thinking and needing on Father's Day: "Woman, give me greasy brisket served on butcher paper while I sit on picnic style seats and watch different sports on huge screens everywhere in the room and do it at least once a month" ...they are happy, I am happy!

Life is good, cancer bites. Need I say more? Blessings to all you fathers out there! Happy Father's Day! I miss my dad.

GOD IS SO GOOD, ALL THE TIME!!

Amy and family

Day 46, SUNDAY, JUNE 20, 2010 10:28 PM

Tom: Random thoughts from a simple mind (Tom's, not the band):

I have it on good authority from several trusted born and bred Texans that Rudy's is THE best barbecue in the state, therefore in the world.

Yes we are simple; I once read that when a woman asks a man what is on his mind and he does not respond with something closely related to either sex, shortstops or carburetors, he is lying...

Shouldn't simple be something good??? There was no planning to be done, no shopping to be done, no preparation to be done, no cooking to be done, no cleanup to be done, no chance of any complaint about the food (or the presentation, whatever that is...) and I paid for it, not to mention dropping off and picking up at the front door after buying everyone else ice cream...What is wrong with this picture???

Q: Why are there no restaurants on the moon? A: No atmosphere.

To all fathers out there – enjoy the remaining 93 minutes of your day, and then remember it is only 364 more days until you are right again...

t

Tom does NOT have a simple mind. Simple needs...maybe, but not a simple mind. That is me and I am sure it is becoming more evident as you continue to read. We make an interesting pair.

Guestbook Note
... seems like God is sending a common theme to folks in Iowa and Texas that "He is good ALL THE TIME" and "ALL THE TIME, He is good." A simple, but important reminder that He remains your source for all

things. Trust that many are calling on Him to provide strength, peace, understanding, and calm for all four of you! Your journal entries reflect HUGE trust in Him and His plan and they serve as reminders for all of us to remain courageous and trusting no matter the issue. Peace and Blessings to you!
Isaiah 40:31; Jeremiah 29:11; Phil 4:13; & Psalm 121 (remember that one Tom?!)

Guestbook Note
Mary just read all the journal entries. They were so enlightening and described so well what you and Tom have experienced. You and your family are in my thoughts and prayers.

> Love,
> Grandma Kathyrn

Day 48, TUESDAY, JUNE 22, 2010 8:17 AM

Tom: Just a quick update this morning…from Tom

Amy is leading her mosaic classes at Forever Faithful Ministries horse camp today. (God uses broken pieces to make beautiful things.) She is not to be touching the tiles since it is very easy to get cut and infections are a major no-no. She is very excited about these and her *Designed To Shine* program – feeling that they are both a part of her calling.

She is still feeling physically very good, but a little more tired – maybe from overdoing it the last few days! However, the dreaded side effect is starting to show up – lots of hair in the brush last night and this morning. This may be the most intrusive and obvious physical reminder of the whole battle. Please pray for Amy's strength and spirits as we enter the phase that will have the constant reminder of the chemo and the cancer.

We are still planning on going to Port Aransas on the 4th and staying for the week. We will be hanging at the beach and trying to forget the events of the world for a few days. Please pray for peace and strength for all and comfort for Amy; it will be chemo II plus 5 days when we leave. Hopefully on the backside of the worst of the impact days.

Psalm 121:8

"…let your light so shine before others, that they may see your good works and glorify your Father in heaven." - Matthew 5:16 (TNIV)

Guestbook Note

Hey Amy... I'm sure you've thought (and wrote) about how the treatment experience this year will be such a great platform for sharing God's love and increasing empathy with so many people. God uses all things for good. I would not ever choose for you to go through this. But what a blessing to witness how you and Tom handle it. And how God is part of your lives. And the wonderful way that you use it to inspire others. It doesn't mean you're strong all the time, or don't need others. In fact, you've been open to sharing how we all need each other. You are truly designed to shine, Amy. Broken pieces assembled into a beautiful life. Thank you for letting your light shine. You're beautiful. With or without hair covering up part of you.

Guestbook Note

Shine on Amy, with a perfect head of hair or with uncluttered perfection!
shine
make 'em wonder what you've got
make 'em wish that they were not
on the outside looking bored
shine
let it shine before all men
let 'em see good works, and then
let 'em glorify the Lord – The Newsboys
I pray that God fills you up, winds you up, and sends you out to amaze those you touch. Big moments or small, keep shining.

Day 49, WEDNESDAY, JUNE 23, 2010 10:28 PM

Amy: Just a brief update on what has been going on here at the Hauser household...

Running every which way with summer activities. I have been carting 5 kids to Forever Faithful Ministries the past 2 days and tomorrow is our last day of mosaic work with the beginner horsemanship day camp crowd. We have had a blast even though it is 95 each day plus humid. We have a huge outdoor A/C unit and a tent over our heads. The kids have been having a blast in the pond after the work is done and making great memories. The running keeps up until dusk or so it seems.

My hair is still there but thinning by the minute. Tomorrow Sue is bringing her head trimmers over and I think Tom and I are going to just get it off. Yikes. Anyway, so many people seem to be worrying about this more than me. God just seems to totally have my back on this ordeal and I couldn't be happier. Don't get me wrong, I am not looking forward to being a skinhead but I am okay with it. Kids seem to be really okay with it so we are good. No worries.

In His grip, in all of it!

Amy

When I look back and see how active I was during treatments and how determined I was to keep my commitments, I am so grateful for God's goodness and His grip on my life. By my previous own nature, I could have easily become stagnant and defeated. The determination to live out Romans 8:28 had been impressed upon my heart over the previous four years. Several "wrong" choices had been made because of my laziness in seeking out His voice. I had decided it was easier to listen to the voices of comfort, selfishness, and pride; and the price that I paid was huge. I now had the opportunity to make some serious changes and I wasn't going to let Satan have the final word. Faith without deeds is dead. Game on, hair or no hair.

Guestbook Note
Hang in there - I know the first sign of hair loss is scary. Everyone is different, but for me the fear of losing my hair was much more traumatic than the actual event.

The one big benefit is much less time spent in front of the mirror :) I am three years out from chemo and radiation this summer - PRAISE GOD! Think on this from the good old Heidelberg Catechisms as you go through the next few days and weeks: Your faithful Savior watches over you in such a way that not a hair can fall from your head without the will of your Father in heaven. (my paraphrase)

Day 50, THURSDAY, JUNE 24, 2010 5:52 PM

Amy: It is 6 p.m. on Thursday evening. I have no idea if I am supposed to be somewhere or doing something. This new "chemo brain" has settled in to my body pretty seriously. If I don't look at a calendar, I have NO IDEA where I am supposed to be or anything. As moms, we usually just KNOW where kids should be most of the time; when practices are, appointments, etc. by instinct. That is no longer the case for me. I live by my calendar and if I don't see it, good chance it will not happen! That is really strange to me. Yesterday I stopped to get gas and pulled up to the wrong side of the pump with the car I have had for 3 years. Things like that happen about 10 times a day now. Bad news.

Sue just came by with the hair trimmers. I am chickening out on doing it tonight. I think I will wait until Saturday. The ponytail seems to be holding things together pretty well. Sue thinks I should wait another few days. We have dinner plans with some of our friends tomorrow evening that have been on "holiday" for 3 weeks ("holiday" is for our South African and British friends' sake). We are blessed to have so many new friends from all over, like the ones we are having dinner with. I think I want hair for tomorrow evening's outing. So...

Today was our last day of doing mosaics with the Cowkids Day camp at Forever Faithful. All 21 kids finished their projects without a single sliced finger!! THAT IS AMAZING!! The weather was so much cooler today as we had a solid cloud cover and then even scattered storms. We were under a large tarp/tent so we stayed pretty dry. Thanks to Robyn, Tamsyn, Lisa, Sara, Avery, Addison, Ross, Gayle and Mich'elle for helping these past 3 days! These are some gals and moms that went through my *Designed to Shine* sessions at The Woodlands United

Methodist Church/The Loft this past school year. They had all done mosaic work with me during our mini retreat and wanted to help with DTS going forward. This is just one aspect of my retreats but God has allowed me even little ways to work with kids and get some of the girls involved in helping others as we go through this journey. I may not be able to do my retreats this summer but this is still wonderful! I think everyone had a great time, learned something, shared their talents, and helped someone else along the way. When we take time to do something for others, I think it can do amazing things for the soul. It is some of the best medicine I have had in years! (And I have had a lot lately!)

Now for those of you that are curious about the mosaics and what they have to do with the ministry...I have always loved mosaics and have been curious about the craft. By nature, I am not artistic or crafty in any way. I think mosaics, especially the ones using broken tiles and pots, drew me in because of the randomness of it all. Nothing perfect, nothing with clean lines, nothing with set rules. Anyway, I took a class on how it was done then decided to start making starfish mosaics after reading the memoir, <u>Ocean Star</u> by Christina DiMari. (This too is another aspect of my ministry, which I will explain at a later time.)

As Tom was preparing our family for a move to Houston with a new career path, and moving ahead of us by several months, I was spending some of my evenings in the garage working on mosaics. During this time, God gave me a story to tell for the various steps in this craft. I felt that I was to use this new skill to work with kids with troubled lives, helping them understand a bit about brokenness in their lives and how we have choices when we have bad things happen to us or when we do things that hurt others. It is a long story as we go through and break tiles, but basically we discuss what the broken pieces of tile represent. The tile pieces are OUR own life events. These are the bad things in our life; like a divorce, death, loss or whatever troubles we experience.

We all have our own different events that make up the pieces before us. Our board/canvas represents our lives. We have choices on how we handle those broken pieces. We can look at them as trash, wasted tile or pottery, and throw them out. We can be angry and hurtful because of our carelessness in breaking them or from allowing others to break them when they were ours. We can crush them and discard them...OR we can allow the Artist/Creator to use them to make something beautiful.

We can lay them on the canvas and watch the pieces come together to make a wonderful masterpiece.

This does not happen overnight though. It is a process and it gets messy again before it is finished. It takes trust when the mortar is dumped on the pieces. It takes refining to come together. It takes gentle hands to smooth out the rough edges, and in the end something unique, unlike any other, is created. And it is beautiful!

This is just a brief overview but it might give you an idea of what I do when I teach kiddos how to mosaic. I like to have a hands on experience going along with a lesson. Kind of helps it stick. No pun intended!

Have a great rest of the week, God is good, all the time!

Amy

Since this post, I have held several more Beauty in Brokenness sessions for a variety of groups. I enjoy the opportunities to create and share about our Father's design for grace and healing in our lives. While the sessions can be exhausting, the fulfillment for me and satisfaction for the participants far exceeds the effort it takes to pull them off. I can't wait to see how this program evolves over the years and hopefully becomes part of horse camps throughout the area!

Guestbook Note

Amy, you wrote: "mosaic work with the beginner horse-manship day camp crowd," So I'm trying to get a picture here, because I don't remember Robert Redford using a lot of arts and crafts in the Horse Whisperer. And then I'm thinking, "What do horses produce that would make good material for mosaics?" Um, no.

Guestbook Note

I LOVE how you're okay with the hair thing. It reminds me so much of how God held all of us during Adrianne's brain mass and heart ordeal this past winter. Although her health challenges were nothing anyone would ever choose to go through, it wasn't as horrible as some might think ... all because God was in control and we had faith in Him. It worked out great. And somehow

I just know the same will be true for you! Go get 'em, Amy and Tom!

Guestbook Note
Amy, I should finish reading <u>Ocean Star</u> today. You were such an instrument of God to give that to me to read this week. Now if everyone would just read it, I can start addressing the group emails to Amy's Pod instead of Amy's Army.
Don't move an inch away from the center of God's mighty hand. Much love to you.

Guestbook Note
I regret to inform you that you are no longer eligible to use this site for your writing. You see, this site is for people to write about their troubles as they battle a significant illness. Then Guests are to write uplifting things to make the sad person feel better. You are the one making people feel better. Hence, all of us will have to write the "journal" entries from now on, while you use the guest book. We are the broken pieces. You are the master artist helping us see the beauty as you put us together. For example, you wrote, "When we take time to do something for others, I think it can do amazing things for the soul." And then you are kind enough to create a succinct how-to manual on mosaics for the rest of us. People pay big money for the type of information you're just handing out, ya know. I love your enthusiasm, love and inspiration, Amy (Tom, too). I believe it's part of a choice you make each day with God's help.
Your transparency through all this is what allows people to see GOD at work.

Guestbook Note
"... the ocean stars that survive the pounding waves and don't get washed up on shore to die are the ones that attach themselves to the rocks and hold on tight!" (<u>Ocean</u>

Star pg. 217) You, our own ocean star, will survive these pounding waves and you will thrive because you are attached to the Rock and He Himself is holding on tight.

9

To Shave or Not to Shave?

DAY 52, SATURDAY, JUNE 26, 2010 10:01 AM

Amy: Maybe...just MAYBE God is trying to teach me a thing or two about the need I have to get my own way. You see, I had decided I would shave my hair Saturday or Sunday AFTER a night out on the town with some of our new friends here, Barry and Karin. I had PLANNED to enjoy my Friday at a leisurely pace for a change. BUT NO! The day started to fill up quickly with busy kids, errands, dog and cat appointments for unexpected swimmers ear, etc. I did however make time to get in the pool to tread water for 20 minutes shortly before needing to run Ross to a buddy's. This is when the crisis began that would throw me into a hissy fit.

As I got out of the pool and went to shower, all was well UNTIL I tried to run my brush through the heavily conditioned locks that remained on my head. RATS NEST is the term that came to mind! Clumps were falling and the remainder was a huge knot. I guess dying hair and chlorine do not mix. Time for desperate measures as my kids looked on with concern. Not the scene I really wanted an audience for. They kindly left me to my own pity party.

I called Tom in a panic and somewhat kindly asked him to get home now to shave my head. Bless his heart, as he was there in short order. Only a few tears were shed but I decided humor was best as he whacked away at my hair then took it to a stubble. Brittany Spears just kept coming to mind. I would rather be me than her, in the crazed state of mind that she was in when she took the razor to her head. At least I had no paparazzi looming to capture the moment for the history books. Believe me though...Tom did ask if I wanted to capture the moment. No words needed to let him know I did not think that was funny. A simple look and he got the message.

Once it was over and Tom returned to work and I had vacuumed up the remains, Sara and I had to run the pets to the vet. I had a load of newly purchased scarves and not a clue how to use them. So what did I do? Grab my old black Nike baseball cap that I have had for 15 years and head out the door. Needless to say, I did not look too good. It is amazing how quickly people look at you then politely turn away when you have no hair! This will take some getting used to. I understand they don't want to come across as staring but it just feels different.

I experienced this at a different level last evening. Tom and I met some friends at Perry's Steakhouse, which is a lovely upscale contemporary place where most folks are dressed quite nicely; while I wore a sundress and heals, with a poorly wrapped scarf adorning my obviously bald head. Though my makeup was of course done to a T, I still stood out as the lady with no hair. I cannot explain the feeling really. It just seems as though people feel sorry for you or something and really...that is the LAST thing I want people to feel. I suddenly went from having cancer, but when in public looking the same as everyone else; then in no time being set apart from everyone, just because of my outward appearance. It gives me a new appreciation for what someone with disabilities might go through all their life. Mine is only temporary but hopefully life changing in how I treat others. Something to think about. Why so many tough lessons to learn in life?

By the way, this public observation of mine DID NOT affect my ability to have a FABULOUS night out. It is simply what I do as a fan of people watching. It is a hobby of mine, loving to observe the human race. That being said, we had a great time and the food was almost as good as the company we kept for the evening. To die for Mojito's at Perry's, by the way!! Thanks for the wonderful treat Barry and Karin!!

Signing off as I get tighter in His grip,

AMY

At first it is so hard to fathom losing your hair and not looking like the rest of those around you, then oddly it can be hard once your hair is back and you are lumped back in with everyone else again. Sounds messed up, I know. The process of standing out as different and "sickly" is nothing anyone ever wants. Yet for me, the transition back, after so much special care and attention, was also very difficult. The focus diminishes as hair and strength return. While not back to "normal," the world begins to treat you as such. Either way, God is with us before, during and after all our trials.

Revelations 21:6 reminds us once again just who we can and ought to lean on when these feelings start to overtake us. "It is finished! I am the Alpha and the Omega--the Beginning and the End. To all who are thirsty I will give freely from the springs of the water of life." (NLT)

Guestbook Note

I was at the altar tonight at The Loft when the candles were being lit. Your seashell is still there. The lovely woman who is the altar caretaker said it would stay there until you, Amy, pick it up at the end of this journey. It is surrounded by melted wax and steeped in prayer. It is there on the altar as our continual prayer before God even when all of us are asleep. One day I hope it will be in a box, maybe one covered in mosaic, filled with cards and scarves and that beautiful pink blanket, all serving as a witness to God's loving care.

10

Busy, but Not Fun

DAY 54, MONDAY, JUNE 28, 2010 10:21 PM

Amy: This week is a busy one but not in the "summer-fun-for-a-stay-at-home-mom" kind of busy that I wish it was. That struck me again today as I was driving myself to and from several health related appointments. I hate missing the freedom and fun of summer with the family. Even though I have been feeling FABULOUS the past 10 days, so much of my time and energy is spent on this PROBLEM. I wish it did not demand so much of my time. Life goes on. As said once or twice before...Life is what happens when we are busy making other plans.

The busy week started last night as I called my go-to gal, Kristie, to see if we could get a few things on the schedule this week for Sara. I hadn't fully realized just how many appointments I had and knew it would be best to keep Sara occupied as Ross is at Edge Camp all week with hundreds of jr. and sr. high kids from church. Between Kristie and a handful of other super moms, we had Sara booked and scheduled in no time. That's when the first pang hit of another week of her doing things while mom is "not well." Sara willingly went to visit her friend Laura, as Laura has been in Brazil since school got out, so I knew today would be a fun day for her. After dropping her off I went to have my blood work done to make sure I am good to go for round 2 of chemotherapy tomorrow. After blood work I returned some not so great scarves to Target, went to Memorial Herman Hospital for my nuclear medicine injections related to a bone scan, met Tom for lunch (my highlight of the day!) then back to the hospital for my bone scan. Not exactly a fun filled summer day. Could be worse.

Tomorrow is chemo again and I have to say; I am not looking forward to it a bit now that I know what follows. I am praying that the last go around was just real hard due to the fact I had minor surgery the day before, as well as all the other stress leading up to the chemo. I ask for prayers that I will be strong and healthy and not as sick as before.

We have been busy planning for our trip to Port Aransas and getting everything in order for a Sunday (July 4) departure. Ross is bringing his friend Kade who is so much like Ross, and Sara is bringing her friend Erin. Erin is flying in from Memphis, TN on Saturday! We are thrilled that her parents (dear friends of ours with whom we travelled to China 10 years ago this November, to get Sara and Erin!) are letting her come to the camp with us. We get to see Erin and her family about once every year or two and this will be Erin's second trip to Houston since we have lived here. Sara and Erin are from the same orphanage in China and are only a month apart in age. Anyway, the 4 kids (all adventurous souls and slight dare-devils) will be doing surf camp during the week of July 5-9 so this will give Tom and I some much needed R&R...as long as no tropical storms (Alex in particular) come ashore that week!! Looks like one is on its way. North Padre is almost four hours drive time and I would hate to get there and have everything cancelled. There is another prayer we could use...that it sends great surf waves but no strong storms inland! Especially toward North Padre/Mustang Island/Port A.

Well, I am going to sign off. I am comfy in my bed with my prayer shawl from Micki and Linda in Des Moines, my Breast Cancer chemo blanket from SO MANY in Granger, Indiana and my Hope book from Jan in Des Moines...oh, and my steroid and anti nausea pills from my oncologist in Houston! Good night my friends and family. Sleep well, dream big, pray passionately and love continuously!

In His grip and soaking in YOUR prayers and verses that you have sent through this journey.

Fondly,

Amy

PS- I will post a pic of my "new hair do" one of these days so stay informed!

I hadn't realized how focused I was on being so busy before the cancer. We let busyness defines us. It unofficially ranks our internal value system. For me, cancer was part of my slowing down and re-evaluating just how I was spending my time and what my priorities were and should be. I still suffer from over commitment in some ways, but the shift has been for the better. I miss the amount of quiet time I had with my Lord during my chemo, surgery, and recovery times, and I long for more than I get today. What a priceless gift it was, once I chose to accept it for what it was. Not a punishment but rather a time to learn and grow.

Guestbook Note

Thank you for your honest record of your cancer journey. I appreciate you sharing your emotions, feelings, up and downs. It makes me feel like I am there with you. What a great group of friends God has put in your life. My prayers will be with you as you begin round two tomorrow and the days to come.

11

False Eyelashes

D<small>AY</small> 55, TUESDAY, JUNE 29, 2010 10:25 PM

Amy: So today was chemo...round II. Piece of cake so far. Tom came and we chilled in the big comfy recliners and had about a 2 hour plus chat with some new friends, Debbie and Randy. Debbie is dealing with a recurrence of cancer after breast cancer 10 years ago. Hers was metastatic then and has now reappeared in her lungs and liver, I believe. Strong in her faith and just seem like neat people all around.

God has put so many wonderful people in our lives since all of this. It has really been a blessing. Like tonight, I went to Wal-Mart and I was looking for false eyelashes since I hear one of the medicines I am getting usually makes them fall out. Thought I should get some just in case I may want to look nice for something...anyway, I asked this worker who was stocking a shelf nearby where they might be. She let me know that she was deaf but we were able to communicate enough to understand one another. While I was looking at the eyelashes, but walking away without any (most were WAY TO GLAM for the no hair look!) she tapped me on the shoulder 'saying;' "you didn't find what you were looking for?" I shook my head as if to say; "no, not really." She motioned me over to her boxes and got out a pen. We had about a 5 minute written conversation about cancer, life, eyelashes and so on. Neat conversation. At the end, she hugged me and said, "I will pray for you tonight." Wow. I was so touched. I don't think I want to wear a wig. I might miss out on blessings like this if I do. Don't get me wrong, many folks (especially women for some reason) still pretend they don't see me. That needs to be their problem, not mine.

Oh, some good news to report! Oncologist called today and my MRI guided biopsy that I had a week ago for another area of concern on my right breast came back normal...no cancer cells looming! Just a fibroid! See...God IS good, ALL the time!!

Praying for an easier time post chemo. The rough spots hit a few days post IV day. I am sure you will know based on me journaling or not AND what I write!

A final note...thanks so much for all the texts, emails and guestbook entries today. You are all so faithful and caring. We all appreciate your heartfelt concern. And Lee, you crack me up so much! You are such a wit! I didn't realize you were so poetic! Karin, Sara had a great time today with you and your daughter. She is excited for the movie and hangout time tomorrow. Kristie, thanks for everything and taking me to my injection/fluids tomorrow and my brain scan. You rock! And everyone else for doing all that you do! Krista, you are on my heart and mind every day and in my prayers and I know you are so strong. I will be thinking of you at your dad's lake house this holiday weekend. Love you. Miss you. Miss all of my family and far away friends! Oh, and to Carole, Joey, Amy and Julie. I am so very sorry about your wonderful dad's recent passing. Joe was like family to us. All of you are. Stay strong. You are constantly in my thoughts and prayers for strength.

I AM FINALLY DONE! Good night and thanks for reading.

In His grip, and so are you!

Amy

I still see that woman at Walmart every so often. I always make sure to tap her on the shoulder and say hello. She always has boxes in her cart so we can write notes back and forth. She has even met my kids and so the blessings continue down the line. Thank you, Lord for teaching me to stop and smell the roses.

Day 56, WEDNESDAY, JUNE 30, 2010 9:00 AM

Amy: Last night in my entry I forgot to mention that Tom's Uncle Bo passed away this week as well. Bo and Doris lived primarily in Sebring,

FL so they could golf and enjoy the sunshine all year long. They still own a home in Union, Iowa right next to the golf course though, as Union was home early in their lives! Doris is still in Sebring and last I knew she was still playing a bit of golf even though she is more than legally blind! What an amazing couple and so much fun to be with! Bo worked for the CIA in Washington, DC and from afar, as did Doris, for most all of their careers. Bo has some amazing stories about the Cuban Missile Crisis, JFK and the Bay of Pigs. Just ask Tom some time as he was quite fond of Bo. Doris was Bob Hauser's sister (Tom's dad who passed a few years back). Prayers for Tom's family and especially Aunt Doris.

PS-still feeling great today so far!

Make it a great day!

Amy

In the midst of personal pain, praying for others does not come naturally. Creating the discipline of putting others' needs before your own can shrink your personal monsters to a more manageable size. For me, I would keep a list of specific needs and pray through these daily. This kept my struggles in perspective and reminded me I was not alone. See James 5:16.

Guestbook Note

I LOVE reading your journal entries. You are such an inspiration. I am learning so much about life by experiencing your cancer second hand via the journal. I love the story about the Walmart clerk and false eyelashes. I think I'd skip the wig too.

Day 56, WEDNESDAY, JUNE 30, 2010 8:05 PM

Amy: Just settling down after a busy day. Karin and Kayley picked Sara up for a movie and ice cream (better really, Berripop!) while Kristie took me to my fluids/injection appt. For that couple of hours, she and I talked and talked and had an amazing conversation. After that, we dashed over to Memorial Hermann for my brain scan. Although it was loud, I was able to catch a quick nap! I am getting used to all these noisy machines and can sleep through the racket. While at the hospital, we had some great conversations and encounters once again. While God is clearly all over this and the reason for all the talks, I am in need of more energy. By the time I got home, talked on the phone, had a few visitors, I am beat. I just wish I had more talk-power. As many of you know, I never have been real chatty on the phone or lengthy in emails or letters. In person is another thing. But right now I am feeling a strong need to talk and listen to everyone and hang on to everything being shared, though I am not real lively by the end of the day. That being said, I am about done typing. Hopefully more tomorrow. I just pray the steroids don't keep me up too much tonight. Tired but can't sleep. Not so much fun. If you hear from me tomorrow that will be a good indicator of how I am feeling!

Blessings from Texas,
Amy

Guestbook Note
The song "Jesus Loves Me" popped into my head yesterday morning and after I had sung (in my head) "Jesus loves me this I know" I thought about you and how Jesus loves you. Than I thought about what you'll likely experience in the next few days and I changed the words for you to sing (Aloud or to yourself).
It is:
"Jesus loves me this I know
for the Bible tells me so.
Gals like me to Him belong
We are weak
but He is strong.
Yes, Jesus loves me.
Yes, Jesus loves me.
Yes, Jesus loves me.
The Bible tells me so."

Guestbook Note
Amy glows with an internal spotlight that is nearly blinding in its pure brilliance. Seemingly everyone whose path we crossed wanted to talk to her or tell me

how beautiful and joy-filled she looks. She smiles at everyone, even people who are barely looking at her, and that smile would make anyone want what she's radiating, the peace and joy of the risen Christ. It is a breathtaking, life-changing sight to behold. Her openness to God's unfolding plans would bring you to your knees on so many levels. I cannot imagine anyone feeling sorry for her. There is still the road ahead to travel, but fear and pity are not invited along for this ride.

God is so amazing. We want nothing but You, Lord.

Guestbook Note

You may be a bright light to us; but the people you know are also really amazing. The experience, wisdom and love shown to you through them leave me awestruck. The faith and trust in Jesus is reassuring and so joyful. I do not pity you, but hate that you have to go through all of this. But, you do shine for Him through all of it. I feel so blessed to know you and to read the wonderful notes in your guestbook.

Honestly, this entry and guestbook is a bit tough to read back on. The reality of it is that life has gone on. The comments of your face "radiating" God's goodness fade. Whatever it is that causes some people to shine brightest for God in their darkest moments, they eventually find out that the glow doesn't last forever in that initial state. Not that the heart isn't still feeling and reflecting Him, it is just not as obvious. This "lack luster" feeling can be a bit troubling on days when your phone doesn't ring. What I now understand is that it is a different type of "refining through fire." For me, it has to do with knowing what really drives me and what distractions I face when striving towards a particular goal. Peace with who I am and WHOSE I am. Of course, this isn't an issue for everyone.

Being driven by the accolades and approval of others is bound to eventually fade and disappoint. The resulting void only leads to a search for the next external "fix." Understanding our value in Christ allows us to break free of the ups and downs of human expectations and enjoy relationship with others as God intends.

Day 57, THURSDAY, JULY 1, 2010 11:23 AM

Amy: Just a quick note to say I am still feeling pretty good! I think I was pretty bad last go around at this time. Not quite sure though. Hope to run to the church and pick up Ross from his return trip from Camp Tejas. Sara will be going home with Rhonda as she picks up Kade from camp. Sara and Mia will visit her horse, swim, and do some fun summer hang out stuff and stay for a sleep over. Sara says, "Yea, one more day without a brother!" Nice. Ross will enjoy a quieter return home with no sissy. All is well. God is good.

Day 57, THURSDAY, JULY 1, 2010 8:34 PM

Amy: I am once again blown away by all the journal notes, visits and food! With all due respect Houstonians, don't you have a life? I cannot get over how much you pour yourselves into our family. I am not sure how to take this all in sometimes. Words do not even come. I think I had 5 visitors today with either food, gifts or hugs. I love you all. I am sorry if I cannot keep up with the emails. I try. Know that you are all so special.

Ross made it home and I was able to be there to pick him up. What a great time had by all the kids. I know several of you that read had kiddos on the trip and I don't know about yours but Ross had a blast. Everything was amazing he said. He seems to be more mature in all ways. Of course, it didn't hurt that his closest 5 friends or so were in his cabin and his girlfriend was on the trip too. Pretty awesome time for a soon to be 15 year old! Great memories and great time to grow in faith. Amen and thank you Lord!

I am getting ready to hit the hay. Tom and Ross went to Sports Authority for something Ross had to have tonight and to buy fireworks after that. Sara is at Mia's having a nice night. Sara texted me and said she got to ride Mia's horse, Prince, and that was fantastic. Do kids seem to have it so good these days or WHAT!!!??

I am going to curl up with a little Ambien tablet and call it a night. Doing pretty well. Can't complain. Feel stronger in my heart than I can ever remember. Thanks to you all and of course, our faithful Father.

I thought I might not ever get back to sleeping without a pill after all the trouble I had through the treatment and healing period. I can honestly say that now I rarely ever need a Melatonin capsule (a natural sleep aid) to help get some rest. It has not been easy but with the desire to stop masking symptoms and instead get to the root of the issues, I have found ways to combat the sleep problems. With scripture in my head, advice from doctors and learning to let go each day, I remember that I am still, and always will be, in His grip.

> **Guestbook Note**
> Serving Amy helps me more than I could ever help her and I publicly thank God for calling me to work for Him. Hoping everyone gets an opportunity to serve our Father today.

> **Guestbook Note**
> With every test, there is a testimony and I know that you will have a great one to share.

> **Guestbook Note**
> After years of trying, you've accomplished what Kirk couldn't...we finally got a computer. I didn't want to depend on anyone else to keep me in touch with you. You're in our hearts and prayers and know that our arms surround you. You are an inspiration, Amy. We're so sorry you have to endure this battle, but know you will win the fight.

Day 58, FRIDAY, JULY 2, 2010 9:53 AM

Amy: It's 10 a.m. It is really dark out. Rain is pounding down. After affects of hurricane Alex looming up and down the coast today I suppose. Get it all out of your system before the holiday weekend and surf camp to follow. Rain away! Just hoping for sun on Monday! Not much else happening at our house anyway. Feeling pretty cruddy today. I think the steroids are fading out of my system and that leaves me pretty zapped and a bit achy and upset in the belly.

My faithful Tess is curled by my side. She is so protective of me that she won't even let Bear cat come up on the bed. They have this look they exchange and the cat just takes off. It is kind of sad but for those of you that know Tess, she is a beautiful and sweet Golden Retriever but she takes no flack from other cats or dogs...or wild animals that have ever crossed her path for that matter. They don't even live to tell about it. She is one protective dog. She is a rescue dog and she is so protective of her family (unless there is a wig on a styrofoam head on the back deck... then she is a complete chicken!! Thanks Sara B!)

Today I plan to lay low as Ross heads to the movies with two buddies. Rhonda will run the boys there as she drops off Sara from the overnight. Sara is then going with Mich'elle, Bebe and all their girls (maybe more moms and daughters too, not sure - from the *Designed to Shine* moms and daughters) to have lunch and then go to a "paint your own pottery" outing. Perfect for a rainy summer day. They are going to a place that they had once made a gift for me at the end of a previous *Designed to Shine* series. Gayle and all the girls made a beautiful starfish platter for me with thumbprint starfish representing each girl in our group. The border of the plate has quotes from our study as well as verses. It was such a surprise and such a unique gift. I was blown away. Now they are going again to take Sara for an outing to make something cool. These are women who just give and give of themselves and it has been an honor to get to know them and their daughters. Funny how God lined up all those relationships before any of the cancer was discovered. Just when you think you are doing something for someone else, it completely comes full circle!

When you get those tugs in life that you need to reach out, do something for someone else. Say hello to someone. Ask someone for coffee. Go to the party. Attend a seminar or class. Teach something. Just do it. God is ALWAYS trying to open doors, guide you to a path that you might not want to take. He always has a much bigger plan for you. So often we just want to do things our way. He is okay with that too. He is always there to catch you when you choose to turn to him to bail you out of whatever mess you turned things into. Life can be amazing when you finally tune in to GOD ALL THE TIME (and let me tell you I have not been one to turn and listen to Him much AT ALL until the past few years). He has such amazing things to reveal. It is a long process but we can do it step by step. You will be amazed at how many people will be there to join in the fun! Time for a little nap.

Amy

Guestbook Note

Amy, it has been such a pleasure having your kids! Sara is such a wonderful, sweet young lady. Such quiet confidence - I bet she could handle anything! Ross, well with all that testosterone, what can you say? You get those boys together and they are loud and fun - they crack me up!! You are blessed with 2 awesome kids! (and a great husband and a heckuva dog!) Enjoy this quiet rainy day.

Guestbook Note

Meeting you during our Design To Shine was an inspiration for me to be a better person, mother and woman. I thank you for your time and dedication that you offered to us so freely.

"Keep your eyes open, hold tight to your convictions, give it all you've got, be resolute, and love without stopping."

12

At the Beach

Day 60, SUNDAY, JULY 4, 2010 9:56 PM

Amy: Just a quick note to say HAPPY FOURTH OF JULY and that we have safely arrived at the beach house in Port Aransas, TX. We had a pretty quick trip here and the kids were on skateboards and in beach clothes in no time. I am feeling really strong and not even very tired! GOD HAS BLESSED THIS ROUND OF TREATMENT SO MUCH!

Tom and the kids bought tons of fireworks but it is almost too windy tonight to light them, at least on the beach. They may do some out back yet. Who knows? Saw lots of fireworks from surrounding towns from all over. It looks beautiful from the beach! Sara and Erin have been chasing sand crabs and screaming like...like...a bunch of little girls! Surf camp starts at 9 and the waves are looking pretty big! Yikes! Better them than me.

All of us firmly in His grip,

Amy plus 5

Keeping active and sticking with prior plans helped maintain a sense of normalcy and kept life on a comfortable plane for the whole family. A balance between the knowledge that mom is going through a tough stage, yet at the same time letting them see that in tough and challenging situations, mom can be, well...tough! Actually practicing what we preach, sometimes you have to be tough, even when you don't feel like it.

Day 63, WEDNESDAY, JULY 7, 2010 9:57 AM

Tom: This is Tom. Amy is feeling good and the kids are enjoying surf camp. Today's daily email from Rick Warren (author of <u>The Purpose Driven Life</u>) struck just the right cord of encouragement to say thank you to everyone for all you have done for us - thoughts, prayers, calls, notes, food, helping, encouraging. To all of you out there, the answer to his question (about having a handful of loving fellow believers who are always there, even if just to sit in silence and share the pain) is an unequivocal "YES!!!" See 1 Peter 3:8; 1 Corinthians 12:26; Romans 12:15; 1 Thessalonians 5:11.

t

Day 63, WEDNESDAY, JULY 7, 2010 10:36 AM

Amy: TWO POSTS IN ONE DAY!

Tom and I are sitting in this really hip coffee place on the island called Coffee Waves. We took the kids to camp, had a great homemade small town diner breakfast at this dive, then came for more coffee (and Dew) and gelato for dessert! What a great day when you have dessert for breakfast. Ladies, the upside of chemo is that you are supposed to eat whatever tastes good and I still think everything tastes good! My oncologist says don't make major lifestyle changes now so I still eat some things that I shouldn't. I am much more aware and am making several healthy changes, but c'mon. The biggest work will be on my whole family. They are a wreck when it comes to eating healthy. I certainly have my work cut out for me there.

Anyway, Tom and I are having some fun while the kids are at camp in the day. I AM BLOWN AWAY at how well I am feeling. I start each day with about 10 minutes of yoga moves and stretches to keep strong, thanksgiving prayer time and a good breakfast...then I am GOOD TO GO! My tasters still work well but I have to say that wine has lost its appeal. Bummer but oh well. Food is more important to me than wine!!! Thank goodness!

We will head back to the pier shortly, where camp is, and do some more video and photos. I want you all; Rhonda, Larry, Kye and Charlie, to know that we are having a great week with your kids. Sorry if they don't call much. We don't get back to the house until about 3 then they clean up and are either playing games, back at the beach or pool or chilling in front of a TV for some rest. We have been either going into the beach town or to the beach in the evenings. Last night we drove on the beach and found a good skim boarding and shelling spot and swam for a few hours. I was the only bald lady in a bikini that I saw all evening! NICE… :0'

They have honestly been out for the night by 10 or 10:30. Anyway, I will try and post again, or download Facebook photos daily, but I love just relaxing and TRYING to forget about cancer; but frankly when I journal, it is on the forefront of my mind. So, no entry means closer to a normal life most of the time. Love that so many say they miss it when I do not journal but know that we are thinking of you NO MATTER WHAT!

Lastly…some of you might get the false impression that Port Aransas is this amazing beach town from what I write. Know that it is not pristine beaches, real fancy beach houses and a beach town like Destin, FL or something. We are just simple midwestern folk that love dolphin, surf, sunshine and sand! I would hate for a bunch of Houstonians to book a trip here and think it is like Gulf Shores or Mexico. It is less than 4 hours from home, great restaurants, fun shops, but just know the bar is set kinda low for us!! It is pretty affordable though!

Love and hugs from Port Aransas, TX!

Amy

Day 65, FRIDAY, JULY 9, 2010 4:42 PM

Amy: Last day at the beach. The kids have been surfing for 5 days in a row and they still want more! We are so grateful that everyone enjoyed it so much. I highly recommend Texas Surf Camps program. The instructors and pros were so helpful, fun and friendly! They worked so hard at teaching the kids, playing with them on the beach and just had a great attitude all around. Fun option if you are looking for something different to do with the kids.

Guys just left to go watch a doubleheader baseball game and fireworks. The Corpus Christi Hooks. Girls wanted to hangout here and do some more shelling and beach walks tonight. I was game for a low key evening.

Tom shaved my head last night so I am REALLY bald now! No stubble in sight! Kojak. Just need a lollipop. Feels really strange.

Got an email the other day and I am not even sure who it was from. All I saw (since I miss some of what is on emails when reading from a Blackberry) was this: LIFE IS NOT ABOUT WAITING FOR THE STORMS TO PASS BUT RATHER LEARNING HOW TO DANCE IN THE RAIN.

I absolutely loved this. It is not strictly biblical; it is not complicated, yet it is profound...to me anyway.

I have had so many of you send notes about me being an inspiration and I find that very interesting as I have never really felt inspiring or anything. What all this journaling really is to me is an avenue to share a bit of the cancer journey in my life as well as my family's. I am thrilled at the thought that this can be helpful to someone and with that, I will keep writing when I can, and give God the glory when I perceive there is something helpful to another.

I do want to clarify that this journey is not easy and it certainly does not define me. I refuse to let a diagnosis in some negative way change who I am, what I feel, or how I see things. I believe that our attitude and reactions affect who we are so much more than we realize much of the time. I have wasted way too much time being in a "bad place" over the past several years, and as a family we have chosen to look at ALL OF LIFE from a more "Christ-centered place;" and that my friends, has made all of the difference.

Since we are at the beach and I happen to feel so at home at the beach (and on a ranch) more than anywhere, I will end with this thought of mine...."Although the storms WILL roll in and wind and rains will come, soon the calm seas will return and only then can some of the most beautiful treasures be found as they wash upon the shores."

In His sandy and salty grip,

Amy

— 13 —

Fear Takes a Seat

Amy: Back from vacation. Laundry is done (thanks to Tom!) and bags are put away. Kade is back with his family. Erin has arrived home safely in Memphis and Tess is home after a "vacation" with Jerry and Nell. All is well. Almost all.

Today is the first day since that first week of diagnosis that I have really allowed FEAR to enter the picture. Today it has crept back in a little. I am not happy about that. You see, a few years ago after going through some very difficult things in life, I vividly recall a conversation I had with Pastor Jane at our church (Meredith Drive in Des Moines). She talked to me about how when we encounter (or bring on, in my case!) trials and have life struggles large or small, we can picture a round table meeting taking place. At that meeting, different emotions and feelings gather for a "meeting of the minds" and I am the one controlling the meeting, so to speak. I decide who can have a seat at that table. For example, humility is welcome, sadness is welcome, courage is welcome and so on...but when FEAR pulls up a chair, I am the one to take charge and say, "there is no room for you here." I am in charge of the emotional outcome and how a situation will progress from an emotional standpoint. I cannot control many factors that are occurring when trouble comes knocking, but I can control my reactions. So when fear continues to pull up a chair, I have to kick him out before he gets too comfortable. Follow me? Pastor Jane has become a dear friend to me over the years and I have probably messed this scenario up badly in her eyes but at least this is what I took away from her talk that day long ago.

Anyway, I have been good at doing this imagery in many instances over the past few years, yet today the bully just grabbed a seat without listening. Kind of like the copperhead snake that just showed up on our patio a few months back. The good thing is, I just grabbed a shovel and it was history! That is what I am working on doing now and journaling helps.

You see, I did a little reading today on my type of breast cancer and saw some statistics that pointed out a few things that have not been brought to my attention by either my surgeon or my oncologist, and that started me worrying again. The main point of what I read talked about how my being "triple negative" has a higher rate of recurrence than other forms of breast cancer. I also read more information on the fact that my form is the most aggressively growing form. Not that this changes anything but certain words and numbers just kept resonating in my head today.

Once you start on a negative path it can just fester. I then started thinking about WHY my oncologist told me last week that he would see me on the 14th and we could talk about my latest test results (remember Kristie, you were there?) and see how the tumor is doing...does that mean something was wrong on my brain and bone scans?? If they are clear, wouldn't he have just TOLD me then? This had not really bothered me at all the past 10 days, why is it now?? Once we lick this cancer the first go around, is it going to come back again and sooner rather than later? This is what my mind has been battling since this afternoon. NUTS, I know. I have been working at keeping this kind of FEAR at bay but today...well today is just not one of those strong days. This is why I don't go on the internet much. I read what I need to know, the basics and I am trusting my doctors to do what is best.

There seems to be a fine line between "knowledge is power" and "ignorance is bliss." Each of us has to find the right balance for us individually I suppose.

Because I was in a bit of a funk this afternoon I decided to go my gym close to home. I thought some light weight lifting and treadmill would be good. I had not been to the gym since I have been sporting the new hairdo. Not a good experience. I had on a cap, a cute little workout deal AND my shiny new Nikes that just so happened to match that "deally" I was wearing and that usually never happens if you see what I usually workout in.

Didn't matter, bald chick doing weights was all the wanna-be athletes seemed to see. (I'm being harsh but so what) Felt like crap. It was like, "You don't belong here, lady because we think you might be sick." I know I am reading into it but that is what the lack of eye contact felt like they were saying. I think I will stick to walks and treading water in our pool. I am fine, please don't think otherwise. I just want to document the journey, remember?!

After the workout, I ran to HEB to pick up some much needed groceries and the feeling of "invisible" comes to mind. Kind of a strike out day except for a FANTASTIC lunch at Tommy Bahamas after church, thanks to the Salerno family. Just one of those days. This too shall pass. I just really don't feel like having "this" anymore. Too late. It now is a part of who I am.

The happy ending to today's entry is this: I have my faith. When I am in a good place or a dark place, I just talk to my Father. He knows my heart. He feels my pain. He listens and He will protect me and comfort me like no one else can. I have learned this well over the years. The hardest part is surrendering to that biblical truth. We want to do things our own way. People will come and go from your life, yet He will ALWAYS remain. He will always wait to hear from you. He will never turn away from your call. Having this knowledge has made all of "this" more than bearable. Of course all of the people He has put in my life are additional fuel for the soul.

Signing off. My apologies if this entry is hard to follow. It was hard to write.

Fondly,

Amy

As I review these posts, I don't want to add much at all but I just have to with regards to that bit on FEAR. As I read it after all these months have passed, I cannot resist the need to mention that as I used the reference of "just getting a shovel and the copperhead snake was history" and that is how I needed to try and handle fear, cut it off.

The part I didn't mention at the time and, as I reflect back maybe should have, is that after I chopped the head off of the snake, I scooped up the head and played with it awhile. I was fascinated with the fact that I was so close to danger. I just had to get a tool from Tom's tool chest, since he was gone, and start fiddling with the fangs.

Intrigued to say the least. Yes, I was aware that it was dangerous...but I was in control, right? All I will say is that it is true that snakes can still strike, even when their head has been severed from their bodies. While I did not get bit, it was a wild experience. Evil, plain and simple. Moral of the story...<u>don't entertain thoughts, feelings or situations you know may come back to bite you.</u>

Guestbook Note

I know feeling invisible sucks. People see a seemingly healthy, beautiful woman with no hair and they need to stare. But they don't want to stare because that would be rude, so they make no eye contact at all. Which is just as rude and hurtful. Please don't be angry at these people, they just don't know how to react. Most women probably feel admiration for you. They think, "wow she's so brave. I could never come to the gym/mall/restaurant with no hair!" Men? well they are probably thinking, "oooh, bald chick... nice butt!" Be patient with these people and try not to take it personally!

Fear is going to creep in and out of your life for a long time. Every time I get my annual mammogram, I think to myself, yeah, this is it, it's been too long, I'm sure it's back. It takes mental toughness to take this journey. Put your strength in God and know He is in control and He loves you so very much!

Day 68, MONDAY, JULY 12, 2010 6:32 PM

Amy: Today is a new day! Feeling great and strong...body and mind. I am grateful for all the notes today. They touch my heart so much, each and every note, email, etc. Rhonda...you made me LAUGH OUT LOUD!! Thanks.

Okay, here is the amazingly great news from my ultrasound appointment today...the doctor did the ultrasound (and has performed the other two prior to this appointment) and the tumor in the lymph node has shrunk by roughly 60%. Needless to say, Julie (my girlfriend that took me to the appointment) and I were thrilled! So was the doctor and the nurse. This is great news for only having had 2 rounds of chemo. The tumor in the breast tissue seems to be smaller yet the blood flow to the area is still evident. The doctor says this is to be expected as she says that takes several rounds to dry up the vessels. The tumor was not detectable during my mammogram and thus difficult to see, period. That in itself is unsettling ladies, as my cancer would not have been found if the large lump had not been noticed by me. Always be diligent with your own health and never ignore things that just don't seem right. Ultrasound is what detected my breast tumor...not the mammogram.

Anyway, time to chill. Been at Forever Faithful all afternoon for a great mosaic session with the intermediate Cowkids camp. Pretty good work by these kids so far. Impressive really. Smaller group and I had three of my teen gals helping today AND they are helping with the whole day camp. They are go-getters!

Make it a great day.

In His grip,

Amy

Guestbook Note

Advocacy is not easy to think about or do when it comes to our health. It is good to know about what you have in order to ask questions and cross-reference thoughts -- truly you are your best advocate for your health. It's definitely a balance -- sort through the info and move on quickly when you need to. You are a fighter...and more importantly you are armed with your faith and God's strong armor.

Give yourself a bad moment and move on. Every day is new! You are loved, you are strong even when you feel weak...and God is your guide even when you feel you are on the wrong trip. Focus on finding your balancing point in it all and remember very simply...God is good all the time, all the time God is good. It is that simple.

Guestbook Note

You are gorgeous, cap on OR off. If anyone makes you feel uncomfortable that is truly their problem. Just don't go there. They don't deserve your company. There are a lot of small minds out there...

I have a goddaughter who has M.S. We were out to dinner and people asked that she be removed from the restaurant because they said she was drunk. (M.S. affects your gait...and sometimes your speech) The owners actually asked us to leave. I was so angry I wrote them a letter. They apologized and sent a gift certificate for $400 to their restaurant. Too late...they could keep it.

Anyway, this "life" experience just gets so complicated sometimes...actually most of the time if we let it. Try to use all your good energy for you...the other small stuff and silly people aren't worth the drain on your resources. Pooh on them.

Guestbook Note

As for reading the mind of a gym rat... I'll forgo a top ten list right now and jump to my guess regarding their number one thought. I'll bet most are thinking that there is one tough, courageous person and that they are in awe of your tenacity. Wow. They may even feel a little threatened if they ever had to take you on in some pound-for-pound contest.

I pray and I trust you'll find a comfortable balance between "ignorance is bliss" and the "knowledge is power."

And I do appreciate the fact that your battle is not easy. I do not ever equate your positive spirit and trust in God to mean that the fight is frivolous or that the journey is not difficult.

Our reactions are our choice... Matthew 6:34 *"Therefore*

do not worry about tomorrow, for tomorrow will worry about itself."

Day 69, TUESDAY, JULY 13, 2010 5:56 PM

Amy: Had a fun (yet hot) day at Forever Faithful Horse Ranch. The Cowkid campers finished up gluing down their individual mosaic pieces of tile this afternoon. Some pretty good work for 8-12 year olds. Thursday will be the mortar. The final touch. The time when the kids get to see what the carefully placed pieces of broken tile will actually turn out to be.

Will it really be nice or what was hoped for? You see, as broken pieces are laid on the plain board and a rough outline of a "planned" picture is followed and contrasting tile is used, the artist must trust that the instructor is guiding them to a final product that will be successful. To the new artist, they might see a lot of empty spaces, dried glue under the pieces and jagged edges that sort of look like random placement from where they are sitting. The mortar is then mixed carefully to just the right consistency and gently smoothed over the project like grace being swept over our brokenness ever so gently yet completely. From the artist's perspective though, they see a huge mess! Over time and steady work though, as they wipe off and remove the smeary mess, they are reminded that this reveals the plan that was originally made for the piece.

Eventually as the crude slowly disappears, a beautifully outlined picture is revealed and all the efforts are realized as TIME WELL SPENT! Doubt and concern becomes a smile of accomplishment. When the artist starts to listen...and do the work, it can be worth the wait.

Mom's flight landed a short while ago. She and Tom should be home any minute. Ross's bus will be back from an outing he's on been for the past two days, visiting Schlitterbahn (a HUGE water park) followed by a river rafting trip.

Once everyone is here...all will be well! Cannot wait to see my mama.

Life is good. Maybe someone should put that on a shirt or something. Better yet (as Pastor Tony in DSM always says) GOD IS GOOD, ALL THE TIME!!

In His Grip, as you know!
Amy

Guestbook Note
Beautiful journal description of mosaic art as a reflection of God's work in our lives with the broken pieces He works with. I've got a couple of shards myself that I've been carrying around for years, squeezed tight in my hand...thinking it is way past time to hand those over to Him.

— 14 —

Mom Arrives

D<small>AY 70</small>, WEDNESDAY, JULY 14, 2010 10:10 PM

Amy: Mom/Nana/Barb is here! We have had a nice first day together. She is trying to adapt to the humidity in Houston. She can't decide if 98 and 100% humidity is worse than the 114 degrees and 10-35% humidity in Phoenix. Luckily the AC is the same everywhere.

Great news today as we went to visit my oncologist. No signs of cancer whatsoever in my bone or brain scans! Oh Yes!!! Get this...not even the slightest signs of dementia in the brain yet! How many of you can say that? Frankly, I thought I had a bit of that going on since I forget everything, but now I have no excuse other than the temporary "chemo brain." I will milk that while I can. Anyway, this is a huge relief nonetheless!

We meet with the doctor on Monday to talk about the inevitable surgery this fall. Hopefully we will discuss what will be necessary and get an idea of a time frame. As for chemo, my next is Tuesday. I would really rather not do it as we have a packed schedule and much to do while my mom is here...shopping, eating out, Wicked on Sunday evening in Houston (all 5 of us) maybe an Astros game, surfing...I could go on and on. Just dreaming. Really, I don't want to go. I will though.

By the way...I think I need to say a HUGE thank you to so many of you. I have not been good about thank you notes in all of this. I have had some neat little gifts, sweets, meal cards, notes, visits, etc. that mean so, so much to me, and I want you EACH to know how touched I am by all of this love and attention. The hardest thing in all of this is how little time I feel I have to just soak it in. Running with the kids, tons of medical appointments, trying to rest a tiny bit and other things have left me little time to screw my head on straight. My apologies for not getting notes out at this point. Again, know my heart is ever so touched. Really.

Time for rest...over did it at Forever Faithful today watching Sara ride all morning. Extremely hot but very enjoyable! Back at it tomorrow but only for a few hours.

Asta La Vista Baybeeeee.

Amy

> **Guestbook Note**
> Happy Birthday Girlfriend! Do you look fabulous in your ball cap or what?! I was so happy to hear your treatments are going well and doing the work they need to do! A real gift!
> Since I can't be there to share your day and a laugh with you, I'm sending it to you in the form of a joke:
> A college class had to write a short story in as few words as possible. The instructions were that the story had to contain the following three things: religion, sexuality and mystery.
> Here is the only A+ paper in the class:
> "Good God, I'm pregnant, I wonder who did it?"

Day 73, SATURDAY, JULY 17, 2010 10:27 AM

Amy: Thanks for all the "Happy Birthday" greetings! I have to admit that I have yet to even get on Facebook to read them all. That is on my to-do list today. I was overwhelmed and thrilled. Beth...you dear and wonderful friend from my old hood in DSM...I CRACKED UP with your short and sweet greeting joke. That was hilarious! I posted it here for those that want to get a laugh and if you don't laugh, you will get a glimpse into what kinds of things I think are funny. Shallow comes to mind but I love it! Just like the movie Napoleon Dynamite. One of my recent favorites. Simple, shallow, yet I almost cry from laughing when I watch it. Sad but true.

So my birthday was busy with finishing up the mosaic sessions at Forever Faithful Ranch. Extreme heat and busy Cowkid campers left me a bit wiped out. Robyn, Natasha, Kayley and my friends, Ruth Ann, Karin and my mom were so much help keeping the campers focused. My sweet Sara was a camper but I think she spent more of her time helping other campers than not! I simply could not have finished that day without all of them! Thank God for the hands that reach out. Serving together is what gets things done! I was super light headed that day and I needed all these gals to work around the group and help them with mortar so I would not faint! It all got done and I was ready for some down time!

That evening we went to listen to a live taping of a women's ministry study, "Named by God." We went a little early to hang out and have BDay cupcakes by who else...Martha...I mean Kristie!!! She made ALMOND JOY cupcakes that were wonderful!

Oh yes, and back to Forever Faithful for a second...Robyn ALSO made cupcakes for a surprise at camp today! She set up plastic horses on them and plastic fir trees to make it like a forest setting. They were wonderful and they all gave me a beautiful floral arrangement as well. Very touching and a great surprise. Thank you girls!!

Okay, so after the taping session that evening we went to a friend's house from LOL and had another little party. A group of us went to Julie's for hangout time. Mom and I left at 10:45 but I hear many stayed until 1:30! Crazy ladies in this group, let me tell you! Have I ever mentioned that Texans like to talk? Just ask my mom! We love it though, please don't get me wrong!

Friday was not much calmer. At 11:30 we had a luncheon with like 10 wonderful LOL friends. Micki treated us to a seat at her table! Thank you so much, friend! Everyone loved it and loved the art show! After that it was back to Forever Faithful Ranch to see Sara's barrel racing show and watch her get a camp award and trophy. Sara got the camper award of Most Kind and Caring Kid! Made momma and Nana proud! Last night was family dinner at Bravo Tuscan. Very good food and family time.

Since this week has been crazy busy, I am taking it easy today. I am actually sitting in my jammies in bed with Tess by my side and a cup of Joe in hand. Life is good. Just going to read Facebook, download some camp pics to it and hopefully to this, and read in the book of Job. I might get in the pool and eat some bday cake that Nana and Sara are going to make today. Some friends might come by this evening and chilled. See, LIFE IS GOOD!

This brings me to a list of the upsides of chemotherapy:

- Women's shower time no longer includes shaving, shampoo or conditioning!
- Any skin conditions are HEALED or BURNED AWAY, really!
- Complexion is great.
- For me, no desire for naps at all! More time to fold laundry or keep busy (this I realize could be seen as good or bad...)
- No need for hair products of any kind!
- Forgetfulness is expected for now!

In His grip - Loving all of the compassion and friendship y'all have shown to our family in your own unique ways. Please NEVER, EVER worry or compare your gifts and ways to the ways of another. We are all created as we were intended to be. When we compare our gifts, talents or lack thereof to another we are allowing fear, regret and doubt to enter into our hearts and that, my friend is not of our God. BE exactly as God intends YOU to be. If you don't know, then ask Him. Find it, unfold it and let IT flourish. IT is not the same as anyone else's. THAT is the beauty in this life – we are all uniquely gifted! 1 Corinthians 12 reminds us that the body is made up of many parts and each is honored.

You see, in the world everyone seems to want to have and act like everyone else in order to be accepted and to fit in. But why? Why should we all strive to "be" and to look like each other? Is that how we where created? NO! You know that and I know that!! So why do we fight that so desperately? Why do we celebrate our similarities more so than our individuality? You may think you don't but lets think again...really, I think we do. We say; "Wow, you just got an awesome new car or huge new home!" but do we say the same thing to the person who says I just sold my car to buy a bike and start to simplify my life and live healthier? No! We say behind his/her back; "That's different. Good luck with that one." Do you see what I am saying?

I am completely rambling on. To go full circle on this "off-paragraph" I will just say this: When you care for someone, just saying I am thinking of you is enough. If one friend brings a fancy meal because they are gifted with cooking or have been blessed with the means to pay for such a treat, it is a blessing to them and the one receiving the gift. If the next friend is one who has so much on his or her plate yet still sends a text as the thought enters their mind to someone in need, that is just as special and just as much of a blessing. Our Lord knows our heart and that makes ALL of the difference. These blessings are for the one in need anyway, not for others to compare! I'm personally not sure that others compare anyway, but rather that the fear that comes from within us is Satan's way of shutting off our desires to become more of the kind of community that bonds us together. It is our job to fight back and tell fear to GET OUT OF THAT SEAT (previous entry noted). If you disagree, I am all ears. So there!

Amy

I clearly remember this being a really good day. I am grateful to have made note of it! However, in my case, chemotherapy had another side effect – it triggered the onset of menopause. It set in after the first chemo treatment and my regular monthly cycle never returned. Another item for others to keep in mind.

As for this list of the upsides of chemotherapy, it is making me realize I need to make one for the upside of post chemo-brain and menopause too. Unfortunately, the list of these changes has meant the onset of more wrinkles, hormone related menopausal acne, stiff joints, skin issues and more hair products than ever to tame unruly strangely new textured hair! Ugh!

While these are real issues that I am facing now, I am certain that they aren't bothering me nearly like they would have only a few years ago. The opportunity to see life through a different lens has put a lid on too much complaining. While I have chosen to color my hair after I was seeing more grey than red (my God-given natural color of old) since it started to grow back, I am consciously working to focus on the blessings rather than the negatives that come from six months of poisoning my body.

Guestbook Note

Do you realize how powerful your words are? You have no idea.

Day 75, MONDAY, JULY 19, 2010 10:40 PM

Tom: Monday night – Tom here. Amy is in bed, hopefully getting some much needed rest for tomorrow's chemo #3. The docs gave her an extra strong Ambien.

It was a fun weekend, capped off by seeing "Wicked" last night at the Hobby Center in downtown Houston. It was excellent and got top marks from everyone – Ross and Sara included. I loved the plot twists and the tie-ins to so much of <u>The Wizard of Oz</u>. It is highly recommended.

Sara had piano today – she is becoming a very accomplished musician, playing more and more from memory, and while maintaining eye contact with her audience. Tomorrow is her horseback riding. Ross was at his good friend Kade's today (Kade went with Ross to surf camp) and is going to "sleep in and hang out" tomorrow.

Today was two doctor appointments: Blood test to be sure all levels are ready for chemo – we got a thumbs up from the nurse on that one. Also a meeting with the surgeon, Dr. S. whom we really like and with whom we have a great comfort. If all goes according to schedule, the surgery will be in late October. The decision is whether to do a lumpectomy, a single mastectomy or a double mastectomy. Choice one would be followed by radiation. Factors we are considering are: Amy is triple negative (meaning neither steroid treatments, nor the new drug Herceptin, will work to shrink existing, nor prevent future growths). This also increases the odds of recurrence as time passes. The other factor to consider in choice one is the difficulty of reading current and future mammograms and/or ultrasounds. Some patients' tissue (Amy included) is naturally denser and with more areas that look suspicious, leading to more concern and more biopsies. Please keep us in prayer as this big decision is weighed and prayed.

Tomorrow is chemo #3 at 10. It will be two IV's of steroids, followed by three IV's of the chemotherapy drugs. One is bright red and is so strong that if any spills on your skin, it can cause damage. The nurses treat it very gently when hooking it up. All in all, it will likely be near 4:00 before Barb brings Amy home. Hopefully this round will be more like the last and not the first.

Thanks go out to meal preparers for this week. We don't want to embarrass you, but we sure want to thank you for your generosity and unselfish giving to us. God has blessed us with a close, new Texas family. Have I mentioned how much the kids and I despise chocolate chip cookies? Especially the gooey ones with lots of milk chocolate chips that clash so badly with a cold glass of milk before bed?

Barb has been taking good care of us all week – feeding, shuttling, cleaning and all the rest. Everyone is a little tired, so please keep all of us in your prayers for strength, patience and understanding. Mainly please lift up Amy for all the above, plus healing, rest and peace of mind and heart.

Love and thanks to all...

Guestbook Note
(From Leukemia Survivor) - Father God, I lift up my sister Amy to You today. Hold her closely as she endures another round of chemo. Work in her body for good. May the chemo do its job. Pour out your mercy and grace on Amy, Tom, Ross, Sara and Barb as they travel this journey with their hands in Yours. Let them feel Your Presence every step of the way. Help them know in their minds and their hearts that You are on the move in and through these life circumstances. Thank you for the people in Texas who have embraced this family and who rally around and support them even now. I praise You for Your faithfulness!
Jesus has opened the way to You. It is in His Name I pray, Amen

Day 76, TUESDAY, JULY 20, 2010 10:35 PM

Amy: It is getting late but I really wanted to get an entry out tonight to say thank you again for all the thoughts, prayers, notes AND a great meal from Pam tonight. I am really struggling with all of this attention right now though. Sara has been with a friend all day and now tonight for a sleepover as they didn't want the fun to end! Girls and their plots to keep the activity going! Gotta love them at this age. Tomorrow the kids are with Kade and Mia S. in the afternoon. So many notes, a meal, kid care...and I just don't know why this is hard for me today. Anyway, I am so grateful and words cannot express how much it means/has all meant. Sometimes it is just really hard to "receive" and so much easier to "give."

Having my mom here has helped in so many ways. I know it was hard for her to know that there are meals coming a few times this week and next but I do have to say with chemo today and more appointments this week and so much to do with laundry, hanging with Ross and Sara and so on for her, it has been great. I feel the meal deal is a real blessing - like today after we got back from my 3+ hour appointment, it just gave us some priceless time to sit as mother and daughter and just talk for a long while, rather than her working away at making a meal while I lay low. When she is so far away, we don't have that luxury to just talk at length like we both want and need to do sometimes. It was really cool to be able to do this today. Thanks for this y'all, from mom and all us Hauser eaters.

Oh yes, chemo #3 was and is well so far. Time went very fast as the nurse was very talkative and informative today and had time to answer several questions I had about treatments and more, and that was great. My new friend Debbie and her husband Randy were also there and came in to visit and meet my mom. BTW, please consider praying for her (if you remember me mentioning her before, once again she is not feeling well and has been very weak). Unfortunately, her cancer has stopped responding to her most recent chemo meds. Her oncologist has now started a new drug with hopes of it making a difference. Debbie has had a long journey with breast cancer, being cancer free for quite a few years, then now there's a recurrence in her lungs and liver. Neat lady. I enjoy talking with her so much. I just hope she stays encouraged and her cancer will start to respond and disappear. Anyway, mom and I go back for my fluids and Neulasta injection tomorrow at 2. Neulasta is a blood cell booster and helps fight off infections between treatments. You might have seen commercials for it on TV the past few years. Anyway, this tends to make me feel flu-like for a day or two but is well worth it in the long run, or so all the docs say! So far so good as far as staying healthy through this journey.

Although I am not the least bit sleepy (due to a bod that is pumped full of steroids), my eyes are tired and my tummy is a bit off so I am going to pop an Ambien and try and get some rest.

Signing off and in His grip...with all of you there too!

Amy

Guestbook Note

It is the gift of dinner, but more importantly, it is the gift of time and of support and of esteem and the greatest of all, of love (1 Corinthians 13:13). You know that doing for others is doing for Him (Matthew 25:40) and what I love most is how everyone brings their best in His name (Numbers 18:12). No one brings frozen fish sticks and that eggplant jello mold that their own family hated. We bring what we think is a lovely dinner that our family and your family would enjoy because Jesus is pulling a chair up to the table, too. Your whole paragraph describing your struggle with receiving and the real time blessings that the "meal deal" gives should be cut and pasted on the front page of all meal calendar sign ups because it just doesn't get any more piercing and plain. How about that switching of gears for me… usually Martha, Mary for a moment. I'm pretty surprised. See… another blessing!

Day 78, THURSDAY, JULY 22, 2010 11:25 AM

Amy: Feeling pretty well today. Very tired but not too sickish (Amyism) at this point which is huge! I pray it will stay at bay. Have heard various survivors as well as others say that as treatments become more frequent, I will likely feel weaker and weaker with each passing one. I hate not to listen to experience, but the power of the mind can be more powerful than about anything. Sometimes I just want to stay in a bubble and just let it do what it will do to me as I am bathed in so much prayer and care. That FEELS like the best medicine I have had through all of this!

Learning so much about life, my family, my priorities and health this summer. Letting go of my ideals and trying to let things fall into place as they will. Very tough.

As I am sitting in my bed right now, I smell burning "toads in a hole," one of Sara's favorite late breakfast or lunch creations. She basically takes bread, uses the top of a cup to make a circle then fries an egg in the center. Tasty. Comes from an American Girl cookbook.

Anyway, I so feel the need to be out there helping. My mom is cleaning my floors and doing our laundry. Tess needs a walk. Tom took Ross to his eye appointment as a parent really needs to be there, and I am laying here. This is my house and these are simple daily things I SO want to attend to. Truly the hardest part of being sick are these such things. My heart aches to be engaged. I cannot imagine being laid up longer than I am. I really have it easy compared to so many that have much more difficult struggles than I.

All is good, just some bumps in the road.

Time for a rest.

Amy

Guestbook Note

From Barb - Since I am here with Amy and her family and can speak with her face to face...this is directed to all of her wonderful supporters. The appreciation I feel for everyone...whether you are one of her "pod" from Ladies of the Loft, one of Tom's coworkers, neighbors, church family or friends and neighbors from the Des Moines area...is beyond words. It is hard being so far removed from her as she walks this path, but just knowing that her needs...spiritually, emotionally and physically... are being attended to by others who care for her and her family is such a source of grace.

Day 79, FRIDAY, JULY 23, 2010 4:08 PM

Amy: Still laying low today. Tess and Bear have been hanging out with me most of the day. Bear the tubby orange tabby cat has been sleeping next to me and has hardly moved all day. Sympathy sickness maybe?

Ross just left with Chance and Jack to run around and long board (latest skateboard style). They love to run to Brother's Pizza in the late afternoon. Sara just left with Ruth Ann and her daughter Laura for a sleepover. Pangs of an empty house in the summertime put a lump in my throat. I cannot complain though as we had a fun time earlier. Mom, Sara, Tess and I swam before lunch. Sara loves to show her tricks to us and Tess paddles around the whole time. Ross and his buddies were here for lunch and we got to chat awhile. It is just never enough for me these days. I cherish every moment with these kids yet at the same time I want to rest. I just hate the conflict of it all. The kids seem so great about everything. Having mom around to buffer and help with shuttling, cooking and overall kid care has been so nice. I love the extra heartfelt relationship around for Ross and Sara. They so need that, whether they know it or not!

Don't feel I have much to say today. Head hurts a bit. Just feel like petting the cat more than writing I suppose. Maybe a post later on. Feeling well, don't get me wrong.

Loving the thoughts and prayers y'all.

Always in the grip!

Amy

15

Reflections

DAY 80, SATURDAY, JULY 24, 2010 11:39 AM

Amy: The house is empty for a while. Sara is still with friends and Ross is on the loose somewhere in the hood. Mom and Tom ran a few errands. Tess and Bear are faithfully planted on my bed nearby. I hate to report that I have not bounced back quite as well as I would have hoped for, this being Saturday after a Tuesday chemo round. I have been up for eggs and toast and some small talk but not much else. I did put on my swimsuit with hopes of jumping in the pool with mom and Tess after she gets back. Treading water feels great on my muscles. The good news is that my mouth feels good and no sores have developed. Food is not the enemy and I am grateful for that! It is a bit hard to keep your spirits up when you spend so much time at home. The past few days I have been in a real brain fog, so my focus is less than it usually is and that isn't saying much anyway.

I want to read a good book but don't feel like finding one. Want to write but then lose my focus or forget how to spell words. Want to walk the dog but know it is just too hot to get very far. Discouragement is more powerful than I want to give it credit for. Sometimes I just get on this site and pretend like I am with each of you that read it. It makes me feel more connected. Some thrive on success or status or whatever, while many others thrive on relationships. I am the latter for sure.

I noticed that mom brought her copy of <u>Ocean Star</u> to read while she is here. She read it once before when I first decided to do a mother/

daughter group on it. I have found it wild how many of my friends have said they went online to order a copy of it to read. I stumbled upon <u>Ocean Star</u> a few years back when I was doing some serious soul searching and talking to God a bunch about who I was as a wife, mother, daughter, sister, friend and so on, BUT I was also at a point where I was unsure of who I was as an individual.

I wanted to go back to work at some level but the desire to be with my kids was stronger than going back to the corporate HR world. Figuring out what would be satisfying and showing my children that I too had goals and abilities that took me beyond our own yard was stirring inside of me. The struggle was that I felt my interests were so juvenile. I am over 40 and want to "do" something. Our family had been blessed by the fact that I did not have to work outside the home but I knew I had too much time on my hands as the kids were growing up. I had been easily influenced and you might say, sucked in, by the "country club" lifestyle, the ease of being a stay at home mom that CAN (not everyone falls prey to this I certainly realize) suck you in and become very comfortable. I soaked in a lot of comfy living that was not a good fit for me or for my family. I knew I needed another focus that was more Christ-centered and others-centered that could still benefit my family and me.

When I thought about what I was passionate about, really passionate about, the list was short. I adore the ocean, everything about the ocean. I am in awe with sea life and diving and every living creature that walks the sandy shores. I tear up just thinking of it now as I long to be on a beautiful seashore right now. Anyway, I also knew I was passionate about horses; just being around them, outside in nature...preferably in the mountains. I am an animal and nature junkie and always have been; not that I don't have other interests, but there's not much else that could make my heart jump, or that I could just go on and on about like these two things.

When I think about it, it is sad, and maybe that is how many adults are, but I just don't feel like settling. Not now. Why do we have to grow up from our passions, why do they have to fade away? Somewhere along the line, the problem has been that I have allowed myself to be far more influenced by those around me, and have migrated to BE and DO what others around me prefer to do.

It was more important to me to "fit in" properly than to be my own true self. Does that make any sense? Probably not to those of you that have always been comfortable in your own skin. I have always felt that maybe I have grown out of my heart's desires over the years (horses, dolphins, the great outdoors…I mean come on!) so instead of pursuing them, I just saw them as childish.

I have stayed on the path I felt was more mature and appropriate for me as I became a mother and wife. The problem with doing that is you are not always sure of who you are. Once you start diverting from your purpose that has been placed within you, you start to do it all the time. You can lose sight of who and how you were designed and I don't just mean horses and the ocean. You begin to place higher value in opinions and forego the blessings emerging in your own life. Not that this cannot work; I just don't think it is the plan. God allows us to make choices along the way and things can work out fine or even really well for us. I just think He wishes we would listen more, be what He has called us to be a little more, and things will work out (maybe, just maybe) even better.

I am speaking not as if full of wisdom here, just hindsight.

I have so gotten off track. I forget where I was going with this… So I found this book (<u>Ocean Star</u>) and had been praying continuously for some time to have something I could pour myself into that really interested ME, and not do something just because it was something to do or the next "right thing" to do. I then found Christina DiMari's website and ordered the book. I loved the story yet it was not exactly show stopping to me or anything. It was not a profound; "This is the best book that will change my life" moment or anything. It was just a turning point. God said; "Here is something to get you started. Look at the dreams I have created for you." Here was a study I could use as something to do with young gals, and I wanted both to share my growing faith and to work with girls. The story hit home as to what I was going through, and I saw how I could use the story of my experiences within my talks. Things were coming together. I just gave it all to Him to use me and the material.

It started slow in Des Moines but I sensed it would grow. I just didn't know how. I knew horses would be integrated and I would be able to do sessions by the sea. I just didn't know when and how.

"Trust Me," is what I kept hearing. We moved to Texas shortly thereafter and the pieces have continued to slowly and steadily evolve. I am amazed at how many of the desires of my child-like heart have been woven into something pleasing to our Lord. It really blows me away. I just keep listening and waiting. I am frustrated with the changes to the *Designed to Shine* retreat schedule this summer and plans for sessions this summer/fall for the Rebel Base youth at church. There seem to be so many moms and teens waiting to join in and do the program that it is hard to understand why I have to wait. I know we don't get to see the BIG PICTURE, but c'mon! I have been so blessed to see things unfold and I am so anxious to keep going with all of this; I just don't like the wait. Thing is, usually He has something better yet in store; more than we can ask or imagine. Trusting; that is the hard part!

Life is a never-ending journey of peaks and valleys. Sometimes they are really close together and it just sucks the air right out of your lungs.

Not sure I ever really got to a point but I feel so much better after chatting with you all today. Not so quiet here after all!

In His grip,

Amy

This was a hard one for me to read and leave as it is. Letting everyone know that I am really not passionate about much of anything is hard to say when we are surrounded by what seems to be a world full of driven and enthusiastically focused people. As I try and let this be about what God wants, and not me, I sense the need to give my post-cancer insights.

When I think back to how HARD it was on my heart when I was diagnosed, because I thought I was finally getting things off the ground with pursuing an interest and a potential ministry (doing something I enjoyed and intermixing my faith journey in a unique way), I struggled with WHY I had to slow down. I knew in my heart God would use the cancer to grow me, but what I had little understanding of was just how PERFECTLY He uses every little bit of our lives in preparation for the next stage. Already, God has opened doors that suit me so much better than what I thought I should be doing.

What I saw as my only interests have grown into things that have been a part of my being that only HE knew I was capable of! Do you get that? When we learn to TRUST Him COMPLETELY with the "what's next" aspects and put our own plans aside, He will offer what is better than we could ever imagine! While I am still working daily to trust that He has better plans for my life than I could ever try and fit together, the outcome can and will be so perfect.

You might be thinking, "well of course it seems perfect, Amy, because you didn't have much in your back pocket to start with." Well, I think sometimes we spend too much time trying to figure out what we or our kids should be doing based on what the rest of the world thinks we should be doing that we forget to stop long enough to listen to what the CREATOR OF THIS WORLD says we should be doing!

Have hope, if you feel you lack direction. Maybe, just MAYBE, that is intentional. God knows you will one day turn to Him and beg for His will to unfold in your life. In that heart-felt pursuit; He will show you things your little earthly mind is not capable of comprehending in any form other than tiny little daily blessings. I hope you will be open to receiving them as they come. They will be there for the taking. Trouble is, they do not seem to come in any way that is recognizable, or acceptable, to our cultural ways of instant gratification.

Guestbook Note
I thought you might enjoy these scriptures today about the ocean and the horse, knowing you experience a connection with God through the ocean and horse created in wisdom by Him:
The earth is the Lord's and the fullness there of, the world and all who live in it...for he has founded it upon the seas.
Ps 24
More majestic than the thunder of the mighty waters, more majestic than the waves of the sea, majestic on high is the Lord Ps 93
Consider the horse:
God says
Who gave the horse its might?
Who clothed its neck with mane?
It can leap like a locust, it goes out to meet weapons,
it laughs at fear and is not dismayed, it does not turn back.
it lives boldly in the midst of the battle around it.
It displays by power. Job 39

$$16$$

Attitude

DAY 81, SUNDAY, JULY 25, 2010 3:11 PM

Amy: Tom gave me another "close shave" today. I love the way it feels compared to stubble. My hat kept sliding around at church today though. Need a slippy pad or something to keep it in place.

Felt pretty strong today when rising, though each day I have been wide awake at around 4 a.m., which is a drag, but I can usually dose off and on again until 8 a.m.

Was looking forward to church as usual but even more so as I had not been out of the house much in the past 3 days.

It was so good to see everyone and I cannot explain how it feeds the soul being there. Not in a million years would I have EVER thought I would look SO forward to attending weekly church services like I do now. I have always attended church, but to say I would find the COOLEST and most funnest (is that even a word?) people there would have been a total stretch. Please do not take offense anyone who I have gone to church with over the past 40+ years...please. What I mean is; I usually like to connect with some or lots of the folks there, just not the overall FEELING of wanting to be there like, all the time. Might be digging a hole here...not the intention to. I just have to say the Loft and TWUMC has blown our socks off that way. MDRC and the Bridge in Des Moines was fabulous as well, but when you are transplanted at our ages and then so quickly get the feeling that you were brought into this hip and fun fold (that we might not have ever been a part of due to our oddness) it feels so great. Oh no. What if it's a cult? I just realized. Fear just entered the picture. Oh my.

I AM KIDDING!!!!!!

If you live around here and wanna check it out. Come with. I think you will like it.

So great to see so many of you. Missing so many of you from afar, too.

Looking forward to the advanced horsemanship camp starting tomorrow at Forever Faithful. I have a Suburban full of helpers from the youth ministries at the Loft coming along with Sara and mom. Going to be much shorter tomorrow due to all the heat right now. Wouldn't miss it for the world though!

Feeling strong in mind, body and spirit today. God is good, all the time you know!

In His grip,

Amy

Guestbook Note

Dear Starfish...From my POV, the cancer just looks like a difficult shard in the mosaic of your life as you truly inspire others. Especially young people, it seems to me. Starting with Ross and Sara, their friends, but then also (obviously) your *Designed to Shine* participants, campers, and many more.

I feel a little badly that God is trusting you with so many struggles the past few years ranging from uncertainties, to living in two states for a bit, to the current medical issues. Obviously you can handle them. Because of your foundation of faith and your willingness to remain in His grip, you are a very powerful witness for God. As I watch this year unfold, the more I appreciate you and your impact on this world, Amy. Have no fear, your role allows for down times and even questions. You're allowed to be human. But I am also sure that your belief with in a never-failing God will remain intact and strong.

Forever Faithful is a spectacular location for a horse ministry and ranch. Ms. Teri has a huge heart for children in need. Having discovered FF was a gift and our time there was and still is a gift. While the location for our family does not allow us to work together closely, we continue to pray for the ranch, its outreach to children in Montgomery County and the plans God has for those that are blessed as they enter the gates of FF.

I look forward to continually being a part of the summer camp programs and sharing God's gift using me and Beauty in Brokenness, a life analogy through mosaics. I especially look forward to continuing this tradition with Sara by my side as she shares the love of the ranch and all it has to offer.

Day 82, MONDAY, JULY 26, 2010 5:45 PM

Amy: Honestly, the emails and posts today have soaked my heart and soul! Wild how that works, isn't it? More great meals. Flowers yesterday. I am so spoiled! The faithful servant hearts of the Texans march on. Can't write much as the entire family is around and the house is a buzz. Wouldn't have it any other way though!

GREAT time at the ranch today. Wonderful group of campers. They did SO good on the project for Ms. Teri and are natural artists! The rain was just behind the clouds but never stormed on us. The temps where down substantially and all my 7 helpers chipped in, connected with the campers and most importantly, seemed to have a blast once again.

Blessings to you all and I will be in touch soon!

In His grip,

Amy

Day 83, TUESDAY, JULY 27, 2010 3:00 PM

Amy: Got this in an email from my friend, Rhonda, the other day and I loved it! Wanted to share today. I'd heard about the last comment it contains (and think I posted once) but the story was a new one to me! I pray daily for my attitude to stay focused on the positive. Feel free to let me know if it starts to shift, as we all need help staying where we want to be mentally and emotionally.

Leaving for the airport shortly to take mom. I will miss her more than words can say. Why do some families get to stay in the same community or state while so many others are spread all over the globe? I know so many that are both. There are blessings in both and some hurts that are in both. It is what it is, right? She will be missed but I know that her wonderful hubby, Parnell (Nellie)...not to mention their Golden Retriever, Dusty...is so looking forward to having her home. It is always nice to get "home." I just hope we get to see Nellie the next time we see my ma. He is a funny, funny man that makes us all laugh so much!

Enjoy the note, below, that I mentioned earlier.

In His grip,

Amy

Attitude (author unknown)

There once was a woman who woke up one morning, looked in the mirror,

And noticed she had only three hairs on her head.

'Well,' she said, 'I think I'll braid my hair today.'

So she did and she had a wonderful day.

The next day she woke up, looked in the mirror

And saw that she had only two hairs on her head.

'H-M-M,' she said, 'I think I'll part my hair down the middle today.'

So she did and she had a grand day.

The next day she woke up, looked in the mirror and noticed

That she had only one hair on her head.

'Well,' she said, 'today I'm going to wear my hair in a pony tail.'

So she did, and she had a fun, fun day.

The next day she woke up, looked in the mirror and

Noticed that there wasn't a single hair on her head.

'YAY!' she exclaimed. 'I don't have to fix my hair today!'

Attitude is everything.

Life isn't about waiting for the storm to pass...

It's about learning to dance in the rain.

A positive attitude, a good outlook, optimism; call it what you'd like. For me, while going through a dark season, the most important attitude-related emotional state has to do with hope. Hope in Christ. Look up the definition if you are struggling with this one, then meditate on it awhile. Ask God to show you what it means for you and your circumstance and how He can give you new perspective.

Remembering back to that visit with my mom, I am so grateful for the love, care, and attention she provided for my family. She was so eager to come to Texas from Arizona and help out and just love on all of us. She did this so freely and willingly as mothers do.

One not so great thing I also remember about this visit was the few heated arguments that took place between her and Tom and even her and I. They are noteworthy because they have been almost non-existent over the 20 year span that I have been married. While it would be easier to leave this part out of the story, the nudge in my soul to mention it is strong. I'm just trying to tell it like it is. While we all want to think a crisis should bring out the best in everyone; emotions are running high, routine is upset when guests (I mean family!) are in the house, and feelings can get hurt in the process. In hindsight, I wish we had all been more willing to offer up an extra dose of grace to one another at the time, but we weren't. The blame game is a tough one to outgrow. We have since made our peace over whatever it was that we lost sight of.

At the end of the day, relationships are FAR MORE important than our egos or the need to be right or to be heard. Disagreements are bound to happen and anger is a God-given emotion. Controlling the emotion and not letting it control you keeps it from becoming sinful. Love needs to have the last word.

(Sorry, Mom, for not living this out as well as we should have sometimes during your stay...thank goodness for GRACE. THANKS!)

— 17 —

No Pity is Allowed

DAY 85, THURSDAY, JULY 29, 2010 10:19 PM

Amy: I am not looking for a response or note or anything. I am journaling the journey, the experience; the cancer walk that so very many in this world have to experience at one time or another. You see, sometimes lately I feel like I shouldn't write because I don't want anyone thinking oddly about my emotions, yet I have headed down this path of honest and personal postings. I am finding myself wanting to not disappoint, and I cannot do that, so don't fret and please, I ask that you just read it like you don't know me or just don't read it. No pity is allowed. I am typing like this is a private diary. Leave it at that please and just zip it if need be.

I am ready for this day to be done. I have had it with kids. Had it with the non-stop "to do" list which is totally my own doing. Had it with having to keep a hat on my head. Had it with all this. I am tired and tired of being tired. I have been a very grumpy mom this evening. Difficult wife I suppose as well; just ask Tom. He just smiles (sort of) and then nods his head or something of the sort. I notice he listens a lot more and talks less. I think he thinks it is safer that way. I hate being grumpy. I really haven't been too much but I do talk a lot. Even Tess is ticking me off tonight. If it wasn't so late I think I would just go out back and scream my fool head off for a minute. A good night's rest is what I need. I just pray this will be gone when I get going in the morning. I just need some time to relax. It is not in my blood, especially as summer wraps up and school is just two weeks away. When I am busy and not feeling 100%, it makes me edgy and I say things that need to be kept in rather than be tossed out. I really hate that more than I can say. This too shall pass and once the kids are in school, much of the stress of a preteen and teen (with them ALWAYS running in out and everywhere) will be slightly redirected.

AND ANOTHER THING. The heat in Houston takes your breath away. My oncologist told me yesterday that my shortness of breath, that I feel almost always, and the tightening in my chest/lungs, is likely to be from the Taxotere chemo. When my lungs feel tight and I am light headed so much, the heat is a bear! Today at the ranch we finished up the mosaic project. I had to sit almost the whole time!! That ticks me off so bad!! I feel like this sick old person or something! That is SO NOT ME! The older girl campers kept pointing the "swamp cooler" outdoor air conditioning-like unit in my direction when I was walking around. Boy. Not cool.

The mosaic looks fabulous by the way. The kids worked so diligently and everyone seemed to have a fun time and learned a thing or two in the process. Worth every hot minute there. Tomorrow Sara and I are going out for the barrel racing event/show, and the campers and I will present the mosaic to Ms. Teri in front of all the parents and family that come for the awards ceremony. What a perfect way to end the summer camp sessions, as tomorrow wraps up the 3 weeks of Cowkid camps at Forever Faithful Ministries. It has been a real blessing to be a part of it all!

Off to bed as Ross has now invaded my privacy of a quiet house. He is watching The Office down here for some reason and won't stop talking. Bah Humbug. I think I will get off the couch and hit the hay.

By the way...God IS good, ALL the time. Regardless of what is written here. He NEVER said life would be easy or fair, but HE DID promise He will be right there to get us THROUGH this life if we ask, and will lift us up and carry us in our weakness, through HIS STRENGTH. We have to read His Book, pray earnestly, and believe in His grace. Some days we do that more so than others.

In His grip,
Amy

Guestbook Note

We can all save ourselves much anguish and suffering in this life by repeating Peter's phrase, "Because You say so, I will..." and finish it as appropriate. God doesn't need my boat, but He chooses to get into it because I am in it. Jesus shows up in our life so that we can overflow into other boats. That's what you are doing, Amy; you are overflowing into our boats. I for one am so very grateful that I got the signal to row over to help you because the overflow has been amazing.

Guestbook Note

I'm glad you left your diary out where I could see it, Amy. I'm also glad to have a few moments when I could jot down some of my own thoughts in private. I trust you will not share these thoughts with a bunch of your friends and family. I'd hate for people to discover the humanness that we all share. Like when our pets bug us. Who does that dog think she is anyway, coming up to me with a big, happy smile when I really just need a little time alone? Scream away. Love you guys. Peace and understanding to you, my friend.

Day 87, SATURDAY, JULY 31, 2010 2:42 PM

Amy: I know my eyesight has temporarily worsened but I think the font size shrinks every time I log on to journal!

Back to normal today. Yesterday too, for that matter. We had a super time at the ranch yesterday afternoon. Sara and I went up for closing ceremonies and the pole and barrel racing events. Teri puts on such a nice event for all the campers. I was able to talk to the kids and families a bit about *Designed to Shine* and *Beauty in Brokenness* and the mosaics. What a neat experience this was for all of us this summer! I am thrilled that my mom got to take part for a few days as well. Now she gets to know what I am talking about and what we do some of the time! The heat was a tough thing but other than that, I think she really enjoyed it.

Tonight we are going to dinner with Nell and Jerry from down the street (this is the guy who went to Hoover High in Des Moines as well but we didn't know that until we met in the hood last summer!). Sara is at Galveston Beach with Ruth Ann and her daughters for fun in the sun and some dolphin watching in the harbor. Ross is at a pool party with some buddies. Tom is in the driveway washing up his motorcycle; taking a dip shortly, then we will take the bike for a leisurely ride in the neighborhood. A pretty nice way to spend a Saturday, I'd say. Make the most of yours, too!

Blessings at every turn.

In His grip,

Amy

Day 89, MONDAY, AUGUST 2, 2010 1:39 PM

Sitting at the Chevy dealership for a few items on the to-do list. I simply love crossing these things off that never-ending list!

The house is empty for 24 hours! Ross is in New Orleans for a mission trip and Tom took Sara on their first annual father-daughter getaway. She made a list of things she would like to see in Texas and they plan to chip away at the list over the next few years. This somewhat impromptu start kept them close to home for a 24-hour jaunt. They went to the Houston Museum of Natural History, out for a nice supper, got a hotel and swimming, then today they are at NASA for some tours. Based on the picture mail I have been getting today, they are having some serious fun!

It has been way too long since I have had 24 hours to myself, I guess. It has been such a treat. Last night 3 girlfriends came over for some wine and cheese and an evening swim. It was such a fun time. Totally spontaneous and those are often the best!

Feeling strong today. Still never 'sleepy.' Resting better at bedtime sans any helpers. Takes awhile but not a big issue.

Car is ready. Time to sign off. Thinking of those that are far away today. May God bless you and keep you and make His face SHINE upon you!

In His grip while I work at understanding the journey that is here before us. Not always getting it but learning to just "be still and know that He is God." Worth it.

Amy

18

Mr. Clean

Day 91, WEDNESDAY, AUGUST 4, 2010 2:47 PM

Amy: My eyesight is getting worse by the day. I don't have my glasses on and I am straining to focus on this screen! Probably the biggest side effect from chemo that seems to remain consistent throughout the weeks. This means the furrow between my eyebrows is deepening by the day and THIS IS permanent!

Have been and continue to be on a bit of a mental hiatus when it comes to writing. So much going on as the summer wraps up. Still having a terrible time with sleeping soundly. I think I got about 4 or 5 hours in last night between midnight and 9 a.m. this morning. Wake at the slightest sounds and my mind seems to drift to any troubling issue pending in life. I suppose this is all the sleep I need if it is all that I am getting. Doesn't seem right but I'm not sleepy in the daytime. There doesn't seem to be time to be sleepy in the daytime actually.

Notice that my muscles are starting to really get soft. Taking the time to workout regularly has become difficult and I am both out of shape and just tire easier thus making it harder to workout. This has got to be a higher priority once school starts.

As I was sitting here on the couch with my laptop, the screen just went to energy saving mode and went dark. I can see my reflection when it does that. I look like Mr. Clean these days. Hoop earrings and a smooth, shiny head. Funny how it still almost makes me jump when

I see my reflection. Half way through the treatment plan and I am still not used to my new look.

Why do women focus so much on the look anyway? Every woman I have encountered that has gone through the cancer treatment process talks about losing her hair as ONE of the hardest parts of dealing with everything. One hates to be vain but it is a big part of how we define ourselves. I can stand tall most days but deep down there is a part of me that feels incomplete, not totally a woman or something along those lines. I don't have the words I am looking for here. I might later as the treatment plan continues. If I end up with a bilateral mastectomy (which is highly probable due to the fact that finding troubling cell growth in my tissue is extremely difficult via mammogram and even ultrasound) I sometimes wonder how it will feel to have lost THOSE and have only beard stubble growing out on my head. Once again, I like my makeup. That will help. Same with the smile. Humor. Smarts, too maybe. I just PRAY my finely tuned intellect (I had trouble spelling that word just now) returns. I have such a dull response mode going on now on just about as regular a basis as the vision blur. Not a good mix.

Look for the Suburban with the bald chick with aviators, driving down any given Houston-area road, and STAY FAR AWAY. It is true and probably well known in The Woodlands that I take my cap off when driving. My kids are used to it by now so I figure I can cool off a bit while I can. It really isn't a "public" place anyway. As long as I don't look at the other people then I suppose they can't see me. Sort of like the baby that plays peek-a-boo, right? If I can't see you then you can't see me... that works. Ross and Sara just may be scarred for life. They should just be glad I haven't taken a Sharpie and drawn on it yet. Think temporary tattoos. It's a once in a lifetime opportunity. You know I will someday. Until next time, God is good, all the time.

Amy

Guestbook Note

I stop by your journal every day looking for an update, and read them faithfully. You are in our prayers and I'm grateful that you have decided to share your journey with us. It is easy to see God working in you and through you, even from a distance, viewed through your words on my screen. He is an awesome and amazing God, so much bigger than any of the challenges we face down here. Let Him lead you beside still waters and rest in Him.

Guestbook Note
I pray that you have good rest. And peace. And sleep. And a laptop with a better battery so it doesn't go into sleep mode faster than you. ha. Kind of ironic, huh? Thank you, thank you, thank you for sharing your thoughts, Amy. Your guestbook is filled with wonderful people and their sentiments, as well. It's a joy to read their notes, too.

Day 94, SATURDAY, AUGUST 7, 2010 10:48 AM

Amy: Saturday morning. It is the kids' last weekend of summer. : (
I can't say it has gone fast but it sure has for them. We are starting the day off in our PJs until lunch, watching Shark Week and Colony recordings from last week. Ross brought us some yummy Bin-nets for breakfast, from a place in the French Quarter, and we are just chillin! We picked Ross up at the church last night as the group returned from their mission trip to New Orleans. What a fantastic week he had! What a difference a week can make. The maturity level has increased, the stories of walking and talking with homeless children and adults, the VBS type afternoons at a run down city park, and the loads of children that would come just to have something to do on the hot summer days. It seems to have certainly notched Ross up a level in becoming a fine young man. What a blessing this is for EVERYONE. He seems happy to be home and grateful for what he has...at least for a day or two.

Sara and I had a special week of school shopping, reading, swimming and lots of time at the ranch with Trinity, the horse she absolutely loves. Sara spent time working with her, doing a few lessons, a trail ride with Ms. Teri, and then the three of us went on a trial ride yesterday morning for a long while. This was simply amazing. Teri has 115 acres that backs to the 3,000 acres of a National Forest so the rides can go on and on. We were able to ride side by side out in the pasture areas (Sara, Teri and

I) and just do what we wanted to do. Not your typical trail riding but free riding. This is Sara's ideal way to have a horse. I just hope we can make it happen. Time will tell. For now, we will just visit Trinity and ride when we can make the time. So many interests that young lady has and so little time to explore them all!

Tom had his men's group this morning as he does every Saturday at 7 a.m.; a group of 6 to 10 guys who meet at the Brooklyn Cafe and are working through a book entitled, <u>The Measure of a Man.</u> He has met some wonderful guys here and felt the need to start an "accountability group" of sorts. The group keeps growing all the time as two other guys he has met at church are starting to come; two of whom he will be golfing with this afternoon. A few of us gals that are friends say they should meet on the golf course at least once a month (Guys, God and Golf) and the group would be huge! Although huge is not the point. Just getting a bit real with some guys on life, parenting, careers, faith, etc.

Tom had a group he met with in Des Moines on Saturday mornings and this group became some of his closest friends. I know many of them read this journal regularly as a matter of fact! I believe for him, leaving this group was one of the toughest parts of us leaving Des Moines. God knew that and has placed some MORE great guys in our path and I just love that he has taken the initiative to start up a group here. Just have the desire for something good and give it to our Lord…then just see where He will take you! Some days it is easier to do that than others. We just have to take one step forward on the easier days and know we might take one or two backwards on other days. Eventually you will look back and hopefully see more progress has been made than you had thought. Much good has been done, and for us, it has far outweighed the bad.

Feeling great and going to do some school shopping with Ross today! Tom will be golfing and Sara will be playing with friends. Enjoy the weekend and your families. Count your blessings…each and every one!

Amy

When I think back to Tom deciding to take the risk and start a small group here in Texas, and realize now that once again God provided an opportunity to bring glory to Him through our sufferings, I am humbled at how so much good comes from such opportunities. As more has happened, I see how God has been grooming Tom to do more and more in leadership groups and outreach for meeting men "right where they are." Men need these connections just as much as women. They just need it in different ways. Thank you, God for showing us more of your ways each passing day.

The need for unique cancer caregiver support has become more and more obvious to both Tom and I during this journey. God is nudging Tom to explore this need as I am currently developing a survivor program (HORSES-HEALING-HOPE) – more on that later.

— 19 —

Still No Sleep

$\mathcal{D}$AY 97, TUESDAY, AUGUST 10, 2010 2:44 PM

Amy: Two posts that were written earlier today while at chemo #4. Didn't have internet access today so I am copy/pasting them in one now, the other a little later after a nap. Feeling a bunch of heartburn after chemo today. That stinks. Time for a nap before Back to School night at 6.

Entry 1: I am sitting at chemo # 4. I am receiving the Adriamycin chemo now (the A in TAC) so 45 minutes to go on this one and about the same for the Cytoxan then we blow this joint. We have officially made it PAST the halfway point! Only two more chemotherapy appointments to go. I have been able to keep all the appointments thus far (meaning no low white blood cell counts or illnesses preventing me from staying on schedule) and if all stays that way, my last treatments will be September 22 or there about. Surgery will be scheduled at a minimum of three weeks past the final chemo and a maximum of six weeks from the last chemo. We are hoping to schedule a Christmas vacation somewhere on a beach or something, as a well deserved trip for the whole family. Tom and the kids have made many sacrifices through all of this, and well, me too I suppose. But that is what we do for family. I still think we need to celebrate what we KNOW is going to be a successful run at this hiccup in the road of life.

I am still not sleeping worth a HOOT but I have been so much better about using my awake time (this means laying there awake because

I am far too lazy to actually GET UP and do something constructive with my time you see) to think about positive things and getting FEAR to get up from the table, so to speak! I pray often about others (many of you AS A MATTER OF FACT...and I mean MANY) just because I love you! I spend a lot of time asking God to let me know just what I am to DO with all of these goings on in my life. I get some ideas and sometimes I just lay there and wait...and think...and wait...and pray... and then I quietly call for Tess in the stillness of the night...and she comes from wherever she might be laying on some cool tile in the house. She always comes to see me. She is like a guardian angel. Just rubbing her ears and her head can calm me and energize my soul. By the way, the Bear cat will hardly ever come when called.

In His grip and I feel it.

Amy

As I read through these entries, Tess is still laying by my side even now. Her devotion to her master (okay, one of her masters) is inspiring. Her shedding and somewhat smelly fur is not.

Guestbook Note
Think positive as I am a 20 year + survivor.

Day 97, TUESDAY, AUGUST 10, 2010 3:48 PM

Amy: Couldn't sleep. Surprise, surprise. Still lying in my bed with Tessie. No cat. Don't get me wrong. I like my cat. I just adore my dog. :) Here is that other post. I suppose I am making up for so little communications over the past week. Brace yourself, it is long.

Entry 2: Monday night the family went out for a spontaneous visit to the camp, primarily to take out all my mosaic supplies that I have been hauling in the truck for weeks. The kids jump at a chance to get out there. The camp was our first home in Houston. Tom's work let us live out there in one of the ranch houses last summer while we surveyed the area for what would be a good fit for us. We were able to help out with some of the summer foster children's camps while we were there, which were some of the best parts of the summer for all of us! We got hooked up with our church since they were in charge of volunteers for all of those camp sessions. Every day we were also able to work with the horses housed at the camp right out side our front door. We could swim, fish, paddle boat and walk trails to our hearts content! It was truly a wonderful first summer here and it will always be a special place to the Hauser family. So again, when we mentioned we needed to run out there...Sara had carrots and Ross had his rifle and target shooting bag ready to go in no time. Ross likes to drive around the property for a bit of practice for driver's education. Most of his experience has been on the Texas beaches and not much else yet (you cannot get your official permit here until 15! He only has 3 days until 15 is here though.)

When we got all the supplies nicely stored away in the dining hall, Ross and Tom took a golf cart to the pond and out to the huge burn piles to do some shooting and for some male bonding time. Sara and I spent the evening with the horses and getting re-aquatinted with our favorite mustang, Stretch. He is the most beautiful horse I have ever seen. He is not exactly wild but he is not broke either. He loves my Sara. He had not seen us for almost 2 months and you could see in his eyes how happy he was to see us, especially Sara. She loves to be around him. I could tell you so many stories of how she plays in the pasture with him, building things out of huge sticks while he stands there and watches and plays too. I would love to share some more of these stories someday.

I was thrilled that Phil and Nancy were home. They are the camp caretakers, for lack of a better word. Phil does EVERYTHING to maintain the camp grounds. Nancy is actually a hospice nurse in Houston but they live at the camp since Phil pretty much needs to be there 24/7. Phil hung out with the guys and Nancy came out to visit the horses with the girls...Tess too! Nancy is a bigger animal lover than me! After our visit, she and I took a walk while Sara drove Tom around in a golf cart. We had such a special time of talking and catching up on things, as we have not seen each other for a few months. She so lifted my spirits and reminded me of all the prayer and care coming to my family and me, from everywhere. She has such a gentle yet direct spirit and I simply love it. She told me she reads my Caring Bridge posts all the time and could recall so much of what has been written here. That meant the world and was just what I needed at that moment. Thank you, Nancy! You and Phil are like family to us ever since our summer together at the camp. Those are priceless moments we will each remember always and forever. Thanks for showing us true Texas hospitality all the time... even if you are from Arkansas and New Orleans (it's been a long time back though!).

Speaking of priceless moments, I have to say that throughout this summer I have cherished SO MANY great email and phone conversations, and person to person talks, with so many amazing folks in my life...more than I can even mention by name. Because I have chemo brain worse by the minute, I am bound to leave someone out that I would never intend to. I have to mention several incredible ones with my favorite and only sister, Deb. She means the world to me and so does her whole family. They are in Granger, Indiana and that is way too far from Houston (especially now) and we all miss them so much. We talk and Facebook and text constantly but it kills her to be so far away. Posting in public is not in her comfort zone. Don't worry, sis. I know your heart and that is all that matters.

Back to whatever I was saying before THAT sidebar...Priceless moments I believe. Yes. So many come to my mind all day long. Why is it that for me it takes something like cancer to make me really stop and appreciate such moments? Because now I just love to listen to what others have to say, soak it all in and file it away somewhere in my chemo brain. I love the time for connecting. I am inspired by other people's stories, words of encouragement, struggles and everything. Maybe it HAS to take a "valley" experience to fully experience some of these moments and get all you can out of them. Part of me believes that such "valley" encounters are really blessings in disguise. Not just when they are over and done with but all throughout...if you let them be.

I could go on and on about the blessings that have occurred just about every day in this one and they almost always happen when I am just out living life and strike up a conversation with someone. Three happened today at chemo even! So, I keep getting off track. My point to all of this was to thank so many of you for the moments. The talks. The prayers. The friendships, old and new. (Talk about incomplete sentences!) EVEN talks with my mom...priceless! (Joking, I have always cherished our talks) She and I have never been short on things to chat about, even when I was a young girl, and I have such fond memories of those days! She is my biggest cheerleader and prayer warrior for this journey.

Anyway, love all of you. You are a huge part of this healing process and DON'T YOU FORGET IT! Could not do it without you.

See...God IS good, all the time.

When I wrote this, I recall an overwhelming sense of gratitude and appreciation. I experienced this heightened sense of God's goodness most of the time I was in treatments. It was as if I was trying to hang on to a temporary seventh sense or something. If I noticed more and wrote about what I was experiencing, it was as if I would be able to capture "it" forever and the feelings would never leave, even once I was out of the role of patient and into the realm of survivorship. Trouble is, it does fade. I wouldn't say it disappears, but it does fade. I choose to remember it as a gift, re-live what I can and cherish "moments" now more than I ever did before. The fact that life keeps on keepin' on is part of the plan. I can't afford to mourn the loss of that seventh sense for very long. There is just too much living to be done!

Even that amazing camp for the foster children has moved on. It has been converted to a safe house for sex trafficking victims. Freedom House is now a place of refuge and healing for another group of God's children. Hard changes but good changes.

20

Proofread?!

Day 97, TUESDAY, AUGUST 10, 2010 4:12 PM

Amy: Oh my gosh! It is out there for everyone to see just how bad my chemo brain is getting. OBVIOUSLY I did NOT proofread those entries one bit. I have this terrible habit of journaling and hitting SAVE immediately! Ignore the wrong words and typos galore. My bad.

Last post today, I swear.

Amy

The chemo brain IS getting better. Wild caught natural fish oil capsules loaded with Omega 3s is a huge help toward optimizing brain function. Natural, healthy diet and lifestyle changes have been my biggest areas of help in expanding my mental territory of late. Chemo brain is real, I don't care what anyone says. I do believe it is temporary though. It takes a good long while to get back to where you were. How long? I am still waiting to find out!

Guestbook Note
I don't believe Paul did a lot of proofing of his letters to people in Corinth, Ephesus, or Galatia, either. White-out was very expensive and even harder to get in prison.
So I'm just going to assume that your words are divinely

inspired. Please continue the habit of not editing your thoughts. :)

Guestbook Note
Following up on Lee's post about your words being divinely inspired and don't worry about hitting "Save", I ran your last post through a website that analyzes your writing and tells you what famous writer your style most resembles.
You write like Stephen King.
I'm not sure whether to laugh or, well, laugh at that!

Guestbook Note
Don't you worry one bit about proof-reading. You're speling and grammer seam grate to me

Day 99, THURSDAY, AUGUST 12, 2010 12:10 PM

Amy: First day of school at Covenant. Wow. Summer vacation is over already. Yesterday I was yearning for some peace and quiet and for my life to just be still for a minute. Today I've got it and I am pulling my hair out. Wait. It is out. Well, you get the picture.

Tom and I drove the kids together this morning. It went so much better than I could have imagined. The staff is incredible, the teachers are so welcoming. Ross's soccer coach, and teacher for a few classes, seems to be a dream. When Ross first talked about wanting a smaller school and feeling a bit of disconnect back in January, I could not imagine having the kids make another change. Sara was not too sure as she was still young but the kids were all welcoming from the get go. She did like the idea of a smaller group and having her brother in the same building, as there are only about 300 kids in the whole school.

Don't get me wrong, Ross was doing pretty well with football, track and other things but the age is a tough one to really connect one-on-one and huge schools make it even harder. We talked as a family, prayed as a family (and as a couple) visited schools and talked to so many friends who have kids both in various private schools here and in the two large public schools in The Woodlands. Anyway, we decided months ago that we would have the kids attend Covenant Christian. As you might imagine, it is a ton more commitment in terms of driving, involvement, etc. We have been concerned that with the health changes since May (okay, I have been concerned more than some) maybe we had made a mistake. (The Hauser's? Never! Ha to those who know us really well.) Well, the past week I was just like, GET OVER IT AMY, it is done and paid for already and it will work out. Today I really believe it will work out. I'm sure God just shakes His head at me; "Chill my child. Chill."

So much more to write but I think I will run some errands then come back to it later. I feel good but tire a bit. Took Tess for a walk when Thomas brought me back this morning. It was so stinking humid though at 8:30 a.m., but it felt great to get out with her. She was beside herself. We have not walked much at all this summer. She NEEDS her walks. Swimming has become her current form of regular exercise now.

Anyway, needed to rest after the walk but OF COURSE could not sleep. I figure I must be getting what I need, which is just some rest. (Phone just rang and the admissions counselor at Covenant wanted me to know that she has visited both kids and they are having a ball! Oh yeah!) Time to run to the store.

Feeling strong, feeling blessed.

"I CAN DO ALL THINGS THROUGH CHRIST, WHO STRENGTHENS ME!" - Philippians 4:13 (WEB)

Amy

Day 100, FRIDAY, AUGUST 13, 2010 11:41 AM

Amy: Friday already. Almost noon. Been up about a total of an hour so far today. Back in bed after a piece of cake. Had an egg while getting breakfast for the kids this morning. Day two of school you know. Yesterday went really pretty well. Don't feel like writing about it all though. Soccer was so hot for Ross but he doesn't complain at all. I will do that for him. Tom took the kids this morning as I was in no condition to drive or even get dressed. He steps up to the plate and gets things done so well.

Last night Bebe brought this wonderful meal over just in time for us to eat. It was so fabulous. The sugar snap peas had Ross diving in for seconds and he NEVER eats those! I need the recipe, Bebe! The cake that Allie made was so, so good. I thought about it all morning and when I finally got up after the kids had been off to school, I served up a big slice. Hit the spot today! Thank you for the love.

Where was I going with all of this anyway? I have no idea. Tess is here. School papers to read. Ross's birthday gifts to be wrapped. If I get these few things done, it will be a good day. Time for a little shut eye. No painkillers, meds or anything but a little Miralax today. That, my prayerful friends, is a miracle.

In His grip and resting in that fact,
Amy

Day 101, SATURDAY, AUGUST 14, 2010 2:31 PM

Amy: Yesterday and today are tough on the body. The hardest part is watching the comings and goings of everyone while I lay in bed 85% of the time. Energy is low and muscles ache. The good thing is I am tired and I can sleep pretty well or at least dose off easily. It is so easy to feel sorry for myself. When I do, I feel worse. When I stop my pity party and push through, it is amazing how much more I can do. It makes me wonder how much of this is mental. I really think so much of it can be. I refuse to let it win, but I am tired just the same. I have been trying to get the strength to get my suit on and get in the pool all day. It is 2:45 p.m. and I have yet to get there. That is my goal for the day.

It is Ross's 15th birthday today. Hardly what I would call a big day for him in a mom's book. No special breakfast or lunch; opened gifts earlier, a pool party tonight at a new school friend's house. Out with two friends at Market Street right now for a late lunch. Tom is running them around. No cake. He is beaming like a teen should be anyway. His heart is so huge. Sara has Addison over. Might do a soccer clinic with her tonight then a possible sleepover. That would be good for her to get out. She has been hanging around here and needs to burn some energy. I am happy when they are happy. Tom gave me another shave today. He is so gentle. He has gotten really fast and good with the old razor. It is very cool to have your husband love you enough to shave your head. I love him so much. He is such a compassionate provider for all of us. I am blessed.

119

Time for a nap, then maybe that swim.
Make the most of the moments....
Amy

Phil 4:4-8. My "go to" scripture, way more often than
I care to admit.

*The transition in our marriage was evident in this post. In our waiting
one year, God began to show us that when we trust and obey, He can do
anything as the Creator of all things. Less focus on the pain that once was
and a new focus on going forward, and it was working!*

*I can now see how a "required" mental mind-set in dealing with
cancer has positive impacts on other facets of life, including the marriage.
Choosing to see and focus more on the positive and less on the negative not
only changes minds, but eventually hearts too!*

Day 102, SUNDAY, AUGUST 15, 2010 5:33 PM

Amy: Much better today. Went to church. Had to sit during a few
songs though. That is new. Usually feel stronger than this on the Sunday
after chemo. I sort of knew it could "build up" in my body but couldn't
really imagine how that would feel or really play out. Now I know. I
have this burning sensation though out my body that comes and goes.
Also just a fatigued or lightheaded sensation off and on. Something
you really cannot push through. It is like being way overheated, but all
of the time. It is like your body just says "ENOUGH" and you have to
listen to it or else you might fall over. That would be mortifying to me
so I listen. Kind of listen.

Sara went with Laura and a bunch of her sister's (Natasha) friends
and folks to Surf Side for a day at the beach. I so wanted to go.

After church, Ross and a group of close friends went to Splashtown
water park. Tom and I had the day to ourselves and I was not about to
spend it sleeping or resting too much! After church we went over to the
mall to make a couple returns and eat lunch. Very weak. I felt like a
cancer patient or something. Weird. Came home after that and rested
a LITTLE bit. Afterwards we (Tom, Tess and I) got on the nice pool

rafts to float and sun ourselves for the afternoon. Very nice, very quiet and relaxing.

Just got back a short while ago from a motorcycle ride with Tom too. Mistake. Way too hot, even on the back of a bike. It felt like HOT oven air blowing on my face the whole time. We only went like 3 miles but it was nasty. Feels good to be in the AC now, and a tall cold water by my side. I think it's relaxing for the evening now. Any minute now Rhonda and Larry are bringing some steaks by for us to throw on the grill. They are special friends and the kids are all friends too. Another blessing in Houston. Rhonda is also a breast cancer survivor...seven years and a lifetime of no cancer ahead! Even same surgeon as me! We were friends before all this unfolded which makes it even cooler. Anyway, a meal during this week is so helpful. Looking forward to seeing them.

Tom is home. Ross is home. Sara just texted and they are leaving the beach. School tomorrow. Destined to feeling stronger than today. I'm sure of it.

My body is a bit weak but my heart is so very happy. Maybe I'll watch a movie tonight. Loving the Lord and how He works. What a ride.

In His grip,
Amy

We went on a motorcycle ride with Larry and Rhonda a few days ago. It was my first time back on the bike since this post. It was a beautiful evening and so special to spend with friends. Oddly enough, we complained that our hair was SO MESSED up and wind blown after the ride as we walked into the biker ice house!

Speaking of Ice Houses (Texas for an open air bar and grill. They started in the days before refrigerators and got their name because they kept their beer cold in huge buckets of ice), I feel the need to speak on the fact that on occasion you probably have noticed I mentioned having a drink in one form or another. This seems like a logical place to address one of my struggles. I must admit that having a drink was often a type of reward or treat that seemed harmless enough over the years. Something that, over time, almost symbolized an attachment to the past and whatever the past represented. Maybe a bit of my own youthfulness. A way to say, "I'm still cool. I'm still young. I'm deserving of a brief escape from my life as it is today and all my 'adult' responsibilities." Ironically, this reasoning is the exact opposite of why youth often begin to drink: in order to feel older and more mature!

During my cancer journey, God began to point out areas of my life that needed to be scrubbed and re-evaluated. My inaccurate and thus personally harmful view of a glass or two of wine came into better focus. I began to see how my taking a drink was taking on an idol-istic (is that a real word, or another Amyism?) significance.

Please stick with me here and don't discount this right away as over reacting. My point is, we all have weaknesses and usually many of them. I do anyway. If I was allowing a glass of wine to be the soothing point of my day or my time out with friends, then maybe, just maybe, I was putting it above what God wants to do with that time or situation. We can rationalize this away all we want. I had for many, many years. Eventually, the Holy Spirit convicted me enough to start asking God to show me how to give this part of my life to Him. I was very fearful that if I stopped drinking completely, I would become boring and annoying to my friends, family and self! How could I change so much on the inside and have to give this up as well?

The beautiful thing is this: over time, God changed my heart and how I saw this little glass of wine. He wants my obedience. Just like we want our kids' obedience. We want our children to obey because we want to protect them from the pain that is the inevitable outcome if they continue their current behavior. We do not want to make their life boring and uncool, just protect them.

For me, God knew I often was not behaving in a manner that was how He created me when I had a glass or more of wine. He loves me and wants the best for me. There are boundaries for me that I must stay within if I want to experience what He knows is best for me. As a brought-to-my-knees kind of grown child of God, I am learning to appreciate His best rather than the best I thought I could be. Why on earth did I have to take so long to get it? I must have a very thick skull. The beauty is that God did not expect my willpower to do the work. He was simply waiting for my heart to align with my desire to ask for His will and His way. Over time, He worked it out. Now my internal battle is over. I was lucky it was not huge, just another obstacle. By choosing to finally face it, it has lost its power.

I can say that the desire to have a glass of wine when I am winding down for the day or when I feel I deserve a break has mostly gone. Will it be gone forever? I doubt it. I know were my help comes from and I am not afraid to ask for help. Identifying what isn't working helps make life work better.

I still have a glass of wine from time to time. Knowing myself and not letting anyone but my Savior tell me what I need is more freeing than any vice ever was or could be. Again, Father knows best.

21

...I Was Told To...

Day 102, SUNDAY, AUGUST 15, 2010 8:46 PM

Tom: Okay, this is Tom – the husband...Amy's husband; the now short haired (sympathy head?) and almost 50, father of her children. Amy asked me to start journaling too. I originally did just to fill in when she was not feeling well enough to do so herself. I am a kind of the facts and narrative type, so don't expect too much of any depth. It's safer in the shallow end, ya know?

When I went to Europe for two months right after Iowa State, my then girlfriend bought me a beautiful leather travel journal. Upon my return, she was appalled that it was filled with dates, places and events – little or no human interest. She obviously had me confused with an entirely different class of geek. Maybe that is why she unexpectedly left for greener pastures shortly thereafter!? Anyway, I expect to get booed down very soon and then it will be back to the main feature of Amy's tremendous, inspired, raw, revealingly honest and inspiring posts.

I am so very proud of her on this journey and her journal is truly a co-authored piece between her and the Spirit. No spell check, grammar check or editor could or should ever touch one piece, sentence, punctuation mark or Amy-ism. The one possible exception might be to parenthetically explain some of them for those less acquainted! Her honesty, both in the positive and the negative, shows the true course of the journeys - both the cancer trip and the life/spiritual one. It is kind of like reading Psalms. One minute David is riding high and praising his Lord. The next he is sick and worried to the point of death, asking for help, wondering why all of this is happening, and then praising his Lord. The roller coaster of life has evidently been going on for quite some time.

I once read it is better to be silent and thought a fool than to speak and remove all doubt, but I have to take the risk. Amy said, actually asked, me something last week that really set me to thinking. In cases like ours and with personalities like mine, the relationship can start to subtly shift from mate to patient. With the emotional stress and the physical demands, I had descended into what I used to call my "busy season mode" when I was in public accounting and working 70-85 hours per week for several months at a time. Busy season mode is a way that geeks of my particular class deal with high stress. We put the emotions on neutral (easier to deal with that way) and go into the "get-it-all-done" mode. Give me a checklist (i.e. audit plan) and I immerse myself, body and soul, into gitten 'er done. Never slow down, never pause, you might not get started again, and of course, failure is not an option (with apologies to Gene Krantz). Come March 31 (90 days after year-end, when all SEC filings and audits have to be done) you crash and pace like a caged tiger because there is not 10-15 hours of work to be done each day, and weekends are terribly empty. I'm starting to drift, but back to the point; you can kind of lose your humanity during this "pushing through" mode and those around you, those you love the most, suffer the most…even if the work is for them.

Bottom line and I will end this…just getting everything done and meeting the physical (and hopefully the spiritual) aspects for the family is not enough. The emotional needs are even greater during this time and shutting mine down to cope is not an option. I was getting along trying to meet all three for the kids, but only about 1.5 for Amy; – sort of like how a patient must often feel in the hospital with the professional medical staff. I am not Amy's doctor, housekeeper, cook, chauffeur, or provider, although I may fill some or all of those functions at any given time. I am her husband and I needed a reminder of that, and am currently trying to right the ship. Fortunately for me she gets tired pretty quickly so my opportunities to mess up, while trying not to mess up, are less!

That is about as philosophic as I get, but I thought it was a critically important point that I had missed through this journey. As James so eloquently pointed out; faith without works is no faith at all. I would add that faith and works without the accompanying human love, or more accurately, tangible expressions of that love, are pretty much worthless as well.

I read Ecclesiastes last night and 10:4c spoke to me – "calmness can lay great errors to rest."

Trying not to evade His Grip...t

Guestbook Note
Tom, don't believe it when people (including you) tell you you're not philosophic and inspirational. After reading your post, I can assure you that you're both of those things and more. Thanks for sharing such an important insight into your journey. I can't think of a better partner for Amy right now. God's blessings to all of you!

22

Brain-Fog-Fuzzy

DAY 104, TUESDAY, AUGUST 17, 2010 9:26 AM

Amy: 9:30 on Tuesday. Tom is right, the chemo brain fog is intense. I am really worried that it will settle in for good. The kids look at me sometimes like I am completely nuts. People probably read this like I am completely nuts too. Tough. Maybe I am. Now if my dad were still here and thought I was nuts...then I would be worried. :)

Feeling so much better than yesterday. Wow, this was a LONG week. The feeling of fuzz brain and heat surges throughout my body was a bit scary the past couple of days. Tightness in the chest, headaches, blurry vision and on and on. The feelings are so hard to explain. The mere fact that they are not familiar is probably the most bothersome. It is so easy to walk around like a sickie and move slow, etc. I often have to stop myself in my thought process and actually say STOP walking so slow! You are fine, you can be stronger than this. When I do, it works. I just have to do it so often.

You see, cancer is not the worst thing I have gone through mentally. Several years ago, I fought a "mental" fight that was much greater. I am certainly not going to get into all that now. I just know that when I look back on the path I had subconsciously chosen for myself; one that felt the need for lots of thrill and little faith when I should have been focused on being a wife and mother, I was more worried about me and my "life" than I was about anyone or anything else. Little did I know, or maybe I DID know, I was ruining my life; one choice at a time. The WILD thing is, after all that grief, heartache and MENTAL TORTURE of getting to a better place...A WAY, WAY BETTER PLACE with myself and my family, after years of work, the payoff has been huge! When we look back on all we have stuck it out through, we see God's hand on all of it and it completely blows us away. Why, I don't know, but it just does. Maybe because we KNOW in our hearts that Christ will walk with us through the fires and will be there when we choose to call on Him, but our simple minds often cannot grasp those truths. Thing is, I finally can! (I am not intending to brag here.)

Maybe because, looking back, I just see it so plainly, and I now know what to look for going forward. I learned so much about the mental game of survival during my darkest days. Days when I didn't want the world to know how messed up I was as a human being. When it was so much more important to me to look the part of "success" than to actually be it. "Screw up" was seeping out of my foundation and it was time to get down on my knees. Christ knew I needed Him and knew I would need Him so much more in years to come.

I am so thankful that my folks taught me how to look up. I hadn't used my faith in a real way until I had nowhere else to go. To me, there is RELIGION and there is FAITH. Big difference to me. One is a study, the other is a way of life. It's like an apple. Religion can teach you about apples. Show you many kinds of apples. Describe apples until the cows come home. You get the picture. On the other hand there's "faith and a relationship"...well, that's my apple. I don't care how much you know about apples or how LONG you have studied apples. If you don't have my apple, you cannot tell me how it tastes. Unless you take a bite of mine there is no way you can discount the taste of my apple and what it does to my taste buds and stomach and body. If you chose to take a bite, why then you just might know. I hope you have and I hope you enjoy.

This has gotten long. As you know, I don't feel like going back and proofreading it. You see, when you type in here, you only get a little box to see so it is not easy to go back. I cannot see the whole doc at once. Bummer. If this is offensive in anyway. Tough. It's MY journal and YOU are reading it.

Did I have a point I was trying to make...Don't recall. Still thinking... still don't recall. Surprise, surprise. Maybe I will remember tomorrow.

Thinking about that grip,

Amy

Guestbook Note

I love reading your "brain-fog-fuzzy whatever you wanna call 'em" posts! Absolutely, don't go back and proofread! The raw beauty, uncensored is what I want! How beautiful, your reference to the apple. You have gone to the core of who you are and you share openly. When you know where your self-worth lies, you don't have to tiptoe...you keep it real, woman!

Did you ever think your ministry would be so far reaching in such a way? The impact you would have on so many? Did you know that I will bug you (and I can be persistent and annoying) about writing a book, when you get through this all this chemo, etc.?!?
I'm not going to proofread...I'm with you!! We must live with abandon! And laugh wholeheartedly!! You are treasured.

— 23 —

Once Again Delivered

DAY 105, WEDNESDAY, AUGUST 18, 2010 1:35 PM

Amy: Just got home from my ultrasound appointment. This was the ultrasound after chemo #4 today. I had prayed many times lately that the shrinkage had not stalled and the tumors were still getting smaller for today's appointment. I guess my prayers were too narrow-visioned or something so I just want to thank all of you who pray so, so much for me. YOU ARE WITNESSES and PART of A MIRACLE!! The cancer in both areas IS NO LONGER VISIBLE!!! The doctor, right then and there with me watching the ultrasound machine with her said, "Amy, IT IS GONE! I CANNOT SEE ANY CANCER AT ALL!" She said this is unbelievable that after just 4 treatments, she cannot see anything. This does not mean that there are for sure no cancer cells still looming, ultrasound cannot pick up one, two or even 100 cancer cells clustered together. Unfortunately, that means I still have to do the final 2 chemotherapy treatments. Small price to pay, I'd say.

As for surgery, still have to do it. This does not change the fact that I have lymph nodes that need to get yanked, at least one cluster with the auxiliary node having been the one with the cancer. They take out the cluster around that main one. I still have the original area in the right breast where the cancer was that needs to come out. Now the 4 doctors will decide or suggest what the options are. Still have tissue that does not show cancer well when doing mammography. Still have tissue that is difficult to read even on ultrasound. Lots to pray about and think through the whole picture. Nonetheless, so many have been faithful and prayerful for me. That is so very humbling. Thanks to so many wonderful people in my life as well as to people I know who have prayed for me that I have never even met. Wow is all I can say.

Still have a long road ahead and still feeling really weak today. Something feels different though. I guess I don't feel so different, even if I look different still…I'm not. My cancer is pretty much gone. My acid reflux or whatever it is still burns like mad after a Chick Fil A chicken salad sammy, but it just doesn't matter as much right now. I am not surprised by God's goodness, just in awe with it and so very, very happy.

I was recently asked by the Women's Ministry at our church to do the opening talk (only like 10 minutes, luckily) at the quarterly ladies luncheon, which is September 10. Julie, the director, and I plan to meet next week for coffee to talk about the theme, 'Hope.' That is what another member of our church is speaking on (Jennifer Sims who works for the Houston area Susan G. Komen Foundation; never met her but have seen her at the Loft once). I think God just gave me a great close for my talk, and of course I will be talking about the journal site and how much HOPE it has brought into this journey as it has allowed all THIS STUFF to happen! Thank you, each and every one.

Time to run to my oncologist for a check up. Hope he has heard the news as the doctor said she was going to call him straight away. Yippie!

God IS SO GOOD all the time, through happy news and hard news, even.

In His grip,
Amy
Romans 8:28

> **Guestbook Note**
> God WILL heal you fully Amy. Claim that and never look back.

While re-reading this post, the statement stick outs that says, "Something feels different though. I guess I don't feel so different, even if I look different still…I'm not. My cancer is pretty much gone." I don't exactly remember how this felt at the moment yet I get the statement completely. I remember when I learned that each healthy individual has up to or more than 10,000 cancer cells active in his or her body at any given time. Thinking back on this day, I realized how much closer to that healthy or normal individual I was becoming with my treatments. I "felt" more like those around me and I liked that feeling.

Ironically, while I was once again beginning to look and feel like everyone else on the outside, it was the inside that was forever changed. Less than two years ago, I longed and strived to fit into the world on both the inside and the outside. Now Peter's words about living as "temporary residents and foreigners" were starting to make some sense. I don't want to feel as if I don't understand or relate to others any longer, but I do like seeing more and more of what God sees. It is a tough transition, although I personally think he wants us to see it in order to spark change, not despair. God doesn't expect us to change things on our own, just to turn to His word and His ways and find hope in Him. He also does not give us His eyes and set us apart from the world's ways in order to make us feel superior or better than the world around. He opens our eyes to empower us with the living, breathing ways of Christ. Christ in us and through us, not US through US.

Day 105, WEDNESDAY, AUGUST 18, 2010 1:58 PM

Tom: Quick note from Tom:
We are once again delivered by God's grace. Still a long road ahead, but the light is much more visible at the end.

> *"I press on, that I may lay hold of that for which Christ Jesus has also laid hold of me."* Philippians 3:12 (NKJV)

Day 107, FRIDAY, AUGUST 20, 2010 10:02 AM

Amy: Still on cloud 9 with the news. Even more so after meeting with my oncologist. He explained that my type of breast cancer, Invasive Ductal Carcinoma, was very aggressive and fast growing cancer and was fortunately caught early enough (stage 2) that the TAC chemo cocktail was doing what they hoped it would do. The fact that as soon as I felt the lump just under my armpit area (walnut size – remember?) I called my doctor and the fact that they got me in the next day or two was a miracle. My doctor has not said just HOW rapidly growing this form is/was but I know that lump had not been there even a few days to the extent that I could feel it so easily. This makes me just want to scream out to women and say NEVER, EVER DELAY when something is not right!! Just go with your gut and check it out! Anyway, the oncologist said that it really is highly unusual that the tumors appear to have responded this well after the 4 treatments. He then went on to explain that I am now in a small category of patients who have had such an aggressively growing cancer that has responded so quickly to the TAC treatments. He mentioned that sometimes fast growing cancers respond a bit faster and then shut down toward the end but can start to regrow once chemotherapy is done. He does not feel I am in that group whatsoever.

Cancer research and classification has become so detailed and specific over the past few years, it is simply amazing. The doctors insist that 6 treatments are still necessary, and that studies show that patients that stop after "thinking and hoping" the cancer is all gone, fair far higher statistics of recurrence if they forgo surgery, etc. I of course, will do all I need to do to stay as clear of that happening as I can.

One friend posted a comment that hit me so profoundly and I loved it. It said something to the liking of, "you still have a long road ahead and we intend to carry you through to the end in prayer and support." That was just what I needed. The prayer has been so important, yet the journey to come is still long and burdensome. Thanks for that note and I know everyone following knows that, so thanks.

Feeling pretty much back to normal now. Finally. Appetite has been strong ever since the first treatment and I am thankful for that. No mouth sores ever; thanks to the Biotene toothpaste and frequent use of the Biotene mouth rinse after I eat much of anything. Huge thanks to Sue for that advice! Doc says my blood pressure has been low the last two visits and that is part of my problem with light-headedness, I believe. When I mention my "symptoms" to my oncologist, he just shrugs his shoulders like, "yeah, we are poisoning your body pretty much so those things can happen." So reassuring. As long as my heart is strong and my lungs sound good, they are not too concerned I guess. Me either.

Time to get in the pool with Tess. She needs the daily exercise as much as me. She is never getting her walks nor am I. 110 with heat index again today. Joy.

Lunch with three special friends today to celebrate the news and the end of summer with them. End of summer break that is, not summer heat. That goes on until end of November here!

Blessings and peace,

Amy

Day 109, SUNDAY, AUGUST 22, 2010 8:59 AM

Amy: It's a hot summer in Houston. I have heard from so many that it is one of the hottest they can ever remember. I love the mornings despite the heat. I am sitting out by the pool with Sara, Tess and Bear having my coffee. The birds sing so many unique songs here. It is quiet. The sky is as blue as can be. The humidity seems bearable this time of day. That won't last long though. I feel strong and ache free this time of day and I love it. As the day progresses, that is likely to change a bit.

We spent a lovely evening with two of our new friends and all the kids last night. We were treated to a fabulous meal, fancy linens and fine wine. Six of us adults spent the evening talking about such a wide range of topics and I felt so blessed to have met more amazing people than I ever could have hoped for. Both couples are from South Africa and are FULL of great stories of travel, dining and sights. They have experienced so much more than Tom and I ever have and it is captivating to listen. The hospitality is second to none. Andra and Ferdi will be moving back to Cape Town in a few months (our huge loss) and we are all trying to plan a trip to go and visit and see even just a few of all the amazing things that are available on that continent. Can't wait!

Friendships...old and new are such treasures. I remember the old camp song, "Make new friends, but keep the old. One is silver and the other gold." I think both old and new are gold, personally.

Ross had a sleepover with a bunch of new school guys Friday night after soccer. Ricky lives on Lake Conroe so they swam, fished and hung out. Huge 14-mile long lake up by the school. Very fun. I hear they have pulled a few gators from that lake on occasion though... : 0

Sara has Laura, her closest friend coming over today to swim and have lunch. Speaking of Sara...the other night she got Tabasco sauce in her eye. OH WOW. Needless to say, it was quite an episode. I think the whole neighborhood could hear her screaming her head off. Sara is not lacking in the drama queen department any either. All this combined made for quite the ordeal. Finally we were able to calm her down and get the running shower water rinsed through her eye. She is well now and was shortly thereafter.

I just had to stop typing now due to one of her many extreme bloody noses. She gets those so often and they are big ones. Time to contact a local ENT for their suggestions. She has had two procedures over the years in Des Moines but nothing seems to help permanently.

Nothing else to journal. Still quite nice out. Still bald when I woke up this morning. Got a heartfelt letter and card from my Uncle Bill yesterday that warmed my heart. He writes such great things. My Dad's brother in Cedar Rapids. I miss them all very much. My grandmother (Just turned 95) too. We talk often though.

Giant (and I mean GIANT) brown and yellow flying/stinging thing looming very near by. Time to go.

In His almighty grip, even when we are not begging for it,
Amy

Photos

The Hauser family, prepared for the battle ahead

In Port Aransas, Texas, just after chemo #2

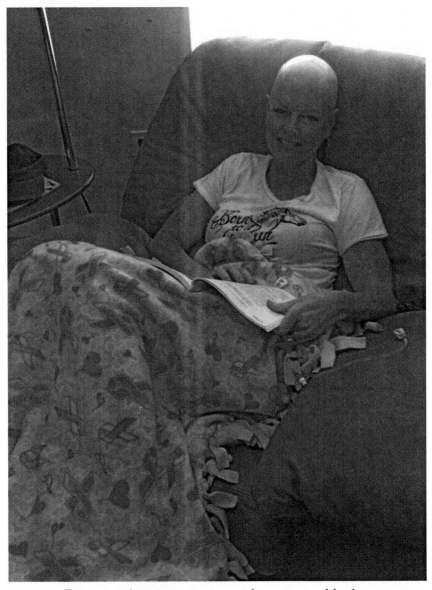

During a chemo treatment, with my prayer blanket

Ross at surf camp – a real beach boy!

The Covenant Christian School soccer team and me. Wearing pink for breast cancer awareness. Ross is fourth from the left.

Ross and Sara having a great time at the camp, our temporary first home in Texas. Hold on!

Sara and her beloved Trinity at Forever Faithful ranch

Speaking at the Breast Cancer Awareness luncheon.
This was just before my belt hit the floor!

My ever faithful Tess, close by during the long
days in bed after a chemo treatment

My very first mosaic, and a pattern used
often during *Beauty In Brokenness*

24

The New Normal

After rereading the following entries, I see that this was the beginning of the "New Normal" that was settling into our lives. Without realizing it, my reality had begun to shift. I had lost touch with what pre-cancer normal was like. As strange as it may seem, the acceptance of these changes, whether temporary or permanent, is essential. If allowed, the Spirit will set new parameters that guide the will to work at improving and healing. He will also balance that will with patience and the peace of recognizing and allowing limitations.

Even now I struggle with this balancing act, as I sometimes long for the old normal. It may return. It may not. As I choose (and struggle at times) to remember that God is in control and He will give us each day our daily bread...the same applies with my current state of physical and mental "normalcy." As I take steps to expand my comfort zones and ask God and Tom for guidance in areas that need expanding without my realization, I can rest assured I am moving forward and not back.

Another unprepared-for change is the shift from what I call Phase I to Phase II. New Normal is a shift in life that has parallels to other major life events – getting married, the arrival of the first child, the last child leaving the nest. This shift has external as well as internal implications. Not just the emotional shock of cancer, but physical changes, both in body and environment. The shift to Phase II is more intense and unexpected and wholly internal and emotional in its impact. It reveals the 'God shaped

144

hole' in each of us with painful clarity, but also opens the door to finally and completely filling it.

During Phase I the needs of the patient are obvious, outward and visible - loss of hair, weight loss or gain, sickness, etc. Everyone rallies around. As a patient, this attention is a lifeline. For those (like me) who thrive on the love and care, it lifts one up and out of the darkness. Prayers are continually coming your way, a plan and a path is set before you and goals are being worked towards daily by doctors as well as other direct supporters. You are enveloped in love, care and attention.

Suddenly, almost overnight (or so it felt), this warm cocoon-like phase ended. I had partially returned to a once LONGED for portion of the _physical_ "old normal" - a growing head of hair and physical strength slowly beginning to return; something you hope will get you back to where you once were, as if nothing had happened. Trouble is, you may start to look like you once did, yet you don't feel like you once did. There are still the consequences of 18 weeks (in my case) of poison streaming through your body, organs and blood. There are new physical struggles and pain, new emotional and mental struggles, and lastly and maybe most importantly...a sense of loss from no longer continually being lifted up in prayer and enjoying the visits and personal relationships that had become the daily custom.

This Phase II presented a whole new set of challenges. Keeping Christ in the center of my needs has made this more tolerable. I know my friends and family still care deeply about my long-term health and I so appreciate that they served when they were called. For me, this new phase required growth, strength and a new level of dependence on Christ as the provider for more of my "earthly" needs and desires. When you think about it, it is truly a beautiful way He paves the path for those that long for comfort. It is not humanly possible for the world (even those we love dearly and that know us better than any other) to meet needs we may not even realize we have. Our growing love for a Heavenly Father that has our best interests in mind is the best source of support for all that Phase II might dish out.

Through Christ's persistent presence in my life, He has taught me that HE is to be all the things that others so willingly shared and did for me and my family during our time of deepest need. HE wants to be that best friend when it is not realistic or possible to depend on others to fill the need any longer. How is it that He knew I would have a sense of loss that way and *would come running as soon as the pangs of "what now" hit? He works in such amazing ways. His mercies are new every morning. Thank You for your unfailing love and desire to connect with your children.*

As I am ebbing and flowing with a variety of emotions and realizing that these are stages and phases of healing that I had not anticipated, I hope to journal this process too, in hopes to share what I am experiencing (and what just might also be happening to people you know and love) on the other side of being a "survivor."

Day 110, MONDAY, AUGUST 23, 2010 8:55 AM

Amy: When does having cancer start to become part of your "new normal?" Just back in May, it was such a shake up to our whole family's way of living. I was not sure I could do it, cope with all the disruptions, handle the stress. The change in schedules and having to plan so much was more than I thought I could bear. The change physically is a handful in and of itself. The exhaustion, lack of sleeping, everything is different.

Suddenly I look back on the start and realize how much adapting has been done. It just has to happen and everyone does what they need to do. No longer is the idea of this illness consuming my thoughts. It is back to school, activities, and what lies ahead. We are created to survive and we kick into that mode almost naturally. Survival of the fittest and we all want to win. Sometimes we wonder what we are really made of. It is times like this in which we get to find out. It may not be cancer, but it also happens when we lose a job, lose a loved one, a marriage ends, a friend betrays, a child goes astray. You can just fill in the blank, really. Sometimes we step right up to the plate and do fine. Other times we have to lean heavily on the strength that surrounds us in order to find what we are made of. Our Heavenly Father has claimed us and called us by name already. We can rise to the occasion and claim it. Unfortunately, it is a choice and not automatic.

Sometimes the "new normal" is conquering and making the best of a situation. Sometimes it is settling for less. Sometimes it is denial and ignoring the reality of what everyone else can see clearly. Not many things happen overnight.

Cancer has changed more than my health. It has changed hearts too; not just mine, but many. In some ways for the better and probably some for the worse. What a ride.

Time for another doctor appointment shortly, the plastic surgeon consultation. Starting to look to the final chapter of this journey. Light at the end of the tunnel! Also meeting with the leaders of the youth ministry at church today. Vision Night is next Sunday and it is a big production of what is to come for the jr/sr High this school year. *Designed to Shine* has a part. I like planning ahead...probably not getting things going until January but it is still a plan nonetheless!

Tenderly in the grip!

Amy

> **Guestbook Note**
>
> You know what I marvel at, Amy? (Well, besides your writing skills and honest journaling.) Your balance. Your ability to continue with family things while doing treatment. The way you allow yourself to lean on others while still leading others. You get rest and yet make the most of every day and minute. You keep faith and hope without ignoring the difficulties. It's an amazing thing.
>
> I started reading the journal because I thought it may help you in some small way. Somewhere along the way it switched to where I now read your journal because it is inspirational to me. Hmm... Good stuff. Godly stuff.

Day, 111, TUESDAY, AUGUST 24, 2010 8:34 PM

Amy: Things are starting to settle into a routine a bit with the kids, school, sports and a little work for me. Carpool is a bit random but that will work itself out soon enough.

Started working with the church youth ministry a bit more and attended a LONG staff meeting today. Nice to start being a bit more a part of things there. Keeps my mind on other things besides me and that is a good change. Looks like retreats and sessions for *Designed to Shine* will really be put off until January and February for the most part, but I will still start being a presence on Sunday things from here on out when I can.

Sitting among a pile of paperwork with absolutely nothing inspiring to say.

Ta-Ta for now.

Amy

Guestbook Note

I like the way you express yourself. I certainly can relate to how the circumstances we are given can influence our attitudes. A saying, "the same sun both melts butter and hardens cement," kind of sums up how adversity affects people differently. We are praying that this experience will strengthen your faith in Christ and your love for others.

Guestbook Note

As I read thru your journals these songwriter's words keep coming to my mind: "... cheering on the faithful, encouraging the weary, their lives a stirring testament to God's sustaining grace!"

Your open & honest words describe a vulnerable, authentic look at how - throughout this ordeal - God has kept his promise to sustain you. And I am certain that He will continue to keep that promise.

Thank you for living out your faith in full view. Thank you for the "heritage of faithfulness" you're passing on to not only your kids but the rest of us, too, inspiring us to a more powerful belief in the One who defends, protects, and sustains.

Thanks for being a blessing. Thanks to the One who provides that blessing.

Day 113, THURSDAY, AUGUST 26, 2010 8:07 AM

Amy: Seasons change. Even in southern Texas. (Technically, EASTERN Texas) Maybe they change in the mind more than the actual temps. I am sitting out back right now. The kids are at school and the house is quiet. I honestly cannot spell anything anymore. My brain does not even recall what the difference between quite and quiet is or which means no noise. Oh Lord, please return this noggin back to "normal" after number 6. PLEASE. Anyway; it is 79 degrees and low humidity and the pine needles are falling from the trees this morning. It smells like a Colorado fall morning. The birds are so active and noisy and it is heavenly. Tess is chasing the squirrels out of the yard and searching for frogs and geckos like she does every morning. Life is good. Really, really good. It feels like a change of seasons is happening and I love that feeling. I, of course know better, that they really don't change here for some time, but I will take a glimpse of it happening, nonetheless.

Season changes are built into us naturally. Especially if you are from the more northern parts. Change is good at times. We are ready for them every so often. Different activities like the shift from beaches and pools to jeans, sweatshirts and football. Next is from jackets to boots and sweaters and basketball. Carefree summers to more reading and schedules. The change is not always easy but you settle in to the new routine with a sense of familiarity and comfort eventually. It is the way we are made. We like to mix things up then get back to what we once knew or experienced before.

Season changes are such memory joggers. Smells long forgotten, sounds we have not heard in months, tastes of foods that are only cooked during the shifting seasons. Comforts of days and years gone by. Seasons are a gift. Memories are a gift. We look to a new season with hopes of creating more memories that will one day be triggered anew. Live every day with the hopes of making "moments" into "memories" that will last a lifetime.

2 Timothy 4:2.

Life has seasons too. Maybe not as predictable of seasons but seasons nonetheless. Many we may not have experienced before - categories might be more fitting. Seasons of joy, fear, loss, growth, numbness, anger, emptiness, illness, doubt, elation and so on. The category content changes with the passing years but the feelings can be familiar as either welcomed or dreaded. They are not always predictable though and we can argue whether they are necessary or not. Just part of the plan for our lives. Use them for God's glory or let them consume you. Once again, it is a choice.

Time for a walk with Tess. This pretend "fall" day may not last long in Houston. Time to soak in the beauty of God's creation on these amazing trails in our neighborhood. Hope I see a few vipers on the trail or maybe even a coral snake today. Yesterday I saw a HORRIBLY huge yellow and black spider in this wild web. The spider was like 5 inches long. It was the size of a rodent. I lost my cool. My two fobias are spiders and wigs. This one was big enough to be wearing a wig. I had to cut my walk in the jungle short because I was allowing fear to pull up a seat at the table. It was not good. I would love to see more snakes, turtles, lizards and the like and less spiders. Off with Tess to start the adventure...then to the dentist.

In His grip and out of the spider's web.

Amy

25

Fobia

Day 114, FRIDAY, AUGUST 27, 2010 8:43 AM

Amy: I CANNOT believe I spelled phobia with an F yesterday! It took me till just now reading Lee's entry to see the mistake. I read his "word for word" quote of my spelling and thought, "why did he spell it that way?" I then went back to my entry and saw it in black and white. This is getting bad (you might notice I am not using big words because every time I try to type them, they are wrong and I cannot figure out spell check on this and then I have to go back and use an easier word so it is not misspelled.) I am sure I am making my momma proud right about now for that college education she and my dad funded! Phobia. It is not fobia. Wow.

Tess is chasing squirrels up trees right now. Another perfect fall like day. The dog is not moving from a locked on-point up a tree at this dumb squirrel.

Last night Sara and I were swimming. Tom and Ross had left to run an errand. The pool gate got left open. Sara and I realized Tess had left the party. We called her, but no Tess. We heard a constant bark from the cul-de-sac next to ours. Surely that was not Tess. I jumped in the truck to fetch her with just a bikini on and a towel around my waist. Forgot a hat. Pale skin, out of shape, small suit, bald woman...you get the picture. Not pretty. Anyway, I drove to the next street and there was Tess in someone's yard staring straight up a tree barking like a freak.

She was the dog that I had heard barking and had been going nuts for like 10 minutes! You could hear her all the way from our house!

There was this woman in the road with a pit bull on a leash just watching her. I jump out of the truck, apologize for my bald head and outfit and start calling my dog to come to the truck. This woman just stares at me like I too am a nut...some nerve! Anyway, Tess comes running to me then she sees this dog. Not good. She bounds over toward said dog and the other dog bears its teeth. Tess attacks. The pit-bullish looking dog attacks. I scream. The lady is tangled in the leash. I scream and take the towel and start feverishly striking Tess with it and finally Tess retreats. I assume 5 neighbors are watching this whole thing in shock by now. I apologize profusely afterwards and this lady actually turns her head and body away from me and STORMS AWAY! She just so happened to live in the house Tess was in the yard of, BUT STILL! I just stood there, bald and bikini laden and looked at Tess, she looked at me then we turned and got in the truck to go home. Some people just have no sense of humor. The dogs were fine. No blood, no harm, no foul. I just hope she doesn't know where we live. :) Time for another walk.

By the way, I will be having surgery on October 20. My last chemo treatment is scheduled for September 21. 95% sure that this will be a bilateral mastectomy. This means both sides. Expanders will be put in place right after the procedure. This means actual reconstruction is a second operation probably after the holidays. I am not giving any more details than that. You get the idea.

Tom and I are taking a mini vacation between chemo and surgery. Still making the plans now. Salerno's have graciously offered to take Sara and Ross to the new Harry Potter park in Orlando for a long weekend in October just so Tom and I can get away alone for a few days. We have not done that since our 10 year anniversary and we are beyond thrilled. Words do not begin to convey our appreciation and thankfulness to what their friendship has meant to us. The kids are becoming very close with Kade and Mia and for that we thank the Lord.

Christmas plans are in the making as well. We are thinking of driving to Arizona to visit mom and Parnell. Deb, Tim, Holden and Hannah will join us. They will fly as they are coming from Indiana. A trip to the Grand Canyon, Sedona and who knows what else will be planned. Looking forward to visiting one of our favorite states! We figure if we drive, we can see more of Western Texas that we have never seen before. The long drive home will not be as fun as the way out though. Time will tell if we chicken out last minute and decide to fly.

Family and friends are the biggest asset we have in life. Figuring out ways to be together is more important than anything else to me, especially now. Cancer is not what any of us want to have to hear we have, but the blessings that CAN come from a potentially life threatening illness opens the door for a gut level appreciation of what we do have and can have. It is eye opening beyond what we strive to see in healthy day to day living that I cannot describe. I am grateful for the opportunity to have this type of "scale removing" from my eyes and I pray every day that it will not fade.

Tess is STILL staring up that stupid tree.

Now it is time for that walk and just for the record, I am not phobic of wigs on others, just touching them and putting them on my head "wigs" me out.

God is good, all the time!

Amy

Guestbook Note
OK Amy here's the plan. I'll go to Sam's and buy enough toilet paper to stock Minute Maid Park. I'll have Kade and Mia at your house at 11:30 tonight, dressed in black of course, and we'll let our four kids take care of Ms. Cranky-Pants!!

PS I'll pick up some eggs too!

Guestbook Note
Great plan, except there needs to be bag full of cats involved as well! And maybe a skunk.

I check your postings daily, and you never cease to amaze me. And just when I think you've powered up as much as you can, you jump to yet another level. Wow. Keep it up!

Laughing and cheering and praying!

Day 116, SUNDAY, AUGUST 29, 2010 10:25 PM

Amy: It's a Sunday night after a busy weekend. Feeling at the top of my game and have been for about a week. Chemo is Tuesday again already. I am dreading it this time due to the fact it took so much longer to bounce back this last go around. Ugh.

Fun weekend. Soccer tourney Friday evening and Saturday. Met MORE great Texans. The parents of fellow soccer teammates were so welcoming and friendly. They just work our family right into the folds of things. Very cool people. The games were good and the team played well. Ross got more playing time than I would have expected given the level of skill some of these boys have. I was pleased...he thought he should have had more. The teams were pretty well matched skill wise except for one team that came really far...almost from Mexico. These boys gave Covenant a butt kicking. They looked like they were straight out of the FIFA World Cup events. Good for the team to see what kind of competition there is out there! Shouldn't run into those kids again unless they make state.

Saturday evening Nellie and Paul showed up with Chinese take out and some great wine. What a fun evening for the kids and us. Sara and Gabby swam and played while we adults got caught up. We are so excited to start seeing more of them once the girls start soccer practices and games again next week. This will be their 3rd season together on the same team. Most of the girls will be back this year and they all play together so well. Fun times.

Sunday was busy at church as I am "working" in the Rebel Base youth ministries for both the 9:30 and 11:15 groups. Tonight was Vision Night for kids and parents as a way to let everyone know what is happening throughout the school year. We had about 300 show up and it was a blast. I got to talk about the upcoming *Designed to Shine* sessions and retreats that will be happening after the first of the year and got to spend a few minutes explaining how I became involved with the youth programs, about my family and the cancer journey.

It was surreal. God has been so good, so faithful and such a great Father. I feel blessed beyond words. I have not felt this cared for or this guided in a long, long time. Pouring out my heart and soul for guidance and direction and then trusting that it will come...not in my time but in His...has all started to bear fruit and I am honored to be entrusted to do that with some amazing people. I will take this season for what it is and what He wants it to be. That is still yet to be uncovered but it is fun so far!

Time for bed. Busy day tomorrow.

Resting in Him,

Amy

Guestbook Note

Your opportunities with youth ministries sound terrific for all involved. I'm sure the same frankness that makes your journal so legit rings true with the young people. And while cancer will be part of your story this year, they will see way beyond that segment to the things that really define who you are. Your faith in God, emphasis on family, your ability to stay focused on positive opportunities, and the way you reach out to others will all "speak" volumes as they search for adults who can actually live out the Scriptures and not just talk about it. You're not perfect; but you're an active student, follower, and believer of Christ. All people are designed to shine, aren't we? You are such a blessing. Praying for an easy round starting Tuesday.

Guestbook Note

I know they say we parents aren't cool, but I thought you were WAY cool speaking at the church last night! I wanted to shout out "I know her! She's my friend!" Rock On!

— 26 —

Kinda Ticking Me Off...

DAY 118, TUESDAY, AUGUST 31, 2010 9:00 PM

Amy: Chemo 5 is done. Went fine. Felt a bit ill afterwards but still went to Wal-Mart with Tom. Been lying pretty low since we got home though. Had a great comfort food meal from Kristie and Jeff tonight that really hit the spot! Some sort of chicken, spinach, tomato and white sauce pasta bake with cheese on top. It was a great hit with all of us! Homemade chocolate chip cookies for dessert withOUT nuts for this family. Very hard for these southerners to understand that preference. Kristie said her family tasted them after she made them and they just looked at each other like, "well, they don't really taste like cookies to us, but if you're sure that is what they wanted...." TOO FUNNY! We loved them and still have leftovers of both for tomorrow.

Tomorrow is fluids and injections. Having lunch with Julie tomorrow afterwards. Have to get out while I can. I know the next few days I will not really be up for it.

Kids are kinda ticking me off today. Neither even asked about chemo or how I am feeling. Turds. That's kids. The world revolves around them pretty much. They are both complaining and so sassy today. I am ready for them to go to bed. One down already and one to go.

Had some good stuff to write today but my stomach hurts. Should have done it when I was feeling better. It might be gone for good. Talked on the phone almost the whole time during chemo instead. Had many calls to make. Check those off the list!

Ephesians 6:1; Colossians 3:20!
Hitting the hay shortly. Maybe more tomorrow.
In His grip,
Amy

> **Guestbook Note**
> LOVE your word sassy! I have to start working that into my everyday chatter immediately.
>
> "Had some good stuff to write today…". Way to leave your audience hanging there, girlfriend! Those might have been the thoughts that pull everything together for me. Now I have to keep reading my Bible and trying to figure it out for myself. If you think of whatever you were going to share, please journal it.
>
> Your pilgrimage through this season is the best example I have ever seen up close that attitude makes the awful bearable. You took a lemon you were handed and made lemonade soufflé and made enough of it to feed all of us with. I will be forever grateful and I am forever changed to have been a witness. Stay sassy!

Day 119, WEDNESDAY, SEPTEMBER 1, 2010 6:50 PM

Amy: Fluids are done. Feeling pretty strong. Food still has its appeal. I touch my head and it is just peach fuzz or stubble. Glasses are on and I can see. Skin is dry. Fingernails still where they should be, have not fallen off that is. Thanks to Juice Plus and tea tree oil daily. Mouth has no sores (thanks to Biotene rinse, I am telling you!). Kids are nicer today and more helpful. Think Tom had a gentle word with them last night. Never hurts. Had lunch at PURE today. Extremely healthy and nice presentation but lacking a tiny bit on taste, if you ask me. "Air fried" sweet potato fries…really? They were pretty good but the side salad option would have been better. I mean, if you can't have the real deal, just skip it. Wonderful time with Julie. We talked way too long.

Had a new nurse at chemo treatments yesterday and today. Donna.

Neat lady. Had a nice visit about the fact that I have not bought a wig. She wanted to know why and thought it pretty neat that younger women are more open to what is going on in their lives than some have been in years past. I actually had a few great comments about my cap yesterday and today. Gives some comfort I guess when women can just take it for what it is. No credit to me just meaning when people can face the facts I guess. I know I am certainly not the only one. Rhonda did it too...6 years ago! Hats off, my friend!

Talked to one lady briefly today on my way out of treatment as she stopped me to talk about my hat. She obviously had lost her hair and had endured chemo as her hair was real short and had very little bangs and all. I asked how long it had been since she had her last treatment and she said over 4 months. Her hair had not grown much. Hmmm. How long am I going to have to keep wearing hats and scarves I wonder?

It appears I am more worried about my hair than the cancer itself sometimes. Old habits die hard. It is ingrained in our culture (especially for women) to worry more about appearances than what is actually on the inside. Not ALL women are this way by any stretch but it is certainly an issue nonetheless. Just look at all the diet fads, even ones that have their own stores and lines of prepared meals. Lose the weight but you have to eat all the prepackaged foods loaded with preservatives, chemicals and low fat garb that will kill you 10-15 years before your time. Short-term gratification. Die early but look good in the coffin. You get the idea. We do that so much. Botox injections, hair and skin dyes and lighteners, chemical peels, tanning beds. The list goes on and on. I am guilty of many of the above. No chemical peels though. I guess it is what we and the rest of the world can see that dominates our thought processes and what goes on in the inside is minimized.

Even with a cancer diagnosis, treatments and pending surgery, I still want sugar. Sugar is the main source of fuel for cancer cells. Old habits die hard. Really, really hard. If I can't see it happening, like I can see fat on my waistline, then I can rationalize it away a bit. I am trying to change my diet and educate myself and my family but it is not happening as easily as I'd like. This body is a temple, and a gift, and a machine if you will. It is time to start treating it as such. Karin has given me a great book on diet and eating to live. Great insight on what our nation has done to our diet and how we can get back to what our bodies are intended to be fed in order to live long, healthy lives. Trouble is, eating is part of who we are and what we do socially and our lifestyles and busyness don't help the matter. Once again, it's a choice. Not an easy one. We owe it to our children and ourselves.

In His grip, whether I feel well or not. He never said the road would be easy but He would be there to see us through it all, rain or shine. I, of course, put that in my own words.

Amy

Guestbook Note
Your words work pretty well!

Reflecting back, my hair started to grow in pretty quickly. This seems to vary greatly from person to person. I have cut my locks several times and have decided to go with the short and spiky look for now. I have been sporting this look for about a year and not sure if I will go back to long layers or not.

It seems cancer has been a springboard for quite a few changes in my life. Better late than never. Sometimes we need a real PUSH to make much needed changes. I wish it didn't have to come to cancer to get me moving. I never did learn lessons easily. I am taking these as some that are long overdue.

27

Called...to Houston???

DAY 120, THURSDAY, SEPTEMBER 2, 2010 11:15 AM

Amy: Running around like a maniac this morning. It is like a game of BEAT THE CLOCK. It reminds me of the nesting process before Ross was born. Get things done before you can't do anything for a while. After 5 treatments of chemo, I sort of know what to expect from my body. Not much after 5 or 7 p.m. tonight if history proves itself accurate. Been to HEB (bought mostly bulk, organic good stuff today), gas in tank, clothes washed, pets groomed, veggies cut and so on. Time to sit and type now then go get in the pool for one more muscle workout as I will likely not get one for the next few days.

Drove the carpool to school this morning. On my way home I was once again hit with the notion that this really is starting to feel like home. This area, just north of Houston (The Woodlands and Conroe where Ross and Sara attend school) is a slightly less congested area on the roads, but not much (especially in The Woodlands), yet it does not feel like a huge city. Houston is the 4th largest city in our nation but from our perspective, it seems so much smaller. I think it is a combination of the people, the fact that you are in a seemingly highly Christian population, that most people drive 69 mph in the fast lane, and nobody uses their horns unless necessary. I realize that is not how it seems to everyone, but Tom and I have really noticed a difference from other major cities (even Des Moines). You often see Christian billboards, KSBJ is a Christian station that is hugely popular here and known among listeners of all types. Blows me away really. Don't get me wrong, not everyone is Christian but they just seem to have a real presence that is not looked down upon or minimized. It is a refreshing change and it changes your day, really.

A few years back, when Tom was searching new horizons and we were seriously considering options outside of Iowa, I remember him calling me while I was visiting my mom in Arizona with the news that he was in the running for two very different positions. One in North Carolina and one in Houston, Texas. I knew he had been to NC a few times and that the potential job there would mean a huge pay jump with a fairly new business venture that would have kept him in the finance industry and mortgage banking. This is what he knew and what he did very well.

It was a great opportunity and a seemingly great area to move to. Problem was, when Tom chose to leave Wells Fargo it was for a desire to do something far more "important;" something that could make a personal difference in the lives of others and not just for a faceless entity. Sort of along the lines of how Rick Warren's <u>The Purpose Driven Life</u> has encouraged so many of us to think about why we are really here, and what our unique purpose is, and so on. Anyway, Tom was not settled with a lifelong career in corporate banking, and the job in NC was different and seemingly a great fit. But was it what his heart was really looking for? Could he settle for just more money and still not really making an impact on others lives? He just was unclear.

Back to when I was in AZ...Tom called and said he got a call from a not-for-profit in Houston. They were looking for a new CFO and came across his resume on a Christian executive search site. They had already reviewed hundreds of resumes and had the deal down to a few final candidates but then saw Tom's resume. Could he fly down soon? I remember sitting in my mom's kitchen and saying, "Houston?" What is in Houston? I had been there once and never thought much about it otherwise.

To wrap this up, after he had flown in to visit the office and we were all back home, Tom basically had two options on the table. Strange thing was, we knew that Houston was where we were supposed to go. Pay cut, hot humid weather, no bonuses, big bugs, Christian based non-for-profit that had a need. We were as good as there. God laid it on our hearts and we really didn't know why. Now we know why. This place {Houston} has captured our hearts in so many ways. I just wish I had Iowa here to mix it all in one big bowl. It would be heaven on earth if you ask me. Mainly the people from Iowa. Sorry but not the other stuff. I miss so, so many wonderful people from so many years of growing, learning, leaning on and laughing with them.

Houston rocks. I don't think I ever want to leave. I find that so strange that I feel that way already. God has such amazing plans and I just wonder how many I have missed over the years where I could have made life so much easier had I learned to be still and know that He is God. Hmmm. Oh well, He seems to steer us on the right path eventually. Nothing is perfect. No job or life is perfect. It just seems to fit nicely for now. Greater things on the horizon still to come.

Ephesians 3:20 and Jeremiah 29:11 are two of my absolute favorites and help me always look to the future. Take a peek.

Amy

I have often thought back to my posts that seemed to reflect how great Tom and I had felt about Houston from the beginning of our move. While it had always seemed good, it was especially good during my illness. While it is still a wonderful place, we now see it through more realistic eyes. Had God been showing us what we needed to see in a new hometown, when we needed it most in order to keep our sanity? While the answer really does not matter, I am so happy He has led us here. While the original purpose had to do with Tom's change to work in Houston...it was only the beginning, a stepping stone and learning stone. We choose to keep our eyes fixed on Him and not look back too much. Thank you, Lord for blessings in various forms.

28

Bored

DAY 122, SATURDAY, SEPTEMBER 4, 2010 2:18 PM

Amy: I am bored. Bored of sitting in the house. I absolutely hate this part of all this. I have been captive inside for what feels like days. Maybe it's only two, but it feels like an eternity. I have all my appetite so I have been eating to pass the time. Watching a few reality shows and even a few flicks. Watched *27 Dresses* earlier today. Yesterday Danette stopped by to bring a yummy egg frittata over. Had some this morning as well. Everyone is gobbling it up. She played me a song on the piano before she left and sang. It made my very quiet and rainy Friday brighten up nicely. She loaned me several chick-flick movies that I have yet to see. I think we will all watch *Cher, the Farewell Tour tonight.*

Tom and Ross ran Sara up to Forever Faithful so she could spend the better part of the day riding and just "being" with Trinity. Not sure what the guys are up to while she is there. Running errands I think. Tess and Bear are still sitting close by. Not sure how they can sleep so much. Ross took Tess for a walk this morning but her activity level has been pretty low this summer.

Don't feel real well to write much here after all. Time for a nap I suppose.

Resting in Him,
Amy

Day 124, MONDAY, SEPTEMBER 6, 2010 11:04 AM

Amy: Happy Labor Day. Feeling better. Glad it is a holiday and I have my family around. Tom ran Ross up to soccer practice. Sara and I have been hanging around, playing with the pets and making pancakes. It was really feeling like a great day up until about 45 minutes ago. That is when the reality of MAJOR chemo brain hit, and it hit harder than it ever has before. So much that it might be something worth filing a medical related claim over. I am not sure I can even relive it again to explain but I will try while it is still so raw in my mind.

Anyway, Sara and I were in my bed and Tess and Bear love to play with us there. Bear is under the sheets, Tess is on top of the sheets and they are playing this wild game of chase. It is so funny and Tess loves to dive under the sheets and Bear runs out...it goes on and on and is so much fun. Well, I decided to get my brand spanking new iPhone and videotape some of the excitement, in hopes that we might just capture a $100K moment for Animal Planet or something. Well, Tess gets camera shy and starts to watch me "watching her" if you will, so the moment quickly fades to just chilling together and looking at our now covered-in-dog-hair clothes and sheets. We cuddled a few more minutes then it was time to get the kitchen cleaned up and start some laundry. The sheets had more post-chemo time than I like so it was time to wash them for the second time this week. It had been awhile since I'd washed the mattress pad too. I think I will throw that in as well. Sara was pitching in so nicely, I was feeling strong enough to get things done. We will have a great afternoon when the guys get back. I think I will call Tom to see how soccer practice is going. Hmmm...where's my phone? "Sara, have you seen my phone?" OH MY &%$?/@*)^%!!!! I run to the washing machine. I KNOW IT'S IN THERE!! I stop the machine and sure enough there is the soggy iPhone on top of the pile, now 15 minutes into a load of hot water with bleach. I grab it and stagger to the kitchen. All I can think of as Sara watches in horror is all of the lecturing I have done in the past week about how the kids have to take care of their new iPhones, or ELSE! And how they (not I) have to have Otter Box covers to protect them from their irresponsible selves. I don't need such bulky covers because I AM THE ADULT - RESPONSIBLE, WISE AND GRATEFUL ADULT. OMG is all I can say. Needless to say, I don't have insurance. I called my "I am available for anything" AT&T guy. He had me pop the SIM card and bury it in raw rice...FOR FOUR DAYS!! I am going there to talk to him later today. I think he feels sorry for me. He should, I know I sure do. Sara has a heart of gold. She wants me to take hers and said she doesn't need one anyway. Tempting but no. Not sure how this one will turn out. I guess I am too young for such a nice toy. If I was clever, I could turn this into a chemo related accident. Hmmm.

Good thing I didn't journal yesterday. Bad day. Our moods and outlook can be so affected by how we feel. When my body is so weak and I am so dependent on others for things, my mind gets weak too. I think my family has learned the pattern and gives me a wide birth. I am afraid they are learning things I wish they did not have to during this journey. Grace comes to mind. They have all learned to give it to me when they would probably rather tell me to take a hike! (That is putting it nicely by the way.) God is working in them just as much as me through all this and for that I am grateful. Teaching us things we would not learn otherwise. Makes me think of the saying; "Be patient with me; God is not finished with me yet."

More great food delivered yesterday. Not even on the food calendar. Thanks Chef Barry. We have been blessed beyond words.

Time to run to the AT&T store then take a rest for the afternoon. Maybe another chick flick. I am going to call for extra fluids tomorrow. The doc thought they might help as an energy boost. Also, Tom and I have a cruise planned for Oct 7-11. Leave right from Galveston and heads to Cancun, Mexico. Short get away and the price was super! So excited for the chance to get away with my hubby for a few days after the last chemo. Debbie is coming Oct 18 or 19th and double mastectomy surgery set for Oct 20th. She will be here about a week to help with running the kids and the like. I am so excited to have her here but wish it was for fun rather than surgery. We will all be in AZ for Christmas though and will celebrate and have fun then.

Getting stronger every day,

IN HIS GRIP, with or without a phone

(For the record, these are the older, cheaper version of the phone. It was a HUGE decision and honor to even get these phones and they are highly monitored by said parent here. Frightening, I know.) Feeling a bit indulged.

Amy

Guestbook Note

Weird how we were just talking about the phones and at what age are we old enough to handle the responsibility. Okay, I know it is not funny, but still! You are just too young!! Sorry it was not caught on video though, you could buy a few with $100K! Also, nice that you have raised a compassionate daughter that wants to share with you!

Guestbook Note

Hello. Anyone there? Just tried to call you but got a strange auto answer and couldn't leave a message. Maybe because of the phone in the washer?? Call me if you can! Miss you!

— 29 —

Relevance

DAY 124, MONDAY, SEPTEMBER 6, 2010 10:04 PM

Tom: Warning - Tom again. Bail out while you still can!

The "long" Labor Day weekend has drawn to a close. Pizza with the family tonight – Ross endured being with us for a full hour. Luckily he didn't know anyone there so his dignity was not too impugned! He and I played a hand of rummy, a game I remember as a kid and that he and Sara both like to play.

Today was the best day of the weekend. Amy, while not near back to full, was much better, both in body (although taking it slow) and spirit. Sometimes we all get overwhelmed by the enormity of this thing called life...did we really move 900 miles, change schools (twice!) think about moving (again!) to be closer to the new school, leave a long standing church family (albeit immediately adopted into our new Loft family), leave the "security" of a decade at Wells Fargo, battle cancer, and in my case, now stare 50 in the face? This movie would never sell. Throw the script on the scrap heap and start again with something that at least has a touch of reality...

There *are* signs of stability. We do not (yet) have any new tattoos, piercings, pink or purple hair (gray does NOT count) nor have we renamed any of the kids; 'Moon Unit,' 'Chastity,' nor 'Achmed.' My 1998 Infinity is still getting me around and last I dusted them off, my golf clubs are the same as they have been for many years.

Some things change, some stay the same. Organ music is now

replaced by a rock band and light show at church, and I think that if it reaches one more soul, then God is quite alright with that. I envision old church fogies around 1200 A.D. or so gasping at the new fangled organ replacing the chanting monks or harps or whatever preceded it, and thinking the cathedral is "going to hell in a hand basket!" Harrumph.

I am sure that I was going somewhere with this…I read a couple of books this weekend and both hit me with some powerful life and faith realities. In his book called <u>Plan B – (what do you do when God doesn't show up the way you thought he would)</u> Pete Wilson (whose picture looks like he may be one of those rock band pastors) asks the ultimate shocker…"Is it possible that you don't really want God? Is it possible that you just want what you think God can give you?" Wellllll, when I read it, that thought just sucked, especially when the other book that I just read hammered at me that one of the key struggles with the true Christian life is "The Temptation to be Relevant." Oh yea! I want to be relevant and I want God to help me find that relevance!!! It was not a coincidence that both of these books – one on my shelf for months, one for days - both shot to the top of my reading list this weekend. I will share a nugget or two and then cease and desist for the night:

> "Winning and accomplishment then tend to become secondary as you begin to focus more on the process and journey God has for you." (Wilson)

> "…when we are securely rooted in personal intimacy with the source of life, it will be possible to remain flexible without being relativistic, convinced without being rigid, willing to confront without being offensive, gentle and forgiving without being soft, and true witnesses without being manipulative." (Nouwen)

The Hauser paraphrase…"get over yourself, your way, your perceived purpose, your relevance and your worth. There is a much bigger plan of which we can only see a tiny corner, during only a nanosecond of His grand cosmic timetable. Don't always look for answers, reasons, human logic, justice, fairness or plain ol' horse sense in this life. Have faith, have hope, trust in Him and do what is right."

I still envision old fogies harrumphing at the new fangled organ...

Guestbook Note
How right you are, Brother Tom! Without giving away my age, I was there! I tried to tell them that the organ would only lead to things like the Doors singing Light My Fire and the Animals chanting House of the Rising Sun.

Guestbook Note
I'm going to cut and paste Tom's last paragraph in his latest post----great words to think about all of the time. The journey is unexpected, but there are so many blessings, aren't there? Laughter is good medicine for the both of us.

~ 30 ~

Perspective

Day 125, TUESDAY, SEPTEMBER 7, 2010 4:39 PM

Amy: Only in the mid to low 80's in Houston today. POURED and stormed most of the day. Humidity...100%. Nasty. No hair, no problem though! House windows are fogged now that the sun is trying to peek out.

Functioning today about 75% of normal. Energy low. Fluids again tomorrow before my regularly scheduled appointment with oncology center.

Rain. Yes, lots here in the last 24 hours. Rained all night. I would know. I didn't sleep after 2:30. Took a sleepy time pill which worked for a while. Then around 2 or 3 it was like an alarm clock was going off in my head again. Tess got a belly rub, brushing and lots of loving late last night. Got on my computer but not up for a journal entry. Hope things go better tonight. I am thinking my body has to rest sometime.

Have a talk on Friday and I am getting nervous. Don't really have a plan on what I am talking about. Could use some prayers for confidence and peace...and strength physically. Tried to go to the mall today to buy some new top or something for Friday. DISASTER. I have not bought anything new for myself since before this cancer gig other than a pair of Nike's. Hardly a fashion statement for a ladies luncheon of 300 women. I could not find ONE SINGLE THING I thought I would like. It is hard to get excited about much when all I know I want to wear is my brown head scarf. Pathetic, really. I don't like the fashions much lately

170

and I think I need help. Trouble is I don't like shopping with people. I am out of touch with what looks good. Nice jeans and a white tee are my favorite, but come on! To top it off, I'm "supposed to" wear pink as it is a breast cancer awareness/hope luncheon. I don't look good in pink. I can't believe this is troubling me. I really could care less about clothes for the most part. Cancer has put things like that into perspective but still, I am a woman. We want to look our best. It is just not real fun to go into a dressing room with nice new, shiny clothes and be bald and lacking muscle tone. It just feels different than it used to. I'd rather save the cash and get something new after all this. It should not be a chore to buy a new outfit. I only have one headscarf I like, that's the problem and I need something to go with it.

Sara is hovering right now, waiting for me to look over her weekly folder. Gotta run.

In His Grip, yet questioning a bit today,

Amy

Guestbook Note

Pink may be the color of cancer but honey you are the picture of cancer. You are a beautiful picture of hope, faith, strength and courage!

Day 126, WEDNESDAY, SEPTEMBER 8, 2010 9:14 AM

Amy: I have to type fast and quick. Anyway, the Apple Store at The Woodlands Mall is the best in the world. They gave me a new phone...free. I can't even write about it as it would take way too long. They blew me away, as did my story to them I guess. If anyone wants to hear, ask.

I just have to say that the power of prayer has blown me away once again. I was overwhelmed with all the gal emails yesterday, on dress and ideas and most importantly prayers for attitude and peace with the talk, and energy, and on and on. I feel like a million bucks today and I was once again wide-awake but not until 4:30. Had a verse in my head and a plan for a talk. Got up and got to work at 5 a.m. God has provided strength and restfulness to get me through the day.

So looking forward to Ladies of the Loft starting up again today.

So much has happened since our last meeting at the end of the spring school year. Doing Prescilla Shriers (spelling incorrect, surprise) <u>One in a Million</u> study. More excited to see everyone. Over 30 registered last I knew. Anyway, once again so many people serving this fight through the most priceless way imaginable...your prayers that are genuinely tender toward someone like me. I am so very humbled beyond words.

All of my love,

Amy

The Ladies of the Loft (LOL) group has ebbed and flowed over the past two seasons with ladies joining in for certain studies then the numbers dwindle down. I think the group has had as many as 110, then down to under 30 for another study. While this can be frustrating, it is the way our lives as busy women go. Again, nothing remains the same. I am finding the need to have a few close friends, and knowing that some months I have a bounty of activity and many months there will be only a few that remain in contact. Again, through it all, a deepening relationship with Christ keeps balance with all the other relationships. Him first, and EVERYTHING else will and DOES fall into place. Figuring out what this looks like is the challenge.

By the way, I don't know if my regular 7 to 8 hours of consistent sleep will ever return. Must be menopause related.

～ 31 ～

Wardrobe Malfunction!

DAY 129, SATURDAY, SEPTEMBER 11, 2010 6:11 PM

Amy: Early Saturday evening. Finally slowing down a bit after a busy couple of days. Been feeling really good. The only problem is that I have tree trunk ankles. They have swollen up like balloons for some reason. My oncologist asked me at my last visit if I was experiencing hand/ankle swelling and at that point I never had. I suppose being in heels for 10 hours yesterday did not help. I looked good though! :) Legs are elevated now.

Yesterday was the Breast Cancer Awareness luncheon. It was such a special day. I cannot begin to explain how much it meant to me. There were 3 full tables of Ladies of the Loft sisters in attendance. I loved that. I met so many wonderful women and the whole program was top notch. I talked for 10 minutes or so. Jennifer Sims (member at TWUMC and Director of Development for Susan G. Komen) was the headliner. Her story was intense. She discovered she had breast cancer when she was 10 weeks pregnant. Her story was gripping and such a testament to God's faithfulness in the midst of a storm. What a neat woman and family. We exchanged cell numbers and I look forward to getting to know her better. She is a funny lady. She was only 31 when she was diagnosed. Similar to Rhonda (36 at the time) and both now in their 40's. Long time survivors, rock on!!

During my talk, which went as well as I could have hoped for, I had a wardrobe malfunction. Don't worry, it was not as bad as Janet Jackson's.

173

My new, fancy belt (strictly for looks, luckily) magically POPPED OFF my midsection right in the middle of my story! I didn't miss a beat as I was reading and said, "*that* did not just happen!" I was laughing SO HARD (so was everyone else luckily) as I was talking about how I have a twisted sense of humor and like to drive without my hat on at times. The timing was perfect. It was actually pretty funny. God has a serious sense of humor and knows just how to break the ice at times. The prayers for peace again covered me through it all, belt on the floor or not, it was well with my soul. I was not the least bit nervous which was OBVIOUSLY God and nothing else, period.

To top off the event, Tom showed up and hid in the back for my talk. It was so special to have him come and show his support. What a guy. :) I am so humbled and honored to have had the opportunity to talk and share yesterday and to be able to share what God has been doing through this walk. My friends want me to post the story I read after doing the scripture and talking part of the talk (does that even make sense? Who cares!). I might just do that one day.

Anyway, after the luncheon many of the LOL went for a glass of wine. My dear friend, Amy drove down 3 hours from Dallas and met up with us there. She and I had not seen one another for 7 years. It felt as if it had only been a week. We worked together at Motorola Cellular in Chicago for several years. When Tom and I moved back to Des Moines she and John moved back to Dallas shortly thereafter. Her stay in The Woodlands was only about 40 hours but we had a blast!! She came bearing gifts for all (even Tess and Bear) like Texans always seem to do! She has ALWAYS had the biggest heart in Texas, I swear. She spoils my family beyond words. After hanging out at home with the kids for a few hours, we headed out for a snack and a drink. Afterwards we crossed over to Market Street and shopped all the great shops for a few hours and listened in to the Dave Matthews Band, playing at the Pavilion.

Market Street was packed, I suppose because of the concert and not because it was a beautiful night or anything. I think it was still 95 degrees at 8 p.m. No outdoor patio sitting for us. All the cafes were packed. Must have been visitors. Way too hot. We ended up having a TO DIE FOR meal (at least mine was) at Jaspers. Loved it. Sad to say that it is 1.5 miles from my house and I had never been there before. Anyway we sat there for a few hours, ate like kings and had the best waiter I have ever had.

This guy was hilarious. He actually wrote a note on our receipt that said he would be thinking of me as I continue down my treatment journey and would be praying for my healing. Never once did he mention the cancer as we talked but we joked about the fact that we had the same hairdo and all. Wow. Houstonians...I am telling you, they are a unique and different breed. Amy even noticed all over the place how nice the people are...even in the fancy boutiques and all. No snobby looks like "why are you here" seem to happen. Amy says they aren't always quite so nice in Dallas.

After a great time of talking and laughing with Amy for hours, we came back just as Tom and the kids were getting back from an impromptu Astros vs. Dodgers game. Tom is always taking them to do such fun things. Lucky kids. Lucky me. After Ross and Sara headed to bed, Tom, Amy and I sat up for a few more hours. We are never short on things to talk about. I love that about her, even after all these years. I miss you Amy!!

Today we all went to Sara's first soccer game. They played great. This team has been together for 3 seasons now and they play well together. Coach Melissa is a saint and such a great coach. She played through college and is the sweetest woman. She loves on the girls, hugs and praises them, yet teaches the game so well. Could not ask for a better Godly athletic influence...and this is club soccer...Houston once again! The girls have moved up to a much larger field, longer game and bigger goals. It was a 9:30 a.m. game, yet it was so hot that all the girls were drenched in sweat, overheated and sick to their stomachs. We all went out to PF Chang's afterwards, but Sara felt so crappy she didn't want to eat. She is fine now though. Amy and I went to return my stupid belt and did some more shopping today. I think my feet are mad at me but I felt fine the whole time. Amy had to leave just about an hour ago. Her husband, John, leaves tomorrow morning on a business trip and her adorable boys (Johnny and Jared) need mama home! We are planning to get the families together sooner than later!

Time to go. Sara is in my room with me and wanting to watch *Good Eats* on Food Network. Her favorite thing to do! Ross is out with a bunch of friends at Market Street. Tom, Sara and I are planning on swimming and cooking on the grill. She has picked a pay-per-view movie for afterwards. Should be a fun night.

Resting in His grip,
Amy and Sara

32

The Transcript

Day 130, SUNDAY, SEPTEMBER 12, 2010 2:00 AM

Amy: Sitting in the dark on my couch. Tess is sitting so close to me, she is the only thing I can see by the glow of my laptop. It is 2 a.m. and I cannot sleep once again. My body is so exhausted, yet sleep will not come. I think I have turned into an insomniac. I worry so much about sleeping that it just won't come. Resting must be enough. My hands and feet seem to be getting tingly these past few days. I know that is normal for many but it has not been an issue for me until lately. Not real bothersome until you are lying awake. I just can't stop moving and shifting constantly to try and get some relief. My mouth dryness is worse after this go round as well. No real sores but a very "hard to describe" sensation all the time going on. These stupid poisons are starting to build up in the ol' system. Good thing is I just turned on the light in the bathroom a few minutes ago to check on my ankles and they are back to normal already after keeping them up most of the evening. That is great! I knew they would be fine.

Just since my posting from earlier this evening, I was listening to my voice messages from yesterday and I had a message from the oncology office. They got the results from my BRACA genetic testing to see if I had the genetic mutations that would reveal that I was at a higher risk for ovarian cancer or not and the results show that I am not!!!!! Praise God once again! This is a HUGE DEAL! Unfortunately, I was at a higher risk to be positive due to the fact I am triple negative in my form of breast cancer. This is GREAT NEWS for my sister Debbie and her daughter Hannah (not to mention, my son Ross). Had I been positive I would have been at a much higher risk to not only develop ovarian, but also other types (per my oncologist's explanation). While being triple negative increases my risk of recurrence, I am in a good position by getting the double whammy in October, and now that the BRACA testing shows that I am not in a higher category for cancers redeveloping elsewhere, my odds seem to stack up as well as can be expected.

Life happens whether you want it to or not. This I can handle. Why waste time worrying about your odds with this news? It is what it is and I am going forward as a warrior. I will read up a bit more but certainly not too much more. I am anxious to call my docs back for details on the results so I can be armed with knowledge for me and for my sister. There is so much to learn on this new frontier. Knowledge is power but there is that fine line where fear can creep in with the mass of information out there. I just continue to pray for a cure for not only BC but all types that affect so, so many.

Time to try for some more shut eye.

Amy

No more going on and on about all these fun things. I feel like a bragger. I guess I am just thrilled when I have a "normal" day or two. Not very nice of me.

Toodle loo.

Guestbook Note
Just a "motherly" comment …that's a privilege that comes with the title! :)…you must NOT feel guilty writing about the positives…I'm sure no one feels you are "bragging". Remember…this is YOUR record of this journey and you are just graciously allowing the rest of us to accompany you by reading your posts.

Day 131, MONDAY, SEPTEMBER 13, 2010 10:18 PM

Amy: Just a quick note to say that today pretty much feels like an "old Amy" day. Stayed home most of the day just catching up on chores, laundry left over from what Tom already did, paperwork and calls. One more week until the final chemo! Lots to get done between now and then. Lots to enjoy between now and then.

Taking in a quiet evening with Sara after a school meeting. Tom and Ross are at an Astros game with Larry and Kade Salerno. Hope Ross doesn't have too much homework as it will be a late night.

Life is good. God is good. Can't complain, so I won't.

Amy

Day 132, TUESDAY, SEPTEMBER 14, 2010 8:49 AM

Amy: I have had requests to post part of my talk Friday. I will attach it here for those interested.

I ran to the mall the other day to pick up something. One of those guys working a cosmetics kiosk said he had something for me and handed me a sample packet...I was in a hurry and stuck it in my bag without looking at it. He smiled at me. As I switched bags this morning, I took it out. It was HAIR SERUM. Nice touch from a funny guy. Wish I'd of looked at what it was before leaving the mall.

Reminds me of the scripture verse, NOT A HAIR WILL FALL FROM YOUR HEAD WITHOUT THE WILL OF YOUR FATHER IN HEAVEN.

In His grip,

Amy

The following transcript was read after a talk (mentioned earlier, with the wardrobe malfunction) about my diagnosis and what is to come. I used a tie in to the childhood song, "This Little Light of Mine" and scripture from Matthew 5:14-16 which states, "You are the light of the world. A city on a hill cannot be hidden. Neither do people light a lamp and put it under a bowl. Instead they put it on its stand, and it gives light to everyone in the house. In the same way, let your light shine before men, that they may see your good deeds and praise your Father in heaven."

So....here is the script from my talk...Guess you will just have to read and hope you can fill in on your own how the transition went...

We hide our light when we:
   1.   Are quiet when we should speak

2. *Go along with the crowd and*
3. *Ignore the needs of others.*

In order for us to shine as Christ tells us to in the scriptures, found in Matthew, it obviously involves a measure of risk. If we are Christians, we should be used to that at some level but do we really do it as He intends? I know for myself and for most of my life, it was easier to just blend in and quietly live out my faith in a way that was comfortable for me, wherever I was on my walk at that particular time. Don't draw attention, it just may come back to burn you.

God had another plan. As a woman with breast cancer, I knew I was being called to take some risks for Christ. You see right away--from the moment of my diagnosis--I knew God had my back. We were fairly new in town but God had let our family know we were exactly where we were supposed to be. I have never been more sure of anything than I was when I was facing this uncertain future. I was in His grip and He who started a good work in me would see it through to completion...whatever that meant. Deal was, He was going to use this and He wasn't waiting until it was all done and over with. He made that clear. He would be glorified in an "up close and personal" type of way. We were starting this journey and I would lean on Him wholeheartedly. I wouldn't feel the need to question too much…it was time to trust. He would handle the rest. Most importantly...HE WOULD GET ALL THE GLORY!

Like the scripture said, in order to shine for Christ, I could not be quiet when I should speak. "I WOULD NOT BE QUIET" the voice in my heart informed me! Fine. Journal! Everyone kept telling me I needed a journaling site. I was not so sure about it, as I HATED to write and have always been very self-conscious of my abilities, or lack thereof, in that area. I did like the thought though of keeping family and good friends informed of medical information as deemed necessary. Tom started a page for me and I soon did my first entry. God had a plan MUCH BIGGER than I. Since June of 2010 I have found my forum for sharing this journey. With almost daily blogs and over 17,000 visits to my site, God has used my story as I have risked much while pouring out my personal story for the sometimes critical world to see. It's funny when we take a route far different from what WE would ever do, and let God do things HIS way, just how amazing things can be. Doing it His way with this journal I have been carried in ways I cannot even explain. The outpouring of blessings, from guestbook entries to emails, to texts and personal conversations, have revealed the body of Christ and His healing power. And it has all been like having Christ's arms around me day and night.

Next, God said; "Amy in order to let YOUR light shine, YOU CANNOT GO ALONG WITH THE CROWD." Well, physically speaking, that's not hard to do when you're bald. I had a platform to be different. I kinda get a rush when I can add some shock and awe into someone's day. Always have and sadly not always with the purest of intentions! If you know me, you know that sometimes I like to take my hat off in the middle of The Woodlands and pull up to some undeserving guy at a light and watch and wait for them to glance my way. I love to just flash a huge grin and wait for their reaction. Some just turn away real fast while others start to laugh and smile. I do have a twisted sense of humor. Talk about not going along with the crowd, I come by it naturally in some ways. Anyway, before the hair fell out, I decided I would not wear a wig--could not wear a wig. Not only because of the heat and fear of it being sideways on my head after bending down to tie my shoe or something (true by the way) but rather because I knew it was part of the need to be real with my journey. This is who I am and part of who I will always be. Good or bad--our life experiences define us and make us stronger or weaker in the character development process. Like the look or not, it's real. Unlike many men I know---at least it's temporary! If I chose to try and "look" like everyone else in the crowd, I would be hiding my light and missing opportunities that God might have intended for good. For me, I had to take the risk.

I have had countless blessings flow from complete strangers because of my bald, cap-adorned head. Conversations and encouraging glances, because I consciously decided I would hold my head high, adorn my face with makeup and hoop earrings, and smile ALL THE TIME. God has blessed me and CHOSEN ME to tell a story. I am honored, not ashamed! Don't get me wrong, this has not been easy...far from it. He never said it would be but He did promise to get us through this life if we would call on Him, trust Him and lean on Him in the midst of our trials. This is the first time I have REALLY done that. I am just sad when I think about what blessings I have missed along my 43 year life journey, due to my innate desire to always do things my way rather than His. I am a control freak worse than I thought. Still working on that one.

Lastly, scripture says we hide our light when we IGNORE THE NEEDS OF OTHERS. This one is the hardest for me to talk about. Through my walk with cancer I have learned so much about serving others in need. Never before have I experienced such support nor seen the Body of Christ rise to the occasion and step up to walk along side a fellow sister SO willingly as I have over the past 4 months. By "allowing" others to see my needs I have "allowed" others to serve and be used by God themselves. I often have to remind myself what my husband Tom says..."*DON'T ROB THE GIVER OF THE GIFT.*" As women of today, it is SO HARD to accept help. I am learning that it is okay. Again, a work in progress.

When we moved to Texas in the summer of 2009 we wasted no time getting involved at this church. I decided to check out the Ladies of the Loft group. Normally I don't think I would have gotten plugged in so quickly, but God knew something I did not yet know, and He was telling my soul I would need to be connected. It is probably the best thing I have ever done. The friendships, meals, prayers and laughs have been countless. I have learned by watching the Body serve so freely. Our family has been lifted up and the whole group has grown closer by supporting a weak link. Hiding my light rather than showing it, flaws and all, would NOT have let Christ's HUGE LIGHT shine on a dark situation. His ways, however, are mysterious yet intricately laid out, and have revealed such beautiful things.

So ladies, if you are not plugged in somewhere in life where there are a group of women that will allow your light to shine; whether it is a study, a team, a book club or special interest group (preferably a Christ centered group), please consider finding one. There are women out there just waiting to bring you in. There are also women out there just waiting to be cared for, blessed and prayed for. It might be cancer. It might be a broken heart or relationship or any number of things. It might just be you - in need one day soon. We are designed for fellowship and for serving. Even serving WHILE we are in need helps us heal and put our own needs into perspective.

Before my diagnosis, I was making detailed plans for a start-up ministry. So much had to be put on hold and my heart was so burdened by it all. Thanks to help from a handful of friends from this church who were part of the Designed to Shine mother/daughter program last winter, I was able to teach a few mosaic sessions that I call, "Beauty In Brokenness" during summer camps at Forever Faithful Ranch. This was no doubt helpful in my healing alongside my TAC chemo plan that is almost finished! By continuing to serve others, whether a little or a lot, the focus gets off of me and instead on others.

I can't imagine going through cancer without my faith as it has grown *so richly because of this disease. I am grateful for that. September 21st is my final chemotherapy. Shortly thereafter my surgery will come and go. I look forward to wrapping up this season in my life. I just pray that the lessons I have learned along the way will have taught me how to shine in ways I never thought imaginable. Shine on.*

    Thank you for this privilege.

Guestbook Note

Note to those of you who weren't lucky enough to hear Amy's speech live and are reading it here: When you get to the part where she is recounting taking off her hat at traffic lights and giving some unsuspecting guy a scalp-flash and big ol' smile, imagine her stylish new belt suddenly and noisily clanking to the ground. Pause in your reading for the gales of laughter, lead by the speaker herself. Amy's devotion could not have gone better. God was glorified.

33

Dear Tom, DUH!!!

D<small>AY</small> 133, WEDNESDAY, SEPTEMBER 15, 2010 11:39 PM

Tom: Tom here again. It's been a busy month – kids starting a new school 25 minutes away, some days requiring three round trips; soccer; piano; church and youth groups; friends, skateboarding and horseback riding. There's lots of good news on Amy's condition, but the final chemos remain plus the upcoming surgeries. As always we are keeping busy; 3 Astros games, 1 Texans game (Indianapolis, Peyton Manning and a Texans win! Thanks again to Barry and Karin for their wonderful hospitality!). Then there was the Mercy Me concert, a visit from Amy's good friend Amy last weekend, and many great times of fellowship with our many new friends.

Some of us guys, many being husbands of the Ladies of the Loft, have been meeting on Saturday mornings for discussion, bible study and prayer. I really don't like the term "bible study" as it has such narrow and stodgy connotations. On the other hand, handles like; "guys spiritual enrichment, burden sharing, mutual support and accountability, prayer time, bagel consuming, sports talking get together" don't have much pizzazz either, nor do any of them have a catchy acronym like LOL… but whatever we end up calling our various gatherings, any male is welcomed and encouraged to attend. We are about to finish our first book and have had some great conversations and hopefully experienced some growth along the way in our walks.

Work has been busy. I really consider it a calling and part of my mission, but I let myself get too consumed with it, so I need to mentally, physically and emotionally step back a bit sometimes. As much as I know it's not my job to fix the world, fix the ministry, or single handedly help every child or even to try to make everything run better, God often has to remind me that these tasks are in is His job description, not mine.

In my last rant I think I mentioned that I read <u>Plan B</u> and <u>In the Name of Jesus</u>, but I believe that there is some susceptibility to chemo brain for close family members, so bear with me…Pastor Andy is starting a series called 'dear John,' based on the letters of John recorded in the New Testament. I read through a couple of versions of 1 John (in conjunction with the aforementioned readings) and have pondered: have I been under the somewhat self-centered, if not self-deluded, impression that this journey (to Texas y'all) was about *my* mission in life? Maybe this entire series of journeys, going back many years (or one journey with multiple segments – layovers in the flight of life?), were all in preparation for the message that Amy is now so powerfully portraying? Is my role in this comedy/tragedy/saga/epic (think I will go with epic, I like the sound of that better) one of support, i.e. servanthood in both the literal and figurative sense?

As I look back on the earlier scenes of life (I am definitely going with the epic theme, then I can meander from literary to cinematic allusions and nobody will be able to pin down what I really mean), my strengths usually were best utilized in a supporting role – a number two, if you will. If I remember my epic conventions (yes, Mr. Geisler, I did pay attention in literature class) there needs to be a journey across water (check), a descent to the underworld (felt/feels like check) and intervention by the gods (using capital 'G' – check).

Don't get me wrong, I don't discount the path upon which God has had me. If one guy got the message at one of Meredith Drive's men's functions, or one guy was saved by coming to old men's basketball night, or one guy changed his walk for the better as a result of being surrounded by fellow Christians on Saturday morning, it is/was the path to be on. We humans believe we are thinking big, but I love the ending of the book of Job (Old Testament, in case you haven't been to a 'guy's spiritual enrichment, burden…' you know). Job and his smug friends rail against each other for nearly 30 chapters on why all this rotten stuff is happening to Job – the supposed friends accusing Job that hidden sin must be the cause for his predicament – Job maintaining his innocence and crying out to God, "WHY?"

In doing so, Job tries to cross-examine God pretty hard. Finally God patiently challenges: "and where were you when I made the earth, hung the moon and built the mountains, Buckwheat?" (my paraphrase). They were all so focused on the current situation that they missed the big picture. Even when we think we are thinking big, we have no clue. Saint somebody wrote that he finally 'got it' when he picked up a seashell and scooped water from the ocean…God told him that the water in the shell represented his (Saint somebody's) understanding. The vast ocean represents God's knowledge and understanding. Must have been a small shell…

I'm rambling, it's late and there is a lot of work to be done tomorrow. The final scene to this excerpt is: the big picture is not mine in which to star, nor maybe in which to have more than a cameo. (Alfred Hitchcock had a cameo in every one of his movies!) Rather so it is that many, many of our friends feel the story to be told is Amy's journey. Let's see how it continues to unfold…

Guestbook Note
Dear Tom,
DUH!!! :)

I have to comment on this whether I really want to or not. From my point of view, Tom is a brilliant writer. I am simply an emotional dumper. While Tom may feel he is only a cameo in this story, I say we are both cameos to an unfathomably star-studded God. How or why we are here no longer captivates my mind. I just want to keep going. We have been handed an opportunity to showcase God's goodness and grace, and together we are going to try and do the best we can. We are getting older, after all. I think we are all handed countless opportunities to showcase our Father, we just often miss the cue. Consciously or subconsciously we decide to take a pass. This time, I want to run with it. I'm not sure how many more chances we might get. I have weighed the costs and I think I feel it is worth the risks. Thank you Lord for showing me the way (again and again and again!).

34

Trust Him in the Wilderness

D<small>AY</small> 135, FRIDAY, SEPTEMBER 17, 2010 10:18 AM

Amy: Met with Dr. S. yesterday. Went through the details of the upcoming October surgery. 3-4 hour procedure. Will likely take 10 days to feel good. Could be longer for me as I will still be dealing with the chemo poisons in my body. That will probably keep me feeling weak longer. Oh joy. My favorite thing to do...nothing. Lord help me please. Good news is that my sis is flying in from Indiana the 19th-27th. This will be a huge help with kids and all. Just having her around will be great. Not sure she has ever been to Houston. Won't exactly be a sightseeing kind of visit though. Maybe next time!

Ladies of the Loft (over 50 women now BTW!) has started the <u>One In a Million</u> study by Priscilla Shirer and I have to share a bit about this week. I love it. Ties in a bit to the "why" of things like cancer, or death, or job loss, or whatever happens in our lives, and I know so many friends have such things in their lives right now.

'When Pharaoh let the people go, God did not lead them on the road through the Philistine country, though that was shorter. For God said, "If they face war, they might change their minds and return to Egypt."' Exodus 13:17

For those not familiar with this story, I will quickly say that Pharaoh had the Israelites captive for over 300 years because he was afraid of their strength as they grew in numbers and thought he would be overruled or something along those lines. God sent many horrible things to get

Pharaoh to let His people go free and finally he did. When the people left, He did not take them the short and easy way toward the Promised Land, but instead in a way they KNEW would take FOREVER (40 years really). This was a real drag for them, as they knew it would only take about 30 days if they took the easy road.

The scripture is still so fitting today as we compare it to how we look at God guiding us out of a troubling or difficult situation. We decide to trust Him but then say WAIT A STINKING MINUTE, this is not what I thought would be the best idea!! What we do next is the big question...the real deal if you will. The sickness has been detected, the person has left, the family member has passed on, the kid moved out... but WHAT ARE WE GOING TO DO ABOUT IT? Get ticked... of course, cry...of course, scream...of course, but what then? Open the Word, get on your knees, call a REAL friend. Ask for help. TRUST what we read and pray about. Shut up after we pray and listen. Day after day and moment after moment, shut up and listen. Forget your ideas of what is best because HE knows what is best for you. I've seen it and I've done it wrong time after time after time. He knows the way out. He knows how to keep you out of the WARS that rage in the short cuts, and He KNOWS if you see war you will go running back to IMPRISONMENT in Egypt. Just keep on keepin' on.

God CHOSE the wilderness for the people of Israel. There are some things we don't know about ourselves until we are put in a position where we have to see God's power within us.

- God will comfort us by His Holy Spirit. Trust Him with the wilderness.
- God wants to develop us, and He uses the wilderness to do it.
- My ears have heard of you, but now my eyes have seen you. Job 42:5
- You can't see miracles unless there is an impossible situation you can't figure out for yourself.

(The last several sentences are straight from the study. Bet you could tell!)

Just had to share this. Love it, feel it, trust it.

Happy weekend.

Going boating on Lake Conroe this afternoon. Whoot, Whoot.

God is good, ALL the time.

Living a miracle,
Amy

Day 135, FRIDAY, SEPTEMBER 17, 2010 2:54 PM

Amy: Here is a medical-ish update for those that prefer that over the other info.

I had a call into Dr. S. after our appointment yesterday, to clear up some unclearness. I have lots of that. Anyway, Dr. S. (breast surgeon) called me back today to further explain what would be happening with my lymph nodes during surgery. I will have all breast tissue removed (99.5% anyway) then as a result of a radioactive isotope injection given the day before surgery, they will test the nodes on my right side and any that show "signs" of cancer cell activity will then be removed. The "auxiliary" cluster that originally had the tumor involved will be removed regardless. Dr. S. feels I have a good chance of not showing any further activity in the others because the chemotherapy has worked so remarkably well BUT they will not know for sure until I am in surgery. IF I have to have more nodes removed than he hopes, I will likely have to do radiation therapy post op. If he only removes the original nodes in question (smaller grouping) then I will not require radiation.

Yesterday at my appointment, Dr. S. was SO THRILLED about the final ultrasound showing no visible signs of the two tumors. It was so cool to see a doctor so happy. My oncologist was not so excited. Pooh on him. Anyway, Dr. S. said I am a "poster child" of why it is best to do chemo prior to surgery. In his words, it provides so much more researchable information on what treatments work best for various forms of cancer and just how nicely they can track progress. Anyway, I did learn that if one was to have a different form of cancer elsewhere in the body, the breast cancer treatment would likely not do anything for it. They are that specific. Scary really. I was hoping I was killing any possibilities of other potential bad stuff going on. One thing at a time. My scans should likely prove that I am in good shape for now.

Also learned that with the BRACA 1 and 2 testing that (as mentioned before) I am NOT at an increased chance (by 50% had I been positive) for developing ovarian cancer. I am the same now as the general population...praise God! Same with my immediate family thanks to that negative test result! My family IS however (mom, sister, niece) now at a higher risk for developing breast cancer since I was diagnosed with it pre-menopausal. Interesting information. They will just have to stay on top of yearly exams, put it on health forms and DO MONTHLY SELF EXAMS (hope they are reading this!)

Lastly, life goes on. I stay off the internet for the most part. I will be FINE!! I look forward to 2011 with hope and a fresh new outlook.

By the way, I called the gal I met at chemo who is dealing with a recurrence after 10 years, and she is not doing well. She has developed lymphedema in her legs due to a new chemo drug they have been trying. She is very ill and the chemo is not doing all that it should. She is positive in her attitude and strong in her faith. We didn't talk long as she was at the doctor when I called. I asked if I could mention her and for prayers...she said OF COURSE! Please pray for Debbie's healing and for God's will in her life to be clear. Thanks.

Amy

35

Adopted

$\mathcal{D}$ AY 138, MONDAY, SEPTEMBER 20, 2010 10:20 AM

Amy: Hasn't been much time to sit and write this past week. This time in life seems consumed with running Ross and Sara to and from social and sporting events. Their lives have become our lives for the most part. They both have changed and grown so much physically and emotionally that it is even noticeable to Tom and me. Impressive for the most part. Staggering at times. A joy to be a part of, all around. Cannot imagine them grown and gone sooner than later. Puts a lump in my throat to even say.

Had some difficult talks with Sara this weekend. Ones I have been dreading. She and I were watching *Extreme Home Makeover* Saturday and a commercial came on about some website that can help track your family roots and genealogy. She said, "Hey, I've been hoping I could do that and find out about who my family in China is and where my roots come from, how can we do that for me?"

Sara is almost 11. She is so very private in some ways and the way she asked this so matter of fact-like caused my heart to sink. My every word was thought out, syllable by syllable. It still was not easy to say, "Sara, there is no way." God allowed some really necessary discussion to take place but Tom and I cannot imagine how that might feel. I am not going into the details of our talks on this matter over the weekend, but they were good. We have had several talks in the past about adoption, but this was another cognitive level of understanding for her.

Oh how I wish I could take the pain away. All the more reason for her to understand the love of our Heavenly Father and ALL of our adoption into His family, and how it is forever regardless of who we are, or where we come from or what we have done. It is the real deal, and so is our love for her as our daughter. It doesn't change the loss she most likely feels but hopefully one day she can fill that empty hole with Him. I imagine that might take more time for her than I would like.

She and her brother have seemed to grow so much during this cancer journey and just in the short time being at Covenant Christian School. Don't think I would undo any of it seeing the good that is so evident.

Gearing up for the final chemo treatment tomorrow. Need to leave soon and go do my blood work to make sure I am in good enough health to have it. I know that I am though! I can tell.

We had a great weekend. Went boating on Lake Conroe with Larry, Rhonda, Kade and Mia. The kids enjoy those kiddos so much. Much wake boarding and tubing done by those 4.

Saturday was soccer for Sara. She played great but the team lost. Sunday was the Astros vs. Reds. 'Stros won!!! They are doing very well this season. Mercy Me concert after the game. They are simply my favorite Christian rock group; 15th row center and like 12,000 people stayed for the show. Made my day. Sara brought her close friend Laura but Ross went out with 12 buddies after church to BWWings for some hangout time. His loss!

Resting and ready as I feel His grip,
Amy

Guestbook Note
I like to believe that someday there will be a DNA bank we can register in and so will someone in the girl's families...just a Someday Thought...God can do anything, in His way, His Time...{Parent of Sara's 'sister' from the same orphanage in China.}

Guestbook Note
I am adopted. There is no greater gift in this world. To me, the term "parents" always means my adopted

parents. I frankly don't even think about the fact that I'm adopted unless it specifically comes up as a topic (like this) or I'm in the doctor's office. (heredity medical history)

I realize Sara's situation is a little different because it's more obvious that she didn't inherit your red hair. So Sara faces the adoption topic more often. But without trying to make all of the non-adopted people in the world feel bad, it is an amazing and solid feeling to know how much my mom and dad wanted me. I seriously never understood the logic behind the running joke where one sibling would tease another by saying, "You're adopted." If people knew what it feels like to be adopted, it seems like young siblings who want to tease another would actually say, "I'm adopted. You're not! So there." :)

I understand Sara being curious. Rest assured that you will always be Mom and Tom will always be Dad. And I know you were not really worried about it. I just wanted to reinforce your assumptions from the angle of a grown adoptee. Ross and Sara have a couple of the best parents in the world. I'm just telling you it's a truth.

Guestbook Note
I just never know what profound and utterly amazing lessons I will learn when I check in here. I am a different woman than the one who showed up at your back door in May and I will forever be grateful to you for helping me. Praise be to God.

Day 139, TUESDAY, SEPTEMBER 21, 2010 4:17 PM

Amy: Home from the FINAL CHEMO treatment! Spent the entire time on my handy dandy iPhone. Texts, emails and phone calls. Did not accomplish anything more than soaking in love and support from so many. When I got home and shut my eyes for 5 minutes, all I saw in that "blackness" (that you have when your eyes are shut but you're not asleep - very familiar to me these past few months) was text boxes and a type screen...very scary. I am addicted to that phone I think. When that is all you see when you try and rest, you KNOW you are on it way too much. I will likely not return any more texts or emails today. I really need to just chill. Sorry if you sent one lately as I may not be getting in touch personally. Just know that I feel so surrounded by love and prayer and just thoughts in general. Thanks ever so much.

My body is seemingly real mad at me today. It is saying something to the effect of, "Really? Are you going to keep pouring that @#$%* in this bod?? Well I am fighting back and slowing you down!" I have usually had more energy on this day than I seem to right now. I have a feeling I am in for a long week. Look out. I just might post more often. Time will tell though.

Starting to feel the steroid effects already. A bit puffy in the cheeks. Hey, maybe that is what we could say when our jeans get tight! "Just a bit puffy in the cheeks." I just might have to remember that one! Anyway, I think I will get the ol' Ambien out again for the next week or so. Hope I don't become an addict. Can't be hooked on that and my phone.

BTW, when I made my last post, know that I, of course, didn't just say to Sara; "We can't do that" about finding her family. I am sure you all know that. I just can't write EVERYTHING about our life here for Petesake. Who is Pete anyway?

Must go. In the grip,

Amy YEE HAW!

I have a theory that Apple might just be the demise of our world! Could it be Satan's sly plan to infiltrate the world with ipads, ipods, iphones and Macs constantly distracting us? The 'bite out of the apple' symbol tipped me off! ;-)

Guestbook Note

I remember the sweet girl who lived next door to me years ago. Now you are a beautiful woman who is a shining light for the Lord Jesus Christ! Amy, I marvel at the way God is working in your life. I pray for new strength for you every day and it's amazing the way you are able to carry on with your family's activities while undergoing chemo treatments. It has been wonderful to see how God is blessing so many people by reading your journal. You give joy when life is tough and encouragement when the journey is rough! Hang in there sweet one and I pray that soon you will be completely healed!

36

That Was You?!

Day 140, WEDNESDAY, SEPTEMBER 22, 2010 3:14 PM

Amy: Home from my final Neulasta injection (white blood cell booster post chemo treatments) and fluids. Probably not the last of those, as I will likely go sit next week for the 2 hours plus to get more saline and vitamins for a boost. May even do it the day before the cruise on Oct. 5th or 6th. I have only done "extra" fluids once but the nurses at the chemo center say they help build strength, insurance covers it, why not do it if it helps out? I can tell this final treatment is slowing me down. Very typical I suppose. Had a 99.4 temp when I went in for fluids today and that is a first. I have to call the doctors if it hits 100.5. Pray that I am not catching some bug!

When getting fluids, I am there for about 2 1/2 hours. In between rests today (I have never slept there until today) I toted my IV stand down the hall to see what food they had brought in for lunch. Mexican. While eating a quesadilla and some rice, I got to talking to this wonderful woman who has the exact same cancer as me. We talked for a while today, shared our stories and talked about family, golf, treatments, etc. As I was getting up to leave she asked my name. When I told her...she said, "I thought that was you!" She has been reading my blog every day! She has a friend who works for her in her office who took my *Designed to Shine* mother/daughter sessions last winter at the church. She told her about my journey and she has been following it ever since...and we had never met until this day as God put us at the same table over

195

lunch. What an amazing journey this has been. Thanks for the talk today, Nila!

Also met a neat lady while out walking Tess today, just down the end of my road. As she was pulling out of her gate, she rolled the window down to ask about Tess as she has two Goldens of her own. We ended up talking for 25 minutes about dogs, cancer and her therapeutic riding ministry, as her property is an acreage, and she and her husband, Dave, are the founders of Panther Creek Inspiration Ranch. I had seen it before but didn't know much about it. Anyway, another couple of conversations I might not ever have had if I felt the need to hide this illness like I some days so desperately want to do. Like now, puffy and wiped out completely. This too shall pass. Hopefully sooner than later.

Too tired to type. The fog in the brain is so thick today.

Resting in Him, before Sara arrives home in 15 minutes.

Amy

Reading back over these entries has been a gift yet again. Remembering how I first met Linda Darnall of Inspiration Ranch is so neat! I can see how God was working that day. I certainly didn't have any idea what lay ahead for our two families' lives as they intersected back then: mosaics created by kids at the ranch for fundraising for PCIR and the recent launch of the pilots for breast cancer survivor programs called HORSES-HEALING-HOPE.

These programs have come from God and we trust HIM to take something bad and use it for good. The same as I trust HIM with the plans for good in my life that will in turn be good for the lives of others. Simple, yes. Beautiful and joyous, yes. It is what lies <u>underneath</u> the complications we make of our lives. His plan can be so simple and beautiful that we actually miss it.

May God receive the glory! Dave and Linda, you are definitely an inspiration. The gradual blending of our lives has been His handiwork. Where it will end up, we will just have to wait and see.

~ 37 ~

Rules of Success

Day 142, FRIDAY, SEPTEMBER 24, 2010 5:02 PM

Amy: As I sit hour after hour and remember that I am done with chemo, all that keeps coming back to my mind is how grateful I am for not having to endure this any longer. As I sit feeling so isolated from the world that is going on outside my fishbowl, I realize how short of a journey this really has been for me. What about SO many that have chemo for twice as long as me or the cancer is not leaving? I wonder how I would handle such news right now? I don't want to know, frankly.

My body aches so much these few days post treatment. All I want to do is eat and lay down. Time passes ever so slowly. I long for company or to talk on the phone but as soon as I start to visit, I get exhausted. I can't win and neither can the friend that calls or stops by. Sorry I laid my head down today, Kristie as we were chatting. :) The bagel was a perfect treat though. Exactly what my tasters were in need of.

I am sitting in my bed and Tess is right here. I am in awe every day at her faithfulness. Why can't we be born as devoted as a Golden Retriever? I don't think she has a self-centered bone in her body. I long for that kind of devotion to my family and to others to come so naturally. Hope we have some insight into that one day. Struggles like cancer do teach one to value what is in the here and now, but our human nature is to always appear more caring, "together" and selfless than I think we often really are. When I look in Tess's eyes, it is so genuine and pure.

Maybe because her brain is not too complex. It is focused on her master. Something to be said for that.

As I have recently been watching more TV than I usually ever had time for, I see all the distractions we have - more than ever before; distractions that keep our focus off our Master and on the things that cause us to strive for the look of having it all "together." Maybe I am just showing my age but it is so intense these days. Surgery for this, pills for that, buy this and have that...it is driving me nuts. I am all for looking good and feeling good but are we hiding from reality more than ever? It seems that everyone on TV has had plastic surgery these days. NOBODY looks older than 50. I am not sure how I feel about this. I am especially fixated on it because I am bald and puffy and about to lose my natural boobs...both of them to boot...and hoping that I have enough tea tree oil to prevent my fingernails from falling off.

Should this make me feel like less of a person? If I turn on the TV...I think so! I mean, we say it is okay and wow, you are strong and have such a positive outlook and blah-blah-blah, but everything "we" as a culture say is, that it isn't okay to not be perfect. When you are sitting in your house fighting the battle for your own existence, you look at all the "rules of success" as hogwash. One could go completely nuts just hoping they are meeting the mark in one way or another. I am choosing not to do that. I don't have the energy to. I am best if I keep the TV off more than I have it on. I wish it weren't this way though.

I am so bored. I don't feel like reading or watching movies nor exercising my brain with puzzles or games. I just want to eat. Nice touch to the sagging muscles. I will worry about that another day.

It is so odd how I feel better when I type here. I don't feel so disconnected somehow. Had a strange lucid dream this afternoon and cannot really recall what it was even about. I just had such a feeling of being so far from home and detached from everyone I love so dearly. I couldn't settle from it and I woke feeling a deep sense of emptiness. Cool thing was, I made myself open my study from Ladies of the Loft (One in a Million) and do a few days of the study. I hadn't had the desire to do it much this week as the whole energy level thing is so off. Since the humidity lifted a bit today, I went outside and opened the book and my bible. God just reached out and settled my soul after that odd dream. He dried my tears of exhaustion and held me right where I was. He is really good at knowing exactly what we need...when we need it. He always waits patiently as we watch the TV, get caught up in the daily self-consumption and even wait for the mail or whatever. He just waits for us to call to Him instead. Hearts tuned in and He is waiting to provide. Amazing...isn't it?

I pray I won't forget how to do that once this journey is over and done with.

Resting in Him and with Tess,
Amy

Guestbook Note

I was struck by your last sentences about wanting to not forget the lessons learned. I think part of why you have written this is so you won't forget. What you went through, how you handled it and what lessons have learned. Also, the love shown to you that certainly validates your place on earth as one of His children who is doing so well. A lesson there for the rest of us.

Guestbook Note

God: make me more like Tess.

Guestbook Note

Don't worry about the boobs! With everything you have gone through at the present time, you DESERVE to have nice perky ones ten years from now!

Maybe that is what has been so hard in this "Phase II" of the cancer journey. More energy but less to draw on from others. The ongoing support fades. It has to. God has not gone anywhere though. As friendships must return to a more normal relationship, He works to move into the role they recently occupied. He continues to wait. He continues to watch and hope that the focus will turn to Him. Just like humans, He does not want to see His child struggle and suffer. Like any good parent, He will let you work through matters in hopes of life lessons making a permanent impact towards life altering change. I continue to go to Him daily and try and learn.

It is different than just one year ago. Already I find myself resorting again to my own understanding, hopes and plans. I just want this experience to change me forever. My Father has carried, walked, and talked with me and now He is placing my feet firmly on the ground. He hopes I will stay close by His side, but knows my nature is to wander.

38

Meltdown

DAY 143, SATURDAY, SEPTEMBER 25, 2010 4:27 PM

Amy: It is Saturday afternoon and I am so glad to say that today is going by much faster than yesterday. It is already 4:30 p.m. Just woke from a little nap so I can try and get a few things done before everyone is home again. Ross is at Caitlyn's house and Sara is at the ranch. Gayle took her up to visit Trinity after her soccer game earlier today. I am thrilled that she is getting to spend the afternoon there. Tom needed some time in the office today and I was able to get outside and swim some laps in the pool. I spent most of the time floating on a raft just watching the huge fluffy clouds. The house was quiet and the pool was still. I just laid there floating and relaxing. Divine. Too bad I wasn't up for much else. Still a very, very slow moving day. The aches are subsiding and the fog is starting to lift. Light at the end of the tunnel. What a difference one day can make. I have been SO GRATEFUL that sleep is coming much easier this time. That makes no sense whatsoever other than the fact that I am really beat. Just a gift. I will take it for what it is. No questioning it, just resting better.

Had a meltdown last night. Pretty much on everyone. It is so hard to keep your cool all the time when you feel like hell. I think they understand that better than I do most of the time. As moms we want to keep everything running smoothly and when I am at home all the time, I see everything that is NOT running smoothly. I have a controlling nature that I cannot seem to tame. Tom is so good for me and helps

201

level the playing field when I am on the verge of losing it. Could not have made it through this season so well without his care and ability to pick up the slack so well as he does. Have been thinking about our getaway that is coming up and looking SO forward to some time alone with him. It seems we get so little of that these days. Part of the hardest thing of not feeling well the past several days has been being alone when I want him to just come and sit beside me. He runs from dawn until after dark some days between work, running errands and running the kids. Someone take that man for a round of golf when this is all done and over with please. He has always walked the talk so much better than me and I admire that ever so much.

Tess just came in the room. It is time to rub her belly. God is good. I am seeing the light at the end of the tunnel. My heart is getting happy.

Amy

After enduring a bout with cancer, it is pretty common to want to do what you can to prevent recurrence and ward off any obvious dangers to your loved ones that may be lurking due to lifestyle. While I have taken on the obvious - diet and other areas where I can educate myself and others that I love - there are the less obvious but equally, IF NOT more important, internal factors that increase the risk of cancer cell growth. Namely stress and other internal struggles. For me, the desire to control my life and the factors surrounding my little world became a battleground for relationships and even my health. During the quiet season of cancer, my Counselor and Friend revealed to me that this was an area that needed attention. While I am still learning just what this means, it has been another gift from my walk through the valley.

Day 144, SUNDAY, SEPTEMBER 26, 2010 3:54 PM

Amy: It's almost 4 p.m. again! Another day under the belt. Have had such a better day than yesterday. Felt well enough to shower and get ready for church. Put mascara on for the first time in 5 days! It felt so good to get out of the house. We made it through the whole service without leaving early. After chemo 5 I had to leave before it was even over! Yeah for today! We stayed a bit long as we love to visit with so many but I tend to over do it. We went to Panera afterwards and ran into like 12 friends from the Loft. Just like in Des Moines...whenever we went to Panera, so many from the Bridge would be there. Ross brought Caitlyn and Sara brought Laura. Fun time had by all. Both are still hanging out at our house now. I can hear the girls upstairs making up dance routines. Silly grills. (Typo on purpose here – old family joke.)

I have been laying down for the past hour. Just trying to replenish the strength used earlier today. I know I need to conserve energy when I can. I tried to sleep but feel very anxious. I think I am just thrilled that I am feeling better and am excited all the time today. Just knowing that I don't have to go back to where I have been has me giddy. I know I have the surgery but that will be different. It's like I feel semi-normal again or something. I know I am far from being back to a real normal but I am excited nonetheless.

Still enduring various side effects. I have noticed more tingling in my hands and feet the past few days. Never had that much before but know many women do. Not enjoyable. Hope it fades quickly. My hearing seems worse than ever before. Also temporary I assume. Dry skin, dry mouth but still no sores!

Now that my body is starting to heal once again, it is time to get positive again. I HAVE to keep my attitude in check. It seems to be the best thing I can do for myself. The mind is so powerful and it scares me how quickly it can shift to the negative. When I surround myself with positive people, it helps SO MUCH. I have been blessed to be able to do that.

Life is good. I insist on living it to my fullest. I think I can say I appreciate the opportunity to re-evaluate what it really means to live it rather than wish it were such and such or more so and so. It is what it is...and what we make it.

What a ride.

In His grip,

Amy

For the record, these troubles WERE temporary. These BODIES are temporary, too! The hearing has improved, the tingling has left and while I am still struggling with wimpy eyelashes, I know this is common and they will gain strength in the months to come. In looking back and in the grand scheme of things, life is going really, really well.

Guestbook Note

And thank you for being a bit of a guru...your words of wisdom really hit home for me. "Life is what it is"... and thanks for reminding me how energy depleting it can be to "wish it were such and such or more so and so." Very astute, Miss Cute...thank you...hero, teacher, "gripped" guru.

Day 145, MONDAY, SEPTEMBER 27, 2010 7:17 PM

Amy: Stronger yet today. Still a ways to go but the sun is setting on this day and a full night's rest brings lots of strength. Woke last night at 4 a.m. Went out to the couch, finally fell asleep around 5 a.m. Still much better off sleep-wise than in treatments past. I am SO GLAD for that.

Sitting out on the back patio before it is dark. I've been able to be out so much today as it is almost a true FALL DAY in Houston. The high was 80 degrees and there was a wonderful breeze all day long. The humidity has broken for the time being and I was able to get Tess out for a walk as late as 10 a.m. today. The time didn't even matter and the temps were perfect throughout the whole day. I actually have a sweatshirt on right now. I doubt it will last but it is a wonderful reminder of fall days in Iowa.

As I sit outside, Sara is watering all the plants for me and Tess is watching her like a hawk. I don't think she trusts her with the hose, actually!

Tom is working late and Ross is hitting the books. The kids seem so, so happy with life right now and I couldn't be more pleased. I had so much doubt about the new school and the trek 20 minutes north. Once again, I seemed to have wasted all my worry as God has taken this matter completely. We did what we felt was the right thing back in December and chose a private Christian school. We knew back then it was the right choice for our family. When the cancer diagnosis came, worry set it BIG time for me (I can't speak for Tom as I was totally consumed with MY worry). I guess I thought this issue was too big for God. Surely He cannot conceive all the trouble I bring on to myself... this must have made Him say: "Oh my Amy, I don't know if I can handle all the stress in YOUR life...you had better take this one back and figure it out with all the useful worry that you can muster. Go for it girl. I am out of here and sorry about the miss-fire on the school."

NO, INSTEAD, God says to me, "Amy, I know the plans I have for you and your beloved family. Did all that worry and fear do any good to you and your health? Will you ever learn, child? I have your back. You are just like the Israelites! I love you anyway and will care for you all of your days. Do me a favor and learn to trust me in all your decisions and let me love you where you are." (Something like that I suppose or I feel anyway.)

The kids are good. So very good. With all our moving I have hated the fact that they have not had a steady "home" or neighborhood like I had growing up. I have worried myself sick about that and have always thought I have been cheating them of something they "deserve." I am finally starting to see that maybe my idea of the perfect childhood for them is not necessarily what God is grooming them for. Maybe, just maybe...He has a better plan than me. Could it be?!

Time to run, Sara wants to use this laptop for some research.

In His grip and now see I would rather be no place else.

Amy

Guestbook Note

What you said about the moving & perfect neighbor-hood struck a chord with me too. I realized that I too, had taken all that on myself to ensure that the right kids & the right everything were right there at my children's fingertips...only the obvious is that it was out of my hands all along! I was trying to protect them after many moves & a divorce but thinking I was trusting God for all of our well being...I didn't see that I was still trying to control it. Thank you for the reminder that His purpose and love are greater & stronger than all. :) I too, feel great to know that it's in His hands. Love to you all.

Day 146, TUESDAY, SEPTEMBER 28, 2010 8:36 PM

Amy: Don't feel like typing much but remember I am journaling all this so my family and I can remember the ups and downs of breast cancer.

This is a downer right now. I am completely wiped out. Went to the store this morning and I think that drains the battery pretty well. I had scheduled an appointment to get fluids today as I have been very low on energy. That took almost 4 hours from the time I got there until the time I left. The huge IV bag of vitamins and saline tasted like a giant prenatal vitamin was stuck in my throat for over 2 hours. Gag. It was the first time I did not have a private room for treatment. It felt really odd to me. I felt more like a cancer patient than I ever have before. I think my attitude about being in that place has shifted a bit. I am real tired of the NW Cancer Center...nothing personal. You just don't feel very "normal" when you are there. I pray I do not have to go through this again. At this point, I cannot imagine having to endure more treatments. My body is completely wiped out from this. I know I can do it but I just don't want to feel like total crap any longer. The side affects are tough. Tougher as the treatments pass. Nurse Brenda gave me quite the praise today though...said she is not used to seeing women handle all the TAC treatment so well and being as healthy as I am/have been is amazing. Great. I am glad my body is stronger than I might have thought it to be.

I am not going to go on and on here about all my woes. It just sucks to be me today. I am at my limit of energy. Better sign off and pray for some more of His.

Limp in His grip,
Amy

I returned to the cancer center earlier this week for my tumor marker and blood work tests. I do this once every six months from here on out, it was once every three months before. As soon as I parked the car and entered through those doors, the old feelings came back like what was journaled on this day back on September 28, 2010. The mind can go back so quickly. Fear started to enter in with the thoughts of: "What if my blood tests indicate a recurrence?" I don't think I could start this process all over again. It took awhile to get calm, but rather than allowing those worries to dominate my long wait, I begged in my mental prayers for peace, regardless, and for God's will for my life to reign.

I am happy to report the results were all in the normal range. You soon learn in the medical PRACTICE world that nothing is a guarantee. Dependence on others to settle your mind is not wise. Dependence on Christ and the Word of God, now that is something to settle in on.

Guestbook Note

All it takes is for me to read your journal and my life gains great perspective. I don't think I could do all you have done. Your body, soul, spirit and faith is so strong. "that little light of yours, you don't let it snore!"

$$\sim 39 \sim$$

The Smudge

DAY 147, WEDNESDAY, SEPTEMBER 29, 2010 6:15 AM

Amy: Slept out on the couch last night. My controlling mind would not shut off until I changed my surroundings from my bedroom to the living room. I do love the sectional couch. It draws you in and is so cozy. Slumber took shape shortly after my arrival. I awoke about 5:45, I am guessing, in a total sleep zoned fog. I forgot where I was. Couldn't get back to sleep and while I was cozy in my down blanket and pillow and darkness all around, I felt the strong sense to get this laptop out. Not what I had in mind.

My focus the past few days has been all about me and my need to control the things around me. Is it because I feel so out of control with everything else lately? Is my mind just weakening with time? Am I already hitting a lull in the faith walk through this time in the wilderness? Or maybe I am just about to have a nervous breakdown?!? That's all we need around here. Mom loses her cool completely...worse things could happen, I am sure of that.

I realized as I was lying in bed that I have not tried to "feel" if the lump is still in my lymph gland since the day the doctors told me the cancer appears to be gone. Oddly, as I laid there thinking about it, I still did not try and feel for it. In the back of my mind I must be afraid I might find it and I don't want to find anything different than the doctors. Why won't I just check and reassure myself? It's a simple movement of the hand. This is completely frightening how powerful

208

our mind is. It will not allow us to go places we just don't want to go sometimes. Think about that for a minute. If I don't PHYSICALLY want to do a simple task of checking for something, I MUST have a fear of "going down that road of possibilities" even if it could mean so much to so many.

With what other things that we can't touch or feel on the outside are we "afraid to go there?" In this instance, I am choosing to believe what experts say...it is gone. I think I just want this to be over with so desperately that the thought of "feeling something" means the road is longer than we thought and I am afraid that would push me over the edge right now. I am CHOOSING to believe what I have heard. Believing to trust what God has said, too. I will feel before this entry is done, just to make myself do it. I know it is gone but the mind is a powerful thing, isn't it?

As I was driving to pick up the kids yesterday, I was thinking about the way I have been focused on little things so much lately and mad that no matter what I try and "hand over" for God to worry about, the more I try and focus on getting better and worrying less...the more I tend to worry. As soon as I surrender things to God, I get tested and fail miserably. The process is long and hard and sometimes we just don't want to do the work.

As I was driving, I kept being bothered by this smudge on my sunglasses. I could not seem to lose focus of it. I was driving terribly as I used my shirt to clean it, then found the sunglasses cloth to work at it a second time. As I continued down the road, I just kept stressing over the little smudge. I removed the glasses and did the hot breath steam bath approach. It appears to be gone now.

As I readjusted my aviators on my bald head, it occurred to me that this is exactly what I am doing with my life right now. I am allowing myself to focus more on the smudge than what lies BEYOND the smudge. Maybe that is what God is telling us every single day. STOP focusing your attention on the smudges on the glass and look out FURTHER! Our focus can be on the little dirt or we can look right past them to the happening world around that is so much better. Same goes for a windshield if you are not a glasses or shades kinda person. When we focus on the tiny parts of the HUGE scene in front of us, we are liable to get into a huge wreck. Not to mention, we see so much less than we are intended to. Here is the hard part. When we are mere mortals, it is so hard to let go of that annoying smudge. Sometimes we wipe and wash and sometimes we just need to readjust our focus for the time being as we might miss the beauty going by. I have no real idea on how to do it but I think I will continue to ask for the ability.

I hear the kids up. Time to "make" some breakfast like frozen waffles or cereal. Great start for their day, I know.

Rested and ready for the day,

Amy

For the record, I still feel the need to clean my glasses from time to time, just not obsessively. If they get too dirty, you might not be able to see what lies beyond, but focusing only on what's directly in front of you is not good either. Like most of life, it's about balance.

Guestbook Note

I loved your writing about the smudge on the glasses! OMG! Have I been in the thick of things lately, it's so hard to let go of those little things and let God do his work...but have to tell you I have handed a lot over to God this week and it helps when the details are taken care of. I continue to be inspired by your words. Keep it up girl. And thanks for listening to me and my smudges... I'm praying for you and look forward to seeing your beautiful smile today.

Guestbook Note

I can't begin to tell you how important and inspirational your journal has been to me. Thanks for helping me look past the smudge. Rest up and heal up so you can go cause more trouble for the Hausers and for Houston!

Day 147, WEDNESDAY, SEPTEMBER 29, 2010 8:33 AM

Amy: Home from running the kids to Conroe. Realized I never mentioned that I felt for the lump. I actually didn't get around to it until I was almost back home from the school run. I don't feel anything but a flabby underarm. Can't wait to start getting back in shape. I am hoping I have a new outlook on what "in shape" really means. It's certainly not just about what appears on the outside but the total mind and body health. I am grateful for that opportunity to see it all in a new light. It is priceless and it is a gift to be able to get out and workout. I can see that today. Ask me if I can still see it in a year from today. God willing and me trying...I will.

Just read two back-to-back guestbook entries. Two of my very closest and long-time friends. Kristi and Krista. Reading your posts and having them there one right after another meant so much. Kristi in Sausalito and Krista back in Des Moines after time in Germany. Me in Houston now. We have so many friends we still keep in touch with but you both have had much loss this past year. Thanks for staying connected through your trials too. God IS good all the time.

It is only 67 degrees right now. I am going to take Tess for a walk. 3rd one for me in 5 days! Might hit 90 today again but it still feels amazing outside. The vitamins and fluids seemed to have taken the edge off for now. Mornings are my strongest part of the day. There seems to be an extra hole in the tank these days though so I can't waste precious time idling in the parking lot!

Cheers to another blue sky day!

Amy

It has been over a year since this post. I check for lumps periodically but not obsessively. We all go to the chiropractor for adjustments weekly and have been learning constantly about a Maximized Living lifestyle of mind, spirit, body, healthy foods and how the spine is the connection from the brain to the central nervous system. Vital information travels from the brain through the spinal cord to all parts of the body, at the same time information from the peripheral parts of the body is being sent back to the brain through the spinal cord. When this information flow is interfered with, problems arise in the body. This new practice is an active movement for our family toward overall healthier living. Regular adjustments, an active lifestyle as well as learning and implementing a changed diet (that is counter to our nation's standards) has provided a plan for going forward as well as we know how. This, coupled with my periodic medical checks, helps me believe I will remain cancer free IF that is in God's plan for my life.

While I know adjustments are not the ONLY way or even the BEST way to achieve health, I know it is more natural than treating symptoms with pills. Chiropractic and diet does not make a bunch of money for a booming medical empire though. Support and growth in spreading knowledge on this way of thinking is not very likely. It is an individual decision.

That being said, I am still working on strength. I workout by doing yoga exercises and walking, but intense workouts still are so hard on my muscles and joints in particular. The lasting consequences of so much poison pumped into my body may continue for some time. I choose to work with the setbacks and try and count the blessings that are in abundance. It is not always easy, but always necessary.

~ 40 ~

Surely This Will End Soon

DAY 149, FRIDAY, OCTOBER 1, 2010 5:22 PM

Amy: It's about time I get some daylight hours in to type in this journal. It is 5:30 p.m. on Friday evening and my high heels are off and my feet up. No swelling today! Only had the heels on about 5 hours so that shouldn't have been cause for elephant ankles anyway.

Today was a beautiful farewell luncheon/party for Micki hosted by Rhonda and Jill. Micki is one of the founding leaders of Ladies of the Loft. Her leadership has been so strong and purposeful. She is moving to Fort Worth and will be greatly missed. I know we will continue to see one another periodically and stay connected but I know too well how hard it is at this busy stage in life. Moving is so hard in so many ways, especially when we as moms work desperately to make sure everyone else is doing okay. Facebook, the internet and cellphones help but there are still only so many hours in a day. We can become so consumed with staying in touch with everyone that there is little to time to just BE. Satan's sly plan, if you ask me but that is an entirely different entry. Balance is not easy to come by these days as there seems to be so much GOOD in what we are trying to do yet killing ourselves in the process. Anyway, Micki will certainly be missed and I have only known her for a year. Change is hard but I know she is aware of how God has a plan and intends it for good.

A few weeks back, Tom and I were asked to attend the Susan G. Komen Race for the Cure event in the Galleria in Houston, by Jennifer, who was the main speaker at TWUMC Cancer Awareness luncheon. We were asked to sit at the table of a generous donor that wanted her table to be filled with survivors of the disease. The dinner was tonight and what an honor this evening was! Tom and I met SO, SO many people. Again, I almost feel the baldness gives you some weird sort of "stand out" status or something. I even was introduced to Nancy Brinker and we talked for a few minutes. If you don't know who that is...don't feel bad. I didn't either. I am NOT going to go into that story in print. Anyway, she is the founder of the Susan G. Komen Foundation. Her only sister was Susan G. Komen and she passed away of breast cancer several years ago. She promised her she would do SOMETHING to fight for her cause. Needless to say, she certainly has.

Over 40,000 people are registered to participate in THE RACE in Houston tomorrow morning. I desperately want to be there. I know in my heart and soul though that my body is just too weak and low in my blood count to go deal with the crowds. I cannot imagine how many will be there that are not actually doing the race so we need to stay home. Next year I will be there rain or shine. I cannot wait to be a part of such a beautiful cause and share in my enthusiasm of HOPE. If we don't have HOPE in all our causes and passions, what is really left?

In His grip,
Amy

Day 151, SUNDAY, OCTOBER 3, 2010 3:38 PM

Amy: It feels like a fall afternoon. Beautiful out and like most days, there is not a cloud in the sky. As soon as Tom gets back from his annual car inspection, we are off to walk the Waterway with Tess and Sara. Ross is away at Mission Waco and I have missed not being in communication with him at all. He is due to be home early evening. Can't wait to hear all about the "homeless simulation" experience.

Yesterday was forecasted to be beautiful so Sara and I headed out to the ranch early to ride. She and I spent two amazing hours riding Trinity and Revelation all over the 100+ acre ranch, just she and I and the horses. There is not much else on this earth I would rather do, nor in a more beautiful place. The property is loaded with fields, ponds and towering pines. The only thing missing was maybe a mountain or two but it was the next best thing. We love it out there and loved just exploring the trails. Sara has become such a good rider! She and Trinity are a great pair. Trinity is only 6 so she has a lot of spunk and get up and go. Sara handles her so much better than I ever could have at that age. Proud momma here. After riding we went straight to her soccer game. She is advancing nicely in those skills. Very strong defender for her slight build. Tough lady inside and out.

As I was driving home from the game, I became completely exhausted and my body began to hurt all over. I had to again come home and go straight to rest for a while. I don't realize when I over do it until it is too late. I bounced back pretty quickly but the feelings that hit are almost impossible to describe. The weakness and surges of discomfort overcome you. This is bound to pass soon.

My mouth has had the feeling of numbness (is that even possible??) for going on 3 weeks. A few sores have surfaced after all this time and I really cannot taste much. My muscles have completely gone and my skin is dryer than ever. I guess this is just the piling on of the chemo drugs over the past 5 months. Side affects wreak havoc on the mind and body. I know my daughter is exasperated with my brain fog, the eye rolling at my lack of ability to remember anything is a telltale sign. Everyone is getting tired of it...especially me.

Surely this will all end soon. It is the price I have to pay for having my health. I dare not complain too much. Tom is home. Time to get outside and count my blessings.

God is good.

Amy

Guestbook Note

I thank God for the faith He's given to both of you. Your journal entries are evidence of His sustaining love for you both. May your love for one another be nourished by His grace as you endure the medical procedures ahead. Every marriage is a challenge and I pray yours will continue to be strengthened. Remember, He holds you securely by His right hand (Ps 139).

I had not noticed the relevance of this reference before! Psalm 139, all of it, is a beautiful reminder that He made us and keeps us and holds us firmly in His hand (grip).

Day 153, TUESDAY, OCTOBER 5, 2010 6:06 PM

Amy: Seems that the past week has been loaded with crazy-busy stuff that keeps preventing me from sitting down to try and decompress and just journal. At times I want to record everything that is happening in this season of life but LIFE keeps getting in the way. I have been strong in the morning hours and keep pushing more than I should to get other things done until evening arrives. Today was a beautiful fall day and I didn't even get to enjoy it much, just doing STUFF and preparing for our trip on Thursday. I was hoping to get Tess out for a short walk but have run out of fuel to get that done. Ross said he would take her before dark.

As I think of all the things that I'd like to accomplish before surgery October 20, some things I know I will have to put on the back burner or wonder what Tom can or cannot do. I have to just let it all go.

In His grip and holding tight to that thought every day,

Amy

Sara and I spent so much time together, just hanging out and snuggling. Ross, growing into a young man, demonstrated his support more along the lines of the strong, reflective type. He is a very kind and caring young man, and is generous with his affections. Still waters run deep. He is growing more like his father each day.

41

Celebration

DAY 155, THURSDAY, OCTOBER 7, 2010 7:43 AM

Amy: The day has finally arrived that we have been waiting a long time for. A celebration of the successful completion of breast cancer treatment! Tom and I leave for the short trip down to Galveston to board a Carnival Cruise ship that will sail for 2 days, spend a day in Calico, Mexico and then head back to Galveston. We return Monday. The kids are heading out with their friends, Kade and Mia to visit the new Harry Potter Park at Universal Studios in Orlando. They fly out today as well. The weather has been perfect this past week and looks to be for the next several days as far as we can tell. What a gift. All this as the nation acknowledges Breast Cancer Awareness during the month of October on top of it all. Our anniversary is October 12 (19 years strong) and surgery the 20th. Big month for the Hauser family.

As I think back to the end of May and the news of the diagnosis, I feel like we have gone through so much - things I was hoping I would not have had to endure in my lifetime. Things I didn't really care to learn about myself or my family just yet. The time has seemed to stand still for me these past 5 months as I have had a one-track mind for the most part. So often my mind just wanders to the thought of those that must endure this so much longer than me. My heart breaks for them as I have met many in such a place. I refuse to let my mind think that this could be me again one day. I just cannot think that way. I have to look ahead to the new and cancer free me! Hair growth will help with that outlook when I begin to see "new growth" on the inside and out, I suppose. I look forward to that more than I can express. I also cannot wait to be able to reflect back on all that I have learned once I no longer feel the active part of this all consuming time in life.

Oddly, I am afraid I will miss parts of it. Much like I still miss being pregnant. I don't miss the hassle parts of pregnancy but the parts that were life changing. Seeing my body grow with new life; the feeling of movement within my own being that only God can get the glory for is a miracle that is so evident; the closeness that the process brings between family members, and the anticipation of finally closing that chapter and moving on to the promise of new things.

Cancer has many parallels to pregnancy. The main difference being; one represents new life and the other potentially death. I was determined that once I did not receive a death sentence...it had to represent a new view of life. That was a gift from God and not of my own doing. He allowed me to do that in very unique way. Just like I don't want to ever forget some of the feelings of my childbearing days, nor do I want to forget the process of cancer leaving my body, even in the most painful of days. God meant it for good, even if it hurts sometimes.

Last night, for a little pick me up, I went to my basket of cards that I have received over the past several months. I only needed to read 4 or 5 before I felt the power of prayer and scripture lift me up to where I needed to be. So many friends have been an encouragement and when I take that in, it does exactly what I need for that moment. Support is a huge part of successfully coping with illness. I think that is exactly what Christ had in mind and He smiles when we do it. In the past, my strong suit was never serving the needs of those who were ill or dealing with loss, and I am not sure it ever will be as much as I'd like it to be, just because I am not as organized or "others" focused - as I am painfully aware.

The cool thing is, I have become aware of how MANY people ARE! I have also learned that there are so many different ways to serve those in need. Some do meals, some by staying in regular contact verbally or physically, some by writing, some by praying and some by various mixes of things. ALL are valuable and appreciated. Doing what we do best does best for the recipient. Enough said. We are grateful as a family that reaps the benefit.

- I MAY BE TIRED, BUT THE CANCER IS GONE
- I MAY BE A FEW POUNDS UP ON THE SCALE, BUT AT LEAST I CAN EAT
- I MAY BE EXASPERATED WITH MY CHILDREN WHEN I AM COMPLETELY WORN OUT, BUT AT LEAST I HAVE CHILDREN
- I MAY HAVE CLOUDY VISION AND BUZZING EARS, YET I AM NOT BLIND NOR DEAF
- I MAY COMPLAIN ABOUT TIGHT MUSCLES OR WEAKNESS, BUT IN TIME I WILL BE ABLE TO RE-BUILD MY STRENGTH WHILE SO MANY CANNOT EVEN WALK.

ROCK ON.
GOD IS GOOD...ALL THE TIME!
Amy

Guestbook Note
Big shout out to friends Rhonda and Larry for taking charge of Ross and Sara so that this get-away could happen. Real friends keep your kids and you are carefree because of who they are with. That's you, Rhonda. I wanna be just like you when I grow up. Or like Amy, either one.

Day 160, TUESDAY, OCTOBER 12, 2010 10:46 AM

Amy: The whole Hauser family is back home from some fun-filled vacation time away. Tom and I had a really great time on our short cruise to Cozumel, Mexico. Not Calica. My bad once again. Didn't really matter to us where the stop was, just wanting blue waters to snorkel in. Next time we will be diving though! Hopefully with Whale Sharks in Central America! Sara says she thinks she is ready to get certified and give it a try...yeah! Ross has been ready since he was a tyke.

Tom and I had perfect weather on the boat and caught up on some much needed R&R. We spent lots of time reading, lounging on the decks, sipping drinks, napping and visiting with some great people.

The water and marine life during our snorkeling were great. No sharks though. Back on the ship, we had a table of 5 couples at our late seating dinner hour and had a blast with all of them. Everyone was from Texas... actually most of the ship was full of Texans. 3 from our dinner table were from the Houston area and we hope to meet up for dinner again one day sooner than later. Thanks for the added fun, fellow cruisers!

Ross and Sara had an equally great time...maybe even better! The Universal Parks and Harry Potter Park met the mark all the way. It was the Halloween-themed time after hours at the parks so they had plenty of Hollywood level scare from haunted houses and all the trimmings to keep them up at night. Great weather, great food and the Hard Rock Hotel to boot! Lucky kids. Words cannot express our gratitude, Larry and Rhonda. Your friendship is such a gift from God.

So, I am finally feeling back to normal, health-wise. I have been taking vitamin C, Folic acid and B12 for about 2 weeks. I had also started on CoQ10 after I researched the benefits and talked to my oncologist for approval to boost the enzymes that help with the DNA of red and white blood cell growth.

Unfortunately, I only took those for about 6 days when the blood pumping level to my heart started going WILD! I could see my veins in my chest popping to the surface and I could not sleep a wink. I realized it was because of this added supplement and decided to stop 2 days ago. I feel stronger and slept so much better after I stopping taking it. Seems just 6 days' worth did the trick though as I am feeling well. I have my pre-surgery appointment for blood work up and pre registration at 1 p.m. today. Getting ready for the big day. A week from tomorrow. Can't wait to see my sister and have her here to help out with things and look after Ross and Sara. She has been recently diagnosed with pleurisy though. She is on antibiotics but prayer that she is 100% before she flies out of South Bend, IN would be greatly appreciated! No idea how she got that other than the fact she cracked a rib a few weeks ago and it can make you more prone to get pleurisy if your breathing has been weakened. Never a dull moment with my family. Time to sign off and get ready for my appointment.

BTW...celebrating 19 years of marital bliss today. Happy Anniversary Tom! Thanks for the trip of celebrations.

Both in His grip,
Amy

Marital bliss...you know I was joking, right? I love to say that we have had marital bliss though! Marriage is such a gift. Television has trashed any real image of a good or normal marriage. Just having someone who has actually put up with me this long and has seen the good, the bad, and the ugly, and still wants to stay by my side, is worthy of my dreams. Tom has known me longer and knows me better than my own blood and that is something to cheer about and to call BLISSFUL! Friends come and go, family moves away, children grow up, but a spouse is there through it all and climbs in bed next to you night after night. My view of what bliss might look like when we where first married compared to what bliss looks like now is totally different. I think we really are in bliss after all!

— 42 —

Unwelcomed Reflection

DAY 161, WEDNESDAY, OCTOBER 13, 2010 9:38 AM

Amy: As the light dims on my laptop screen, I don't like the reflection I see staring back at me today. I see a furrow-browed woman with glasses frames too wide for her hairless head staring back at me. Some days, I don't welcome the reflection. Today seems to be one. Working on that. I woke this morning around 5:30 and moved out to the couch. I had that feeling again where I had a story to tell and I felt the nudging to get my laptop and write. I chose not to listen. I was more into getting rest. Doing things MY WAY. I rolled over and took the opportunity to snooze for another hour instead. God was giving me the chance to tap into His abundant gifts of cleansing and renewal for a glimpse into what He wants to reveal or renew...knowing I needed it, yet I chose to say "No thanks. I am in a crappy mood and I prefer to stay here because I am rather comfortable in this place of misery, and my family is used to it more than the happy-go-lucky cheerful place that I have been in so much of the time lately..."

What I want to know is why? Why when we are really working on our faith-walk as Christians...trying to learn more, understand more and trust in our Heavenly Father more...do we sometimes FEEL HIS PRESENCE and KNOW He is guiding us and our actions, and then sometimes (even in the same season of life) we feel He has backed away a bit?

Our hearts are the same, we still trust and love Him the same, yet we FEEL differently somehow. Almost abandoned. As if our Father is saying, "I have carried you when you needed me most, now I need to see if you have learned what I was whispering in your ear. You need to walk MY talk a bit on your own and see if you have grown and learned from My ways."

Problem for me here is I have done this so often and I usually fall quickly on my face. He just shakes His loving head and picks me up, dusts me off and stands me up again. I know He will always be there to help me up but I would like to please Him one day and say, "Look Dad...I didn't fall this time! You've taught me well!" I am not sure if that is what He is striving for as the goal (like we as parents try to do with our own children) or is His goal completely different and quite the opposite?

Could it be we are supposed to yearn for that "feeling" we have when the Spirit is so indwelled in us that we are to cry out for it? As believers we know that we have to walk in the wilderness at times but I am not really talking about wilderness here as much as just a feeling of presence. Some people may not even know what I am talking about but that is okay too. Years ago I would have thought I was nuts, but now, it is the greatest feeling I have ever experienced and one I wish for everyone to experience. I have learned to seek it out. Matthew 7:7 says; *"Ask and it will be given to you; seek and you will find;"* I think this is what the scripture is talking about.

I am pondering much today. The mystery of faith baffles me sometimes. The certainty of what we know and trusting what we do not see. Why the tests of our heart? I suppose our faith walk can be much like the relationships in our own lives. We can reap the benefits when we are physically close and be full of energy in one another's presence, but when we are far apart...though we know the love and caring and thoughts are there, the connection is different. The heart has not changed although the momentary joys are not there quite like they are when we see one another face to face. You can talk, text, Skype and so on but the intensity will vary. The knowledge that you will see each other again (sooner or later) keeps the relationships intact and ever growing and changing.

In His grip as His arms are long and strong,
Amy

Guestbook Note

You have no idea how powerfully you have touched me through your journal. You already know Tom is one of "my guys." He is one of those 2:00 am friends. You know the ones, if they called at 2:00 am and asked for help you'd say "I'm on my way" and reach for the keys. Even if it's a long way to Houston. But you have touched me every bit as much as your knucklehead husband. Your post today hit me straight on, like many before it. Sounded like you were channeling me and my feelings/ questions.

I'm glad you and Tom had a nice escape. Terri and I will be praying for all of you as you take the next step next week. And thanks for putting yourself and your faith out there for the rest of us knuckleheads. We need it. We all want to make Dad proud, even if that's not at the top of His list.

Day 164, SATURDAY, OCTOBER 16, 2010 2:11 PM

Amy: SIMPLY BEAUTIFUL day today. Not much time to journal. Busy living life! Sara had a rockin' good soccer game this morning and now she is getting ready to head to SCREAM ON THE GREEN for a BBQ, pumpkin patch and carving and dancing at TWUMC. Tom and I are off with Rick and Vanessa to a winery to listen to several great country rock bands, including the Kyle Hutton Band that happens to be Vanessa's brother.

Trying to rest up for surgery a bit. Tom and I walked earlier today and I've been trying to do that each day and doing some hand weights as my body is getting stronger. Slowly but surely.

The care has been great here and Deb flies in Tuesday evening. We are looking forward to having her here to fill in the gaps. Life is good. God is good.

I will be reading the old prayers and notes that I have of course saved over the months to provide strength before Wednesday morning. Prayers for a quick recovery from the 6 hours of surgery would be greatly appreciated. Tom could use a few prayers as well for the ability to keep all the kids activities and school deadlines straight!

Happy weekend.

Amy

Guestbook Note

Anna has been asking about you almost daily. We drove last night past your old development. Anna said she would cry if she saw your old house. She misses you (and so do I). We will pray for you and your family as you prepare for and undergo this (hopefully) final step.

Guestbook Note

I can't tell you how much your journal entries have inspired me. I am part of a house group through HOPE {Lutheran Church} now. I lead a group of sophomore girls. I never imagined that I would be able to do such a thing. I prayed about how I could possibly be more a part of the lives of teenagers. It was only 3 days later when our youth pastor asked if I would be interested! I thought to myself, "Wow did I say that out loud or something!" I was so taken back by the call. There was no way I could turn that down. I explained to the Pastor where I am at on my spiritual journey. He said it was OK and that we want you right where you are at! God was definitely trying to get my attention. I pray that I continue to listen with open ears and heart. I couldn't but help think of you and all that you are doing now. Times and priorities change! {lifelong friend of Amy's}

43

Not On Our Own

DAY 165, SUNDAY, OCTOBER 17, 2010 8:55 PM

Tom: The spousal unit here. I thought I would give an update on the proceedings and maybe a thought if it survives through the update.

It is Sunday evening and I am sitting on the back portico enjoying the temperature dropping towards the 70's. Sara spent last night at her friend's so the rest of us slept in a bit and then enjoyed Andy's sermon – it followed up well on yesterday morning's men's group discussion – the world likes the gray, but we are called to be on the extremes – light or darkness, black or white, believe or don't believe, right or wrong. I am looking forward to the rest of the series. Some may think I live too much on the extremes as it is!

In case we aren't able to update much this week…Tuesday night Debbie flies in, Ross has a soccer game - they are to wear pink. He and I went to Academy and bought pink socks, headband and wristbands. He manned up and didn't seem bothered, but then the whole team will be doing it. The keeper is even going to look for a pink jersey. He is a neat young man and Ross says he is definitely the "dad" on the team – a leader who everyone looks up to. Seeing role models like that helps take some of the anxiety out of being the parent of a teen.

Amy has her pre-surgery injection Tuesday as well. Some type of isotope (not the Albuquerque baseball team) that will be an indicator of whether radiation will be necessary after surgery. We are hoping and praying that it won't!

Wednesday we are to be at the surgery center at 5:30 – that would be a.m. Oh-dark-thirty in military time. Surgery is scheduled for 6 hours – 4 for the double mastectomy and 2 for the reconstruction surgeon to lay foundations for maintaining the health of the skin, tissue, muscle, etc. until they are ready for the reconstruction surgery. I have said it before and repeat it now, I want to see the catalog and have a say on the replacement parts…fat chance of that!

The schedule is for two nights in the hospital. We will see how Amy feels to see if the kids will come down Wednesday night or wait until Thursday – same with whether I spend the nights there or at home. The hospital is only 5-10 minutes from work and only 20-25 from home, so we don't have to battle Houston traffic and parking – a huge plus. We are as comfortable with our surgeon – Dr. S. – as any doctor either of us has ever had. Calm, professional, and a great bedside manner – he just exudes competency and excellence in a subdued, humble way. He has also been the surgeon for several ladies we have met and all give him top marks. Having that confidence in the surgeon is huge.

As always, the outpouring of help has been unbelievable. Jesus has no shortage of hands and feet in north Houston. Sara is covered to and from soccer Thursday and Saturday, Ross and Sara both are covered to and from school Wed – Friday. Meals are coming and I have had numerous, pull-me-aside, genuine 'whatever-we-need--just call' offers. You hear that a lot, but these were each and every one heart-felt and heart-received. Thank you more than I can express guys (and gals) – you know who you are and so does the Man who sent you. Amy and I, and the kids, are forever in your debt.

I did have a thought that has been rattling around my addled brain this week and won't go away; so I feel compelled to write but am not sure where to start, so I guess I just blurt it out. I know that surprises all of you who know me well! :/ It is the phrase "God does not give you more than you can handle." To which I respectfully want to reply; "horse hockey!!!" (With thanks to Colonel Potter for coining such an apt phrase.) I have read the Bible a bit over the last few years, and nowhere (to my limited knowledge) does it utter such nonsense – at least not with that emphasis. Maybe in Hallucinations 3:16!

To be more precise, the prevailing sentiment is that He does not give, cause, allow, nor permit Satan (read Job sometime, and follow up with C.S. Lewis's <u>The Screwtape Letters</u>), or "life," to give us more than we can handle. I beg to differ. The only way most of us meaningfully grow in our faith is when life (from whatever quarter) does hand us more than we can handle. Is this not the essence of growing in our faith – when things are beyond us and we have no hope but to trust in Him? None of us are getting out of this world alive.

We can get out of it and to a better place, but not due to our own efforts. It is only when we realize that we cannot "handle" life, or certain facets of it, that we turn to the One who can. Yes, the Bible does state; "I can do all things..." but that is only the first part of the promise. It finishes by telling us *how* we can "do all things;" "I can do all things <u>through</u> <u>Christ</u> <u>who</u> <u>strengthens</u> <u>me</u>." So no, He does not give us more than we can handle...as long as we know that the handling of it all depends on partnering with Him for the victory. Better is the claim that, "Nothing can happen to me today that together God and I cannot handle."

Having said all of this; God frequently has to use a 2x4 to get my attention, if not a 4x4. In each and every case, the realization eventually comes that this is more than I can handle – *on my own*. These are the times I grow, by reaching out to Him and to others and understanding just a little bit more of the grand plan that is so frustratingly revealed one frame at a time. I prefer the old movie speed of 18 frames per second with the ability to fast forward, but those buttons don't exist in real life. The only one that does seem to occasionally work is the one that plays it even slower.

Where I am going with this...? Don't know...other than if you, or I, or anyone thinks they can do it on their own, then they have another think coming (credit mom for that one). Amy can't and hasn't and won't be able to. I can't and haven't (although not without trying) and won't be able to. No one can effectively, for any length of time, handle life on his or her own. Many have tried, some have done better than others, but none have accomplished it. Even the Lone Ranger had Tonto, the Green Hornet had Kato, and John Wayne needed his horse, dog, or Jack Elam...

Please keep us all in your prayers this week and beyond. There has been incredible strength given to us through life's series of episodes, but that does not mean it has not been without its periods of dark despair, angry questioning and sometimes feelings of hopelessness and meaninglessness. Through it all we have somehow made it through it all, *but not on our own.*

Guestbook Note

Tom, my response to your great post is "Amen, Brother!" In other words, I agree with your horse hockey assessment of "God won't give us more than we can handle." He may not give or cause things to happen to us, but we can take comfort in knowing that in every situation, He wants more than anything for us to turn to Him to meet all our needs, and He is faithful to do that. In fact, He designed us to be 100% dependent on Him so we don't take things into our own hands and screw stuff up. In the occasional moments when I remember to rely on Him, He has taught me that life is WAY easier in that mode than when I try to figure things out by myself. He has to remind me often, but I'm starting to get it.

One of my favorite quotes is something I learned in Christ-Life Solution (I don't have original material either): "The Living God, Creator of the universe, lives in me, and He has a complete and perfect solution to every situation I face." There's such peace in that.

May you, Amy, Ross and Sara rest in the knowledge that you're in the hands of the great provider and He is carrying you toward His perfect and beautiful solution.

Amy, you're closer and closer to emerging from this year's medical cocoon with wings and a life even more beautiful than what you've experienced in all your years thus far. Maybe it's hard to believe and I know this week isn't going to be easy. Prayers are with you. I know you've got to take one day at a time, but I'm really looking forward to seeing everything unfold for you in the coming months/years and the way you and the family will impact others in positive ways.

Guestbook Note

Parenting brings me to that point of realizing I do have more than I can handle. It is good to be reminded this is an opportunity to let go and let my faith grow. You all are in my prayers. I thought and prayed for Amy as I stood at TCU's stadium on Saturday and paid tribute to her battle with cancer. May victory be hers as she fights back!

44

In By 8 and Out by 11:30!

$\mathcal{D}$AY 166, MONDAY, OCTOBER 18, 2010 2:30 PM

Amy: Another shorty. Love reading the notes. Thanks for all the thoughts and prayers. I can SO FEEL THEM all! I feel stronger than I have in 5 plus months and the vertigo and tingling in my legs seems to have subsided for the most part. I am about to take Tess on another walk as I have been trying to get that in each day for the past week or so. I feel much better about my physical strength going into surgery now and I am so happy about that! The little trip away was just what I needed!

This whole journey has been such a group effort and I love that! The online journal has allowed me to feel a connection that I TRULY NEEDED to beat this thing! By letting others know what I needed in prayer and YOU ALL BEING WILLING TO PROVIDE it has helped HEAL me! This is community on a grand scale! Community from all over this country and beyond. There have been so many emails from friends and family of friends, saying they have put my needs and cancer healing prayer requests out there and on church prayer chains, and I can SO tell! I feel at peace about the surgery Wednesday and I know it is because God is pleased when we come together and care for others. Thank you.

Now I just need a timely recovery so I can get doing whatever it is I am supposed to do going forward. Pray that I don't allow FEAR to pull up a chair to those "meetings of the mind," saying that a recurrence is in my future. I guess a normal feeling once chemotherapy is now over, but I don't want it to rob the joy of the new found role of survivor-ness. That completely makes no sense but hey. Tom is much more eloquent that I. That's why we make the perfect pair. Two ships passing in the night... or he a plane that just flew over my head in our case. I am still the ship in the water just floating along... We are ok with that visual.

Will write about our Tulip the hamster story later maybe. Never a dull moment here.

Still bald in His grip,

Amy

Day 168, WEDNESDAY, OCTOBER 20, 2010 12:51 PM

Tom: In by 8 and out by 11:30! Not 6 hours after all!

Amy should be to her overnight room any minute now. The surgery went very well and both surgeons were very pleased. No visible or physical signs of cancer and only 2 lymph nodes showed the dye/isotope marker and had to be removed - both on the right side where the tumors were found. She is resting comfortably in post op and is expected to have a good recovery, maybe only one night if she feels up to it!

Ross called from school to check during the surgery, worried about his mom. I called the school after surgery to let both he and Sara know all went well; then sent notes to family, friends and co-workers. If I overlooked someone, I apologize. I was trying to get as many notes out as I could as fast as I could.

Many thanks for the infinite prayers, notes, calls, visits and texts the last few days (actually through the whole time). They were and are felt, appreciated and treasured. No shortage of His hands, arms and feet around us...

t

Day 168, WEDNESDAY, OCTOBER 20, 2010 2:44 PM

Tom: Update #2

Amy is in her room and resting. The post op was closer to 2 hours, but all was well. She is very sore and can't move much and it hurts to open her eyes. A few ice chips, spoonfuls of broth and small chunks of red jello made up lunch - no Rudy's barbecue!

She can hit her pain button every 10 minutes and we are doing so on the button.

She looks beautiful, good color, no signs of swelling at all. She said she feels like her chest has a lead weight on it, and it is wrapped up pretty tight. Lots of tubes still - oxygen, pain med, monitors, pressure sleeves, but she seems to be resting fairly comfortably.

We may bring the kids down so they can feel reassured. They have had to do a lot of growing up lately, but I believe much of that will be used for the good of being prepared for life ahead. I have tried to stay true to one of my earliest parenting pledges; my job is not to remove the potholes and boulders from their road, it is to prepare them to successfully navigate through them, finding the strength the Lord offers them, on their own (or at least without Amy and me) someday. I know - mean dad. And, yes, I have broken up a few of the larger boulders on occasion.

t

Guestbook Note

God is so good. I see that so clearly through both of your posts, even though I stand on the periphery of your current trials. He shines through you in your posts, in how you parent, in how you love. I adore that you can see Amy's beauty glowing even right after surgery. I love how you are so aware of your children's fears and their needs--and the educational opportunities. You both are such inspirations. I've been praying for you since the note from Pastor Jane arrived this morning, knowing that today is probably one of the most important days in your lives. You're amazing disciples, and I thank you for sharing your experiences and faith with us all. God bless you. I'll continue to pray for strength, healing, and most of all, that His love continues to be revealed to you. You've got an AMAZING future ahead of you! Xoxoxo

Guestbook Note

I said a prayer for you as I drove across the Golden Gate Bridge. Today was sunny and it was hard to miss God's glory when I glanced at the oceans horizon. From sea to shining sea, people are sending their love and well wishes to you. Heal fast! This chapter is almost over. You did it! I am so proud and happy for you.

45

A Different Reflection

DAY 169, THURSDAY, OCTOBER 21, 2010 2:26 PM

Amy: It's 2:30 pm Thursday. I'M A JOURNAL JUNKY!! I just wanted to touch base with everyone and say I am doing REALLY WELL! No more morphine drip and only pain pills here and there. Not near as much as they have offered up.

Deb stayed the night with me last night, which was so nice. Tom was able to hang with the kids and get them off to school this morning. Early out at Covenant today so Tom brought them here awhile and the four of them just left. Tom looked wiped out and I think he is going home for a little snooze. They are all coming back for a little visit after supper tonight. I'm going to try and nap soon myself. The pain pills seem to be wiring me a bit. Just like my momma.

I just want to say that I am living proof of the amazing power in prayer. I handed this stress over to our Heavenly Father and with your diligence in prayer He handled everything. The surgery went smooth and quick and the shortage of pain seems to have the nurses a bit bewildered. I am so grateful. Now pray for hair.

Guestbook Note
My prayers have been answered. Have been working at church replacing heating system last two weeks with you on my mind saying prayers for a successful outcome. Blessings from GOD, for all of us who love you Amy.

Guestbook Note

Haley and I are working at the Des Moines "Race for the Cure" tomorrow in honor of YOU! We're celebrating your life, all the good things about your cancer journey, and how you have glorified God so greatly on your journey! We will be handing out water bottles and holding signs toward the finish line. We are putting bright yellow duct tape on the back of our volunteer shirts that reads "CELEBRATING AMY HAUSER!" I'll try to get someone to take a picture for us!!

Guestbook Note

"....*The joy of the Lord is your strength.*" Nehemiah 8:10

Day 171, SATURDAY, OCTOBER 23, 2010 2:31 PM

Amy: It is Saturday afternoon post surgery week. Feeling pretty well. Better than I thought I would be. Yesterday Tom and I came home from the hospital around 11 a.m. With a new oral antibiotic and pain prescription, my stomach was not a happy camper. Tossed my lunch a few times. Not pretty. I have to say that was the first and only time I have been physically ill during this entire cancer shindig. Hopefully the last. I am not a good patient when vomiting is in the picture. Debbie has been such a great nurse for me. She held the bowl for me, wiped my mouth, has dumped my 4 bloody drains more than once, and has filled in as "mom" for Ross and Sara; by helping them study for tests, watching movies, and even helping Sara bake a Welcome Home cake for me! She completely rocks!

Tom and Ross are at an ISU vs. Texas football game and Sara is with Peyton and her family for the day. She has a 5 p.m. soccer game that the guys should be back in time for. Deb and I are sitting around visiting and she has not stopped cooking and doing laundry during all of our visiting. It is so good to have her nearby this week.

I am getting real bored of sitting so still. May need to try and walk tomorrow or something. I have only taken one Vicoden pain pill today as I hate the spacey and sleepy way I feel on them. I'd rather be a bit sore than falling in and out of sleep all day. I will take them before bed again though for a good nights sleep.

My hair is a thick fuzz on my head now. Actually somewhat matted when I sleep on it! Colorless for the most part at this point. All glory to God that the cancer seems to be gone. That is all that really matters now. My chest is tightly bound with white hospital bandages. Drains are pinned to my dressings.

When I look in the mirror I do not really see the same person I used to see. In some ways, I do not recognize the refection looking back at me, yet over the past 6 months I've gotten to know her. I wonder if the old reflection will come back or if it will ever be the same. I am not sure which I want. A blend of the best qualities would be ideal but I will leave that up to my Maker as He knows best.

I am relieved that when I look in the mirror and see my physical state today, I am ok with where I've been and what I have had to go through. I've been provided with just what I have needed to get through each and every obstacle. Soon the hair will grow and I will be able to have reconstruction and to the passerby, I will no longer have a label saying CANCER. I will always have a label saying CANCER SURVIVOR in my heart. I pray that it is one everyone who meets me will be able to read without seeing the physical signs. I pray it is something I can use for good from this day forward.

Romans 8:28
A bit sore in His grip,
Amy

***ALL THINGS WORK TOGETHER FOR GOOD FOR THOSE WHO PUT THEIR TRUST IN THE LORD!** Paraphrasing Romans 8:28*

This has been my favorite scripture for about the past 9 years. Someone sent it to me when we were going through some REALLY rocky valleys in life. I have since memorized it and prayed for clarity and understanding of it. I truly believe it now. He has revealed His faithfulness so much over the past several years as we as a family have learned through trial and error… over and over again…what TRUST really looks like. It has been the best gift I could ever ask for and one of the hardest to accept, yet worth the endurance and fight to gain. Well worth the quest, I might add!

Guestbook Note

New Cruising friends...I've been thinking about ya! I walked 18 miles today to prepare for the 3-day walk. Only 2 more weeks before I walk 60 miles in 3 days all for boobies. :) I'm glad to hear all is as well as can be. Family is such a blessing. It sounds like your sister is your angel on land. Brian and I will continue to send prayers your way!

Day 172, SUNDAY, OCTOBER 24, 2010 12:04 PM

Amy: Sunday around noon. Been sitting out back for the past few hours reading <u>Secretariat</u>. Family is at church. Nice day still. Humidity seems to be down a bit. Tess and Bear sitting on the patio with me. Life is good. Sore but good. Stiff back and chest wall muscles more today than they have been. Keep making the effort to take deep breaths every few minutes to keep the lungs healthy and using the muscles. Did decide to take a pain pill again about an hour ago. Takes the edge off a bit.

I put one of those cotton tube top long summer dresses on earlier so I would not be so hot. Look like I am ten years old in the chest. Creepy. That will change as the weeks pass and the weekly visits to the plastic surgeon happen. I know, but still. I am not letting it get me down though. Again, the cancer is gone and that is all that really matters. Time to get back to my book and enjoy the quiet before everyone gets home and Ross shows up with 3 friends for the afternoon. Love getting back to some normal activities for them. Love that they all want to be here with us. Sara stayed the night at Gabby's and they are playing for a while still. The kids have some amazing friends, especially their parents, and we are thrilled that they are so well cared for.

Until tomorrow. In His grip,

Amy

Guestbook Note

Okay, so... Mom gets a cancer diagnosis. Endures effects like losing hair. Has surgery. Is in recovery after beating cancer. What kind of home do kids want to visit under these circumstances? Must be a home where Mom has a faith and strength that makes others comfortable. A home with a lot of love. A place where caring for others is bigger than a medical battle. Pretty cool kind of place. God bless your home.

Day 172, SUNDAY, OCTOBER 24, 2010 12:14 PM

Amy: I BE WRITING LIKE I AM ON DRUGS OR SOMETHING!!!

I just re-read my post...after posting, of course and like yesterday's post it is laced with more typos than ever! I will TRY and proof before hitting "post" this next week. I see my brain is still a bit fried. They will likely be short and random. If they appear long over the next few weeks...please do not read them for the sake of my and my family's dignity. One never knows what one will do under the influence. I apologize ahead of time!

Amy

46

CPR - Complete Pathological Response

DAY 173, MONDAY, OCTOBER 25, 2010 7:37 PM

Amy: DR. S. JUST CALLED. HE SAYS I AM WHAT THE MEDICAL FIELD CALLS A CPR...COMPLETE PATHOLOGICAL RESPONSE!! 100% CLEAN PATH. REPORT. NO TRACES OF CANCER IN THE 3 LYMPH NODES TAKEN AND NONE IN THE BREAST TISSUE. IN SURGERY, 2 NODES SHOWED THAT CANCER HAD BEEN PRESENT. ZERO REMAINING. CLEAN BILL OF HEALTH. ALL GLORY TO GOD. THIS JOURNEY IS OVER. THE HOME STRETCH TO COMPLETE HEALING IS WELL UNDERWAY.

Ross just took the T-bones off the grill. Time for a celebration meal. Wish you were here.

Blessings,

Amy and family

Guestbook Note

Yahoo! Well we've come to expect nothing less from you now! You are a walking MIRACLE. We join you in praise. Keep going my friend, you're on your way to getting stronger. You are amazing, especially when your face is always smiling and your words are always praising our God.

Guestbook Note
To all of you faithful prayers, friends and family...as Amy's mom I just have to write my heartfelt thanks and appreciation for all of your amazing faithfulness, not only to Amy, Tom, Ross and Sara but to our loving heavenly Father. You have been so diligent in the prayers, the loving notes and visits, the showing of love through meals, visits and helping hands in more ways than I can list! You truly have been the hands and feet of Jesus...I know He is saying "well done, good and faithful servants"!!

Day 175, WEDNESDAY, OCTOBER 27, 2010 11:37 AM

Amy: I'm sitting on our couch on a hot, humid end-of-October day. Too hot to sit outside and post. Cool front is supposed to hit soon. Looking forward to walks again. Tom just came and picked Deb up for her flight back to South Bend, IN. The eight days she was here flew by. Words won't seem to come in order to express what it was like having her here. She is my only sibling and we have grown so close over our almost half century together on this earth. I am aging us by a handful of years you realize. So much has happened in our lives yet we are still so closely connected. Always have been except for those jr. and sr. high school days. Deb and I have not even lived in the same state for over 20 years yet we talk at least weekly if not daily and our lives are so different yet so much the same. We talk the same, have many similar mannerisms and shop the same, decorate the same and fight the same. There is much comfort in our bond. Sisters are a gift. Her willingness to drop her hectic life with high schoolers Holden and Hannah and her busy Secret Agent Man, Tim, to come and single-handedly take on my family and my MOM job, means more than words can possibly convey. I miss you, sissy.

Now it is time for a rest. Started my exercises today. Not too bad. Feels pretty good actually. Two drains came out yesterday and plastic

241

surgeon says everything looks great. I go back Monday to get the other set of drains removed and a bit of saline inflation in the expanders. Boobies, here we come!

I just want to say thank you from the bottom of my heart for all the notes, witty posts, emails and cards, flowers, food and so on sent from so many. Please know that each and EVERY one has meant SO, SO much to me and my family. It is hard to not spend day and night just replying back in detail to everyone but I cannot possibly do that the way I would like. My replies might be brief or even non-existent if the time I see it is not good. You all have been food for the soul and we could not have done this without you and our Father in Heaven. I will continue to post periodically yet it will have to end soon.

Before my diagnosis I was working with a co-worker of Tom's to start up a website for a ministry. All we were able to accomplish before all this was a domain name. We now have a plan to get something started as soon as we can. I plan to use that as a blog at some point. I will also be using it for *Designed to Shine* retreats, sessions and the like. We are starting sessions at church for jr. high moms and daughters in January...print material going out now, and a rescheduled retreat the last weekend in February for Elizabeth's Place (teen moms group in Montgomery County sponsored by our church) and hopefully a cancer support foundation or ministry of some sort, all wrapped into the one ministry some way or another.

God gave me the name before all of this but that is all He would let me have at the time. We locked in the domain name, but I guess I had to go through all this before I could move on. Now we need to get the site put together soon. Not too soon. I am excited to see what lies ahead. We plan to do it our Father's way and not our own.

Time for a nappy.

Safe and peaceful travels sis, you are in His hands,

Amy

47

So This is the Day the Back Pain Began

DAY 177, FRIDAY, OCTOBER 29, 2010 4:00 PM

Amy: This patient is losing her patience. I am bored of not doing much. Problem is, I can't do much.

I feel strong in the mornings when my muscles are well rested. After a few hours of doing something like, oh say, walking to the mailbox, running a quick errand and sitting around reading, eating, talking (and getting up 96 times as a low level activity for me) the mid and upper back begins to ache to high heaven. My pits sweat as I cannot use product under my arms due to the fact that I have drains and drain holes in them. Today it is somewhat cooler day so I am wearing one of Ross's hoodies to hide my drains pinned to the inside sides of it. It is a relief to have a little break in the weather so I can do this. Shorts and flip flops and a sweatshirt and hat...sitting in my house (out back in the shade now) is driving me nuts but Sara has a friend from school over and I don't want to freak her out like I do my family with tank tops and baldy mom walking around. I am just ragging about it now to get it out of my system. Hailey's mom is picking them up any minute to take them to do their nails and have dinner. I will jump in a cool shower the moment they leave.

As soon as these last two drains are removed, I think I will mentally feel so much better. I feel like I am carrying a couple of hand grenades around. That is what they look like but unfortunately they are clear and if one of the kids gets a glimpse of the bloodied water, they go nuts. I think I have scarred them for good with all the drama. Hilarious, really. ;) They just might make good doctors someday. Sara since she gets into all the medical detail and Ross more as a counselor with his level head and compassionate nature. We love seeing these traits in them.

Anyway, as each evening nears, my discomfort grows. I am still pretty much only taking Tylenol in the day and take one or two pain pills at bedtime, often coupled with Tylenol PM or Ambien. I STILL cannot sleep well and now with the fact that I am on my back and sore it seems to have made this a bit worse. Last night I actually went back on the couch for the first time in weeks and did get some rest. Who knows why that seems to lull me to some peaceful rest...but it does.

My mind is the problem. I just cannot shut it down. The funny thing is, it is not worry or stressful stuff but just STUFF. Maybe it is time to start getting the laptop out again when I can't sleep and see if getting it out helps...whatever IT even is. Not entries, just stuff in a document like; "You know what I would like...a place to get a mani and pedi that is not a fashion place but a place for healing chemo-laidened dry skin, and a spa with special chairs for weary bones after a bilateral mastectomy, and not just fancy rooms with massage therapy tables." BTW, this may exist as I have not even tried to find one. Places are happy to accommodate such needs but certainly do not cater to, if you get my drift. Second BTW...I have had two pedicures during all this so I am not AFRAID to go out like this, I just want a SPECIAL place for us SPECIAL PATIENT FOLK.

Back to why I decided to journal rather than watch Oprah this afternoon. I want my family to know that having had this bilateral mastectomy...which although the cancer was appearing to be gone and the nodes seemed to be clear...it was something Tom, Mom, Deb and many friends felt was the right choice (first and most importantly I too thought) for me. My tissue was proven to be very dense (don't laugh) and cystic over many years. I am still grateful for the choice I made for me. It certainly is not for everyone. I have a great team of doctors and know my next step will prove to be very pleasing. I hear some women cannot mentally stand the thought of losing their God-given gift(s) but I am here to say that it is not as bad as one might think. Having an attitude adjustment and having gone through chemo BEFORE the surgery just might have helped with that.

I believe that women who get a diagnosis of breast cancer and then are told that they need a double whammy the next week might certainly have a harder time wrapping their mind around all of the sudden changes. Time, prayer, support, growing faith and attitude all wrapped into one has made all the difference in my opinion. Having the knowledgeable medical staff directing the plan for THIS specific cancer, and determining to treat with chemo first, did allow me the option of a lumpectomy or mastectomy. After all the tests, mysterious spots after chemo started, more tests and all the hoopla, I went for the more drastic choice and I don't think I will regret it. I am a woman no matter what my boobs are made of. BTW #3...Texas state law requires insurance companies to pay for breast cancer survivor reconstruction. They say, "Everything's Bigger in Texas!" and they see to it in all situations!

Ross is in San Antonio for the night...soccer tourney. He is playing so well this season and I wish I were well enough to be at more of his games, but they are often far away. Thank goodness Tom was able to make most of them. We are both so proud of him.

Sara and Hailey just left. Time for that shower.

Proverbs 3:5-6

"Trust in the Lord with all your heart and lean not on your own understanding; in all your ways acknowledge him, and he will make your paths straight."

In Him,

Amy

So this is the day the back pain began. I was wondering just when it all started. Through reflection on the whole cancer journey, I have to say that the back pain that started and carried forward intensely for roughly ten months was almost more difficult than beating cancer itself. The back pain does not seem to be a common complaint of most breast cancer patients. An unusual side effect of us select few! Likely stress related.

I am happy to report the pain has subsided, although it still accompanies me, and my back is now a very weak part of my body.

Chronic pain is not visible to the rest of the world, but can be agonizing to the patient, and have an even greater impact as one has to sort through the effects almost silently. What an appreciation I gained for others that endure such ongoing struggles as I walked through this aspect of the illness.

It is funny that I chose to write Proverbs 3:5-6 on this very day. This summer I started memorizing certain verses and meditating on them for over a week at a time. This became one that God chose to use for my current life verse. It is so simply stated and so often used. I had no idea how much my Counselor and Healer would reveal to me in these words, and continues to do so today.

Day 181, TUESDAY, NOVEMBER 2, 2010 6:21 PM

Amy: Today is a real fall day...again. Yesterday was 91 and today was like a high of 63 or so. Finally rained last night...first time in maybe 35 plus days. You could almost hear the ground sigh with relief.

Was able to take Tess out around 3 p.m. today for a short walk. Very short. She loved it as she has been waiting for days.

Today was a very difficult day, pain-wise. I have to say that the past 3 days have been just as hard if not worse in some ways than post-chemo days. I have been suffering from constant middle back pain that really will not subside. I completely hate taking the pain pills and 3 Advil or Tylenol don't seem to do much. Today I laid in bed flat on my back for most of the day getting some relief. The huge struggle for me is not doing anything and not being the mom I so desperately want to be.

Today is good enough mentally that I am able to type and read my LOL book, <u>When a Woman Trusts God</u> by Sheila Walsh. It is a great book that I recommend for anyone (man or woman) who wants a glimpse into what God CAN do when we let Him into some of our darkest places. Sheila suffered from major depression, and a childhood of abuse. Then, her life as a Christian co-host on the 700 Club came crashing down before she was able to face some of these issues that she had worked so hard, for so long, to hide from the critical eyes of many "believers." She has been on the Women of Faith tour for 14 years AND she will be at our church this December for our Christmas Tea, and I CANNOT wait to see her!

Anyway, off track again. Just wanted to post before we devour a great meal from Sonya and family, and to say hello and please say a quick prayer for relief of back pain. Good otherwise. Have not returned many emails or calls today due to pain. Hard to concentrate when there is this dull, constant pain. Hope to be at LOL as I need the diversion tomorrow. In His grip but wanting Him to loosen it ever so slightly, seems to be a bit tight in the chest and back today. I should be grateful, I know.

SO NOT proofing as I want to shut this thing off and get out of the chair.

Amy

> **Guestbook Note**
> I so appreciate you being real. I wish the pain was gone but know you will turn it into some sort of life learning lesson. Living outside of my comfort zone in a new town helps me relate to your words of not being the mom you wish you were. I struggle with that too these days. I almost feel like I don't know who is living this life inside my body that used to be mine. Maybe these are days of total surrender where we both should allow God to be the "mom" He needs from us. It may not be the mom we are accustomed too so that can be a bit strange for us. I will pray that you get to see our precious LOL sisters today. And that God will do your living for you in this day in His perfect way. Peace my friend!

Day 182, WEDNESDAY, NOVEMBER 3, 2010 4:55 PM

Amy: Doing better by quite a bit today. Thanks for so much prayer. Wow. Went to Ladies of the Loft today for 90 minutes and was doing well but a bit restless sitting. Not bad. Well worth it. Great ladies and great discussion. Lots of laughs too.

Tom met me at Chick Fil A for an impromptu lunch, came home to rest for 30 minutes on the heating pad and popped a few Advil then we went to the oncologist for my 3 week post chemo follow up. Doctor seemed puzzled by the back pain but not too concerned. One cannot ever tell what he is thinking though. He was pleased with the path reports, hadn't heard the results. I asked him about what we do from here...periodic scans and tumor marker blood work about every 3 months for a while is all. I re-mentioned the "few spots" that showed up on my CT scans in my lungs back at the start of all this. At the time he said they were of no concern and seemed to be shadows and nothing else and that we would keep on top of them. Since I mentioned it again he said we should probably try and get insurance to cover a PT Scan of the lungs in 3 months. PT scan vs. CT because PT scans are more thorough and just a tiny bit of radiation exposure. Problem is our insurance would not cover one before and may try and fight one now. Oncologist says he will work to get the coverage.

I hate that I had to be the one to mention the lung thing but if I have learned nothing else in this journey from a medical standpoint, I have learned that you HAVE to take charge of your own health and NOT expect the doctors to do it for you. You have to ask questions, probe for meanings and make suggestions otherwise you will get the basic care. I really only feel this way with the oncology group, not my surgeon, radiology or plastic surgeon. Oncologist also said that triple negative cancer that is more aggressive can also come back with higher odds than other estrogen receptive cancers. It is also one that is more likely to never return IF I can remain clear for 5 years post treatment. That is the big number here. Now we will work toward that goal! I am confident that we are done with this journey! I am good with whatever God's will is yet praying this was all we have to do. Tomorrow is never guaranteed but rather a gift. Celebrate every day for what it is.

Today was a tough day but just a day nonetheless. Tomorrow is a new day.

God is good ALL the time.

Amy

Guestbook Note
Fellow cruiser - can only imagine how much of a blessing your journaling is and has been to so many. If nothing else while praying for you, we are all learning a life lesson regarding taking care of our selves when it comes to our health. God has been and will continue to use you for His glory. You are so right tomorrow is not

promised or guaranteed to any of us. So let's make this day a "God" day for this is the day that He has made and we shall rejoice and be glad in it! I love you all with the love of the Lord!

Day 184, FRIDAY, NOVEMBER 5, 2010 6:15 PM

Amy: The fact that I have not written in several days is proper indication that my back is still in pretty constant pain. Had Mary, a friend of mine who is a great Massage Therapist, come do a 20 minute chair massage today. Helped for about 30 minutes but I do know it helped loosen some knots and things. She has had several good suggestions on other ways to help alleviate the stress on my back and neck as well, which is so very appreciated!

Decided to take my gym membership off medical hold yesterday. Tom and I went and it helped walking in with someone else. I decided it is time to get in the pool and start slow, regular stretching and (after a few stiff laps) it felt great on my back!! Went today and was so looking forward to getting in there, hitting the sauna and hot tub with powerful jets for my back. It was the first time in 6 months that I have felt I looked a little like everyone else, if even for just a short while. I had my racing suit on (and boobies look pretty normal if not darn good in a chest-flattening suit!) and a swim cap and goggles. The feeling didn't last real long as I could only do laps and treading for about 15 minutes then it was off to the sauna. I left the swim cap on at first as there were 4 others in there but as I started to feel the rubber melting to my scalp, I thought I'd better peel it off.

Time to run, meeting friends for dinner while Ross is in Waco for soccer regionals and Sara is with Mia at The Woodlands High homecoming game. Missing more of his games hurts my heart, but there is no way I could endure the 3 hours to Waco.

Amy

Day 188, TUESDAY, NOVEMBER 9, 2010 10:43 PM, CST

Amy: Is it the fact that I am getting so tired of all that is involved with healing from breast cancer or is this really that difficult to get through the reconstruction process and heal completely from surgery? It is probably a little of both.

I did not anticipate the back pain that I am having to endure. I honestly think this might be worse than the chemo...or have I blocked some of that out already? The pain shifts to different parts of my back on different days. I have not been able to type or even read due to my need to get up and move, stretch, lie on the heat/ice. Today I decided to take half a pain pill and I have had more relief than I have had in two weeks. Wow. I took another a few hours ago and I actually was up for a little journaling! I think I will take another tomorrow! The plastic surgeon did another "fill" in the expanders yesterday. Said that the expanders are why I am having so much pain. Said they are hard plastic, bulky inside and likely pushing on various nerves that just so happen to affect my back. Said the sooner we finish and get the regular implants in place, the better I will feel. I have a tentative date set for Dec 10 but if all continues to heal as well as I have been and I continue to tolerate the fills as well as I have, we just might move that up by a week.

Much to be grateful for in all of this. Trying to keep my eye on the prize. This will soon be behind us and I cannot tell you how much I look forward to some "regular" days ahead. Just feeling more mobile today felt like a HUGE gift in and of itself.

God has been so "present" in all of this. I have learned much about trusting Him and His will for my life. He does not always let us know much of His plan for our lives but wants more than anything for us to just follow Him. That trust does not come easy and often at a high price. After all of this time in the valley, I have decided I want to just "follow Him" rather than try and lead my own way in the dark. Why not follow the Light rather than stumble and fumble along? Don't get me wrong, I often start off on my own path but still see the glow of that light from afar and work my way back to a brighter trail. Isn't that the adventuresome nature He put within us humans anyway?

I think when we do that wandering, He just slows the pace and waits for us to turn around and seek the better path. He is the keeper of the light and is always there in our darkest nights. Choosing to look up long enough to see where that light is coming from is the choice we have to make. Maybe I'm looking down too much and that is why my back hurts. What if I get hooked on pain pills? Oh the worry that comes back so easily. It's late. I'm tired.

Resting in His grip,

Amy

Guestbook Note

All I can say is I predict that by February you will feel better, stronger and more grounded than ever before. Thanks for sharing your honest journey. Dec. 16 will be 16 years cancer free for me!

It took me a few months longer than predicted, but I DO FEEL STRONGER THAN EVER ONE YEAR FROM THIS DATE! Time can seem like it is standing still at moments yet when you look back on just how far you have come, it is remarkable! That is the perspective that must stay in focus.

— 48 —

NOW She Tells Me

$\mathcal{D}$AY 191, FRIDAY, NOVEMBER 12, 2010 7:50 AM, CST

Amy: I want to post the contents of an email I received earlier in the week that has been a huge relief for Tom, mom, Deb and I. This was from Sue who was clearly a gift from above from the moment of my diagnosis. Sue goes to the Loft. Last year she experienced a similar diagnosis with the tender care of both Dr. S. and my same plastic surgeon leading her through. Sue was also a nurse before her choice to stay at home and raise her beautiful children.

I decided to post this as my sister suggested I do, reminding me that this will hopefully help others down the road as they encounter the situation to help another going through the same diagnosis and aftercare.

> **(E-mail From Friend Sue…)**
> Amy,
> I couldn't pluck up the courage to tell you how bad the reconstruction is! After everything you had gone through I didn't have the heart to tell you the worst is still to come. You wouldn't have believed me anyway and written me off as a whining pessimist.

Here's the bottom line:

After about 3 weeks the pain settles a lot, and then is only really bad for 36-48 hours after each expansion. DO take your pain killers. Mentally this is a killer. You are not having the discomfort because you are killing the cancer cells, you are not having the discomfort because of recovering from surgery. You are having the discomfort because you want 3D boobs. The guilt that comes with that knowledge is ridiculous. Forget it. You are having the discomfort so that next summer the children will see you in a swimsuit and not remember this year. To them you will look 'cured.' That is why you are doing this. You will have hair, you will have boobs and you will be cancer free.

When they are fully expanded you will have solid bowling balls stuck to your front. They are heavy, they are spherical, they are big and you will THINK the whole world is looking at you knowing you have oversized false boobs (your friends will be fascinated by the process but the rest of the world won't notice). You will keep these for about 3 weeks.

Back massage is critical to keep the fascia layer 'fluid' and to remove the knots you get once you start 'hunching' because it is the most comfortable position to be in. It makes sense - the fascia layer is thin but fibrous. It covers your whole torso and has been cut and now being stretched from beneath as the implants expand. Your back muscles are having to do the work that your chest muscles normally do, and you are carrying extra weight in front.

I know this sounds all doom and gloom. I never regret having reconstruction and would repeat the process if I had to. The surgery to change the expanders is easy-peasy.

You probably fccl likc you havc used a life supply of 'brave faces.' It's ok to feel fed up. This has gone on forever and you want life to return to normal. It returns to normal really quickly after the expanders are changed out.

I do worry that you are still trying to do too much. Please, please try and take it easy the day after expansion. Remember the pain of childbirth? Exactly! This will all be a numb, distant memory once you have those CCs.

You know where I am if you need me.
TAKE YOUR PAINKILLERS!
Hugs.
Sue
(I copied Jill and Rhonda on this so that your close buddies truly understand what you are going through. I hope that's ok)

Amy here again...Sue and Rhonda have prepared me for more than I would have known otherwise and it has helped me not feel so alone in the uncertainty of what is to come. They are gifts that are truly priceless. I was warned my eyelashes and brows will likely come out AFTER the chemo, as my hair on my head starts to come back. It happened. I now LOOK more sickly than I actually was before. This has not been easy on me. They are completely gone.

I have verses that I say in my head over and over as I am swimming laps with stiff muscles--struggling to make it to the other side as strong swimmers lap me. *I CAN DO ALL THINGS THROUGH CHRIST WHO STRENGTHENS ME...FOR I KNOW THE PLANS I HAVE FOR YOU... PLANS TO GIVE YOU A HOPE AND A FUTURE...* (Phil. 4:13 and Jer. 29:11)...they have to go on and on like a broken record. If not, I feel the need to explain to perfect strangers that really, I do know how to swim, and that in 6 months I will be back to kick their butt in the pool or to explain why my boobs look bigger than they did last week and that really I am not sick any more or why I .....

It is simply crazy, I know, but you should see some of these pumped up people. They seem to live for how they look. Anyway, so I take a deep breath or two then start to focus on Whose I am. I am performing for an audience of ONE and only One. I can do all things through Christ who strengthens me (repeat). By the end of the episode, all is well.

That reminds me, I was at the gym yesterday swimming and when I got out of the shower, I went to my unlocked locker to put on my sweats and front zip hoodie and low and behold...only my sweats were there! I wigged out. Someone had stolen my new Target hoodie in the 40 minutes I had been in the pool area! Problem was, I came in my swimsuit and sweats and hoodie only! Thank God they didn't steal my bottoms! I was livid. I had to take my suit and dry it under the hairdryer then put it back on, walk through the gym in sweat bottoms and my lap suit. I was so very tempted to just go out in my towel through the gym yelling, "Thanks to some thief that might still be in here, I am leaving the gym naked!!" Needless to say, I voiced my frustrations to the check in ladies. Not cool. So not cool. Luckily my gym bag was in the pool area with me or my car just might have been gone when I reached the parking lot.

In His grip without my hoodie,
Amy

49

Live Like You Were Dyin'

Day 191, FRIDAY, NOVEMBER 12, 2010 1:43 PM, CST

Tom: Tom here. Amy has had some rough weeks these last few days, as you may have gathered from her last post and the great hoodie caper. I recently downloaded <u>The Complete Adventures of Sherlock Holmes</u> on to my Kindle, maybe some deductions from the great detective could solve the crime and return the garment!

Amy is going to a luncheon in a few minutes but I took away her driver's license and will take her. Too much pain and meds and chemo brain side effects to be driving when I can drop her off. Lots of new pains and issues and, as our treasured Dr. S. says, we are in a new world and need to check out everything that is out of the ordinary. If you are up for a little cancer ward humor, take a guess at the colo-rectal Dr's name at the clinic where Amy has to go to have some issues checked out......Dr. Butts!

Although a lot of new issues come with the territory, it is nonetheless always a little (or a lot) disconcerting each time wondering, what if...??? It all keeps us grounded and more comfortable with His sometimes tighter grip.

Before I forget (I do a lot of that lately). Please lift up our dear friends the Simon's. Steve's dad was having trouble with his balance a few weeks ago and a baseball size tumor was discovered in his brain. Surgery at Mayo got a lot of it, but at 80, there are some extra tough

256

decisions to be made. Please pray for peace, healing, understanding and acceptance of His will.

Kind of like with my dad just before he died suddenly a few years ago, Steve (my fellow bucket-lister - even before the movie) has had some great quality time with George recently. Whether he is being called home sooner or later (or much later), we both realize what a gift these times are and how we need to make more of them every day with those we love.

Three songs run through my mind a lot recently and all have a similar theme – *Live Like You Were Dying*. Amy gave me one of them by Tim McGraw. After his friend got back "the x-ray," he was asked "what didya do?" He replied; "I went sky diving, mountain climbing and bull riding; I loved deeper and spoke sweeter; and gave forgiveness I was denyin'; and I hope you get the chance to live like you were dying..." There are worse ways to live one's life.

Final thoughts as I have been pondering the many growth opportunities presented in our lives these past several years (can you tell I reread James again?!). We are to be thankful for the trials (aka opportunities) and it seems we have had our share the last few years. It is easy to get down, get angry, throw elaborate pity parties or get bitter towards others who we perceive as slighting us (real or simply perceived). It is a slippery slope and downward momentum is quickly gained and not easily reversed. In my more lucid moments I have discovered an inkling of a thread of how to start to dig out (or stay out) of the pit. I/we can use all the prayers I/we can get to help me/us out with this one.

Take it to God continually. Like gravity, the pull of the dark, negative side never turns off. We need the equally constant counter influence of our Maker.

I am committed to examine where I have made mistakes and learn from them for the future. Things I am learning; no matter what the situation or even how apparently un-based a criticism appears, there is almost always at least a minute kernel of truth or wisdom there. Find it, accept it, admit it and learn from it. Ask God to remove the bitterness from your heart and keep it out. Harboring resentment, a grudge, anger or hatred is like swallowing poison and expecting the other person to die or the situation to improve. It might feel good for a minute, but the effect is not what you really want!

As if all this is not hard enough, then comes the biggie, we are supposed to let go, love and pray for the other side. Sometimes this is a person; sometimes it is a situation (which likely means that we are angry at God for "letting this happen"). Either way, ya gotta let go, smile (fake it for awhile if you have to) and start the process of clearing out the bad and letting in the good.

Who knows - maybe we will get to make 8 on Fumanchu someday!

t

Day 196, WEDNESDAY, NOVEMBER 17, 2010 3:35 PM, CST

Amy: Sitting out back on a beautiful fall day. About 79 degrees in Houston today but a front is coming in for a few days. I love sitting poolside with my feet up and taking in the quiet before the kids get home...which is any minute now.

Finding the time to write has been tough. Back pain is still there but much less intense than in weeks past. I am sitting with an Empi-Electrode device on my back now. Karin and Barry loaned it to me and it really seems to temporarily relax the muscles.

Great news...I am having my final surgery to replace the expanders a week from today! November 24. Outpatient. Salerno's are taking the kids for the day/night, which is a huge help. Sure hope I feel okay to go over to Nellie and Paul's house for Thanksgiving. If not, Tom and the kids will. It was the only time that worked out (for surgery) and the sooner the better. As the expanders are expanding, so is the pressure on some of my nerves...literally and figuratively!

Had my appointment today - all is well. Not giving any more details as Tom gave enough already. Bummer is she wants me to do a colonoscopy in January. Says that former cancer patients should move the normal screening up by 10 years and that makes me over due by 3 years. Can hardly wait.

November 15th was Sara's 11th birthday. Her primary gift was one she has been wanting so badly...to officially sponsor Trinity (6 year old chestnut mare quarter horse) and she is thrilled! She has a show at the ranch this Saturday and is looking forward to having her own horse in the show...no loaners anymore. She is feeling pretty cool about herself these days…in a good way that is! Straight A's on her report card didn't hurt either.

Ross just started driver education this week. Soccer is over and was a great experience. This fall, being on the Varsity team gave him some great opportunities to shine and to learn from some great players. Report card had all A's and B's and we are happy to say the homecoming dance at The Woodlands' High was a huge success!

Chemo brain and pain killer/muscle relaxer meds are a nasty combination for me. I can't seem to do much and certainly not more than one thing at a time. Tom is picking up so much slack, it isn't even funny. He has more on his plate than I ever have at one time. He is so very good at juggling multiple tasks. Wearing the mom and dad hat suits him well.

No other interesting things to report at the time.

In His grip,

Amy

Day 200, SUNDAY, NOVEMBER 21, 2010 10:46 PM, CST

Amy: Today was one of those Sundays that seemed to go on and on. While it was beautiful here, probably 80 with blue sky and a gentle breeze all day long…inside my head it was cloudy and cold. I had an edge brewing inside me, even from the start of church today. I am sure people that I talked to might have felt it. I just wasn't all there. Lately my mind seems to be overwhelmed with all the activity brewing around me in public or busy situations. I assume this is a new chemotherapy related withdrawal but it is real bothersome. It's like I get overwhelmed when more than one conversation is going on or when more than one person asks something of me. I cannot compartmentalize like I normally do. It flusters me and causes anxiety that I have never experienced before. Hope this fades after the holiday season and we can experience the start of a new year all the way around.

Enjoyed a special lunch after church with friends at Tommy Bahama's. We sat outside and it felt like we were all on vacation. The Market Street area was a buzz with activity and shoppers and diners. The Huge Christmas Tree was up in the center on the green and all the other decorations were so festive. Fountains running and kids in shorts and all seemed odd against the wintery backdrop, but no complaining here. No need for a White Christmas for me!

Stopped over to the mall quickly after lunch to get a few items for the guys and me. Nice just hanging out with the family all day. Came home and we all took naps and cleaned rooms, etc. Boys went to Wal-Mart while Sara and I watched *The Bucket List*. Good movie. Reminds me of things I have been pondering so much over the past 6 months. What are some of the things I want to accomplish before I kick the bucket one day? By say 90 or so...Take Sara and Ross to China, dive the Great Barrier Reef, gallop a horse bareback in the wide open fields, take a safari in Africa, tour the Napa Valley, take a Mediterranean barefoot cruise, and on and on. I also want to know true JOY and live it each day, regardless of my circumstances. Not sometimes but in ALL times. I also want to know that I was a source of joy to others. These both are quite complex if you ask me. I mean, what does true joy really even look like? It is completely different than happiness. It is more like peace and contentment regardless of your circumstance. Not easy when things are more in the valley than on the mountain top.

Getting tired as I took a muscle relaxer before bed. Should continue this later before my jaw drops to my lap and I cannot pick it up again.

Ready for final surgery Wednesday. Not looking forward to outpatient surgery but they say it will be fine. Back pain is letting up a bunch and after Wednesday, should really start to subside. Hair is about 1/4 inch long. Soon the caps will be put away and the Annie Lennox look will take over. May even dye it orange like her for a hoot!

Have not made the time to journal much lately as we have so much on our plate and some that I have been hesitant to even put here. Will try to write more as I sort through this next phase of breast cancer. Many new emotions surfacing these past few weeks with a new sort of pain to be dealing with. Having an underlining "edge" has required much focus on attitude. It doesn't come easy either. It is feeling like a metamorphosis in some ways. Sorting out the good and the junk and dealing with a transformation of sorts whether I want to or not. So many physical, mental and heart changes happen after this kind of experience. Many I could never have anticipated. Irritates me kind of. I didn't ask for this. Never would have. Deal is, it's what I got. It's what Tom, Ross and Sara got. I just hope I learned whatever it is I am/was supposed to learn in this process. I am sure I won't really know for some time. One thing I know as I was pondering back to the first weeks of my new normal. (I can barely remember some of the details that at the time were so overwhelming and so foreign.) I can clearly see how I was carried by our Lord and that takes my breath away every time.

If the God of the universe could sweep me into His grip so obviously during a time when He wanted to reveal Himself to me (in a hard but necessary way) and show me He is present when I cry out the most and beg for His fatherly love to cover the pain...doing it so gently and getting me to my feet on the other side...then I should be able to do anything and feel His kind of acceptance in all things.

Problem continues to be that; LIFE GOES ON. We forget and start trying to control our destiny the next moment. That does not work well for me. I then have to humble myself and hit rewind. This will soon be a memory. Life will go on whether I am a changed person or not. Strange that I am making such a conscious effort to analyze all this. Remember this is just a rambling journal of someone whose pain med has clearly kicked in. Time to sign off and re-read the insane post in the morning.

One last "top off" fill in the morning with the plastic surgeon.

Thanksgiving is the day after my implant swap surgery. Much to be thankful for...so, so much.

In Christ,

Amy

Guestbook Note

Life Goes On. Yep, it does. But life in America (and hence, the world) has been altered this year due to your actions, Amy, and the window of enlightenment you've provided through your writing. Your strength. Your compassion for others in the midst of all this. And your willingness to admit the source of this goodness is God - in the form of the Holy Spirit - and that Holy Grip. Has the entire culture changed? Well, no. The greed and anxiety that pull us away from God still exist. But you and the people you touched this year having definitely moved the pendulum toward the good and Godly end of the spectrum.

Guestbook Note

I wanted to make sure I took the time to say "thank you" to you! Just two words but I felt God tugging on my heart to tell you. Because you needed to hear it. Thank you for the time you take each day to share your incredible experiences to all of us. Your honesty, your genuine willingness to expose your feelings and every ounce of what you are going through is truly remarkable. Not everyone would do this. But I'm thankful you are! It's beautiful to see how God has and will continue to use you as a tool to show so many others that may not know our God how wonderful and caring He is - even though He has thrown a curve ball into your life. It's how you handle it and get through this that molds you into the person God wants you to be. And, again, you are willing to share it because you have the gift of writing and your heart weighs heavy with the overwhelming love you have for Him as you are trying to figure all this out. It's truly amazing to see it all unfold in an on-line journal.

Keep the grip tight ..... and this too shall pass!

— 50 —

Not Your Typical Thanksgiving

$\mathcal{D}$AY 203, WEDNESDAY, NOVEMBER 24, 2010 9:33 PM, CST
Tom (via phone app): This is Tom. This is kind of a weird day so I
will try to give the update on my phone…{from operating room waiting
area at a nearly abandoned hospital on Thanksgiving eve}.

Surgery at 2 to replace the expanders and to put in the permanent
prostheses silicone implants. All went well, Dr. pleased, sent us home
at 5. Amy is not feeling too well - usual post op lousy feeling, plus still
an extremely sore back. She ate a little, took pain and muscle relaxer
pills. I ran to Walgreens to get prescriptions.

When I got back, Amy's left side was all swollen, from the bottom
of the breast to her neck - very hard, very swollen and very painful.
Called the surgeon's service. Got worse. Quickly loaded up for ER.

Got to ER, surgeon met us there. He thinks there is internal
bleeding, need to reopen left side to see, fix and drain.

Amy has been in OR for about 30 minutes now. Will definitely be
spending the night in the hospital - Memorial Hermann, since it was
the closest.

Will update later when I hear more.

t

PS - haven't told the kids yet, they are at friends (who know) for the
night. Want to wait until tomorrow when we know more facts.

Day 203, WEDNESDAY, NOVEMBER 24, 2010 9:53 PM, CST

Tom (via Phone app): Now out of second surgery; it was internal bleeding. They drained a lot of blood, but no evidence of what caused it; said that it happens on occasion and often seals itself. Shouldn't need transfusion, but will check levels in morning to be sure. I will see her in a little while. Spending the night here under care.

Day 204, THURSDAY, NOVEMBER 25, 2010 9:44 AM, CST

Tom: Happy Thanksgiving!!! Lots to be thankful for.

It is now about 9:30 Thursday morning. Amy got some rest, despite it being 2 a.m. before we turned in and having had the usual parade of visits all night long. The swelling is gone - it was blood from the internal bleeding and the second surgery took care of it. A drain was put in that will stay in through next Tuesday. We will be going home this morning.

It was quite a scare; swelling to twice the normal size, terrible back pain and her heart racing at 130+ for over an hour. The doctor said about once a year this happens and it often has already sealed itself. Amy lost a lot of blood, but they don't want to transfuse - just let the body rebuild. Amy will feel very weak until the blood replaces itself over the course of the next several days.

The Salernos will drop off the kids this morning at the house and we will fill them in on the overnight - mainly the good results, not the drama of the time!

We felt all the prayers through this all and were reminded that as you look around the Thanksgiving table, everyone has, or had, or will have, trials of life that require patience, understanding, love and prayers. Kind of like conditioning for track, the tough times prepare us for the long haul - that back stretch when we want to give up but instead need to kick it up a notch.

As usual, God knows what He is doing and has it all under control. I guess that is the advantage He has of seeing (and developing) the big picture, rather than just today's section that we get to view. We would likely mess it up if we had more of the pieces than we need for today... fortunately He never does.

Have lots of turkey for us! Blessings to all.

Guestbook Note
Thinking of the past month. A month ago today was the news of your being a complete CPR-complete pathological response. As I re-read posts today, the enormity of the journey hits me, and so do three other things: your persevering spirit with eyes and ears of your heart focused on listening and looking to the One in whose grip you are, the depth of the love of Tom beside you, and the friends walking with you---both words of grace and encouragement and truth (like I think it was Sue who wrote about the reality of expansion pain).

Your words on hope and joy echo through this and in the midst of this day, and in midst of pain and recovery from surgery, praying this morning for relief for you from pain, blessed encouragement to both you and Tom in a way that speaks to you of the Lord's presence and love.
Thinking of Oct 25 news
Thinking of today Nov 25
And I am struck as I think the next 25 is Dec, and reality of the Lord's presence with us today because of what we mark on Dec 25.
With love for you both.

Guestbook Note
I decided this year to look at what the Thanksgiving holiday is really about and focus on the true reasons to celebrate. As an ignorant foreigner (South African) I set about reading up on the history of Thanksgiving, about the pilgrims of 1621, or was it the rainfall in 1623, or was it when Abe Lincoln proclaimed it in 1863? Here is one definition of why we celebrate it:

The practice of remembering the blessings we have received throughout the past year began from that very first Thanksgiving with the Pilgrims. Within the country that is now the United States of America, the first National Day of Thanksgiving was announced by the 2nd Continental Congress. The third Thursday of November was set aside by President Lincoln for people to give thanks for all of their blessings.

However you look at it, it is clearly a time of being thankful for all we have and all the blessings we have received over the past year. 2010 has been a tough year for many people, so at this time I wish to spend the holidays focusing on all the fantastic things I received during 2010, to say thank you to those who gave them to me and to start thinking about how I can return those blessings during 2011.

So, I would like to give thanks that God brought you guys into our lives this year, that has changed my life forever - You are very special and treasured friends. 2010 has been a trying year for you all I know and I also know there is still some way to go, but I think there is a reason Thanksgiving Day falls the day after the final surgery! I will continue to pray for you guys but just know that it is going to be all up from here.

Take care and have a wonderful Thanksgiving weekend!

Guestbook Note
You and Tom are humble examples of how to face adversity and grow through it. A blessing to all of us who know you. Look forward to seeing you soon!

Day 204, THURSDAY, NOVEMBER 25, 2010 6:13 PM, CST

Amy: It's Amy. It's Thanksgiving 2010. I am on the other side of this walk with breast cancer and I have much to be thankful for. So much that it is hard for me to see through the blur of tear filled eyes. It is after 6 p.m. and Tom, Ross and Sara are probably sitting at the Thanksgiving meal table at Paul and Nellie Mitford's. (Josh is Ross's friend and Gabby is Sara's.) Tess is sitting next to me on the couch and it is starting to rain a bit. Mid 80's today and now a cold front is moving in for the next few days.

I am so, so glad that Tom and the kids have some way of celebrating this holiday rather than sitting around home ordering a pizza. I need the quiet and they need some normalcy.

I have thought much about family that is spread out so far all over the country today. So many memories of Thanksgivings past, yet mom is in Arizona with Parnell, Deb and her beautiful family are in Indiana celebrating with Tim's folks that flew in from Maine, Bill and Janice are in Iowa City with Janice's folks and brother, Mary and Ray in Comanche, and Grandma Kathyrn with friends at home in Cedar Rapids. Tom's siblings are spread out this holiday in Iowa, Montana and Florida.

With the thoughts of each and every family member comes a flood of holiday memories. So much fun: like being snow-bound with Grandma Kathyrn and my folks while visiting Deb and Tim in Maine, to having Thanksgiving in Des Moines out on the deck with all of Tom's family at our house. Dozens of get togethers that make me smile. Makes me miss my father. He loved the holidays. Thinking of you - Bob Savel, Milo Savel, Chuck Elliott, Ruth Elliott, Bob Hauser, Lucille Hauser, Bob Paglia. Bet you're having a super feast today!

I am Thankful for:
- My family, near and far
- The returning of my good health
- My friendships, old and new
- My freedoms
- My growing relationship with my husband and kids
- My Heavenly Father who loves me, guides me and challenges me all of the days of my life.

(These are not in any particular order of course)

BTW, I am feeling pretty well. Left side of chest and armpit are real sore and I have a drain in again on that side. Tender from opening me up a second time in 3 hours, I suppose. Bruised a bit there too. Tired of this but hey, life goes on and I will continue to praise my Father in heaven and count my blessings every day that I have been given!

In His grip, this I am sure of,

Amy

Guestbook Note

You absolutely amaze me!! One night we're crying with worry and the next day we're crying with joy. What a fighter you are, and you will win this battle. We pray that the light is finally being seen at the end of the tunnel and the rest of your journey will be easier. Your faith and strength is so inspiring!

We love you and are so sorry that the road has been so long and painful. We pray that every new day you will be stronger and more comfortable than the day before.

As I re-read this entry, I completely recall the feelings that were experienced that evening. If you are wired at all like me, you are driven by your emotions and feelings much of the time. This can be a dangerous way to live if you are not in tune with how to focus back on truths from God's Word. For most of my years, I did not know how to do that and am still learning continuously. In thinking back on this day and on many holidays without extended family, I would find myself in a funk. Longing for the past, wanting to recreate what once was.

After this season of stillness (meaning the cancer season), God revealed to me in another moment of sadness and sulking that if my eyes were truly in tune with Him (and as Tom and I were working to start a ministry called MADE FOR MORE), then it was due time that I started to understand just what MADE FOR MORE really meant.

This is what the Lord shared during one of my pity parties, and it has completely altered (ok, I still have moments, but they are much shorter lived) my outlook when I start to go down that road of "remember when." What I heard from Him...

"My child, I have given you so much in this life. I have given you family that loves you and so many memories.

These are gifts that have strengthened your relationships. Gifts that have strengthened you and them. Please do not see them as losses but as jewels in your crown that makes you who you are today. As you begin to unfold the gift of ministry, using both gifts you know of and gifts you are uncovering for both you and Tom...you already have the name that I have given for you. Use what you <u>know</u> of MADE FOR MORE, yet also be willing to learn and share, and see as a gift, just what else it truly means to <u>be</u> MADE FOR MORE! You must see that in ALL THINGS we <u>are</u> made for more - our relationships, our actions, and our gifts. Start to focus on ETERNAL things and less on what you see and what the rest of this world sees right in front of them. Amy, the relationships you think you are missing out on that are going on in other parts of the country or that have been cut short because of earthly death...they are not lost. They are eternal and are gifts that will be yours FOREVER. Nothing is wasted when you trust Me completely. Go forward in truth and with the understanding of My promises. I AM the creator of the universe...so I think I've got this covered."

I have found a peace that surpasses MY understanding now, and I am good with that. Again, another gift in times of trouble. Who would have thought?

~ 51 ~

It HAS Gotten Better…

D AY 205, FRIDAY, NOVEMBER 26, 2010 12:42 PM, CST
Amy: Me again.

Sitting on the couch, but the other end of it for a change of scenery. Watching W on cable. Pretty good story (although a liberal sided slant, if you ask me) of the local boy gone president. Tough road for him. Tough roads for most of us.

Feeling really spacey today. Probably a combination of the pain level (which is pretty high especially on the whole left side of my chest wall), and pain killers, and the fact that I lost so much blood (though they chose not to do a transfusion). Feel shaky a bit. Hopefully this will all pass soon.

When I look in the mirror I am humbled beyond words. The pale, scarred and swollen person looking back at me is not a familiar face. Maybe because I cannot see worth a hoot now or maybe it's because I tried to dye my stubbly head a darker shade so it was noticeable and now it is a mix of dark purple and brown (all natural, fades in 20 washes… thank the Lord!). My eyelashes are slowly growing in but a ways off from looking at all normal. My fingernails are loaded with ridges and remind me of how my grandmother's looked when she was in her 80's. The top of my left hand is black and blue from IV's being forced into veins Wednesday and Thursday morning. My neck and back are still stiff. I think the muscles have completely forgotten how to relax by now. I might consider investing in a weekly massage therapy program until things feel back to normal! My physical self has changed so much but I know it will return back to normal over time. "Time heals all wounds," or so they say...whoever they are. This is bound to get better, I just know it.

I don't want to sound like a sad sack, just using this as an outlet and a way to connect when I feel disconnected. Would love to be with family today. I cannot wait until our get together over Christmas in Arizona. Praying I will be strong enough to really enjoy our time together. Hope. That's what it is that keeps me going. It's a light at the end of my tunnel. When I don't have the strength to keep my mind and heart focused the way I know it needs to be, I call out to my Father who always hears and gives me just what I need; not anymore than just what I need, but enough.

When Tom and I were waiting in the emergency room late Wednesday night, I asked him to pray and he did. I think it was the only comfort I had all night long. He asked me as we were waiting if I wanted him to look up and read any specific scripture and the one that came to mind first was Jeremiah 29:11. Tom read the surrounding verses out loud as well and these are the words I had going into my second surgery of the day...

Jeremiah 29:11-12 *"For I know the plans I have for you," declares the LORD, "plans to prosper you and not to harm you, plans to give you hope and a future. Then you will call on me and come and pray to me, and I will listen to you."*

I am not sure how much it changed my situation at the moment but there is something in just processing these truths in our subconscious. Promises from above. When I read through this today, I can find comfort and hope for my tomorrows. Funny thing is, I never thought I'd be the type to remember ANY scriptures by "heart." I suppose I really haven't. God just gives them to me when I need them. Love letters, really.

Time to take a pill.

In His grip,

Amy

Once again, as I reflect back, I am aware that it HAS gotten better, so much better. When we can look at life and how far we have come versus how much has gone wrong or isn't working the way things used to, we are bound to be in a better place. God has His hand in every detail of our lives, we just need to stop and recognize the work for what it is...and give thanks.

Day 207, SUNDAY, NOVEMBER 28, 2010 3:08 PM, CST

Amy: It's late afternoon on Sunday. The days have blurred together as I am so out of any sort of routine. Have not left the house since I was released from the hospital on Thursday. Released...sounds like I was a psych patient or something. If I don't get out of the house soon, I will be one for sure.

Had a horrible day yesterday, as I am experiencing some not so pleasant side affects from surgery. Not going into details. Let's just say I experienced cramping and other pains that are RIGHT UP THERE with child labor, I kid you not. Almost ended up back in the ER. So much for this part of the cancer journey being a walk in the park. I think I am worse off than I was after the mastectomy. I realize this is not normal but it is "normal" for a person that experiences complications after surgery. Lucky me, I win the "about once a year this happens to someone" prize. Better go buy a lottery ticket or something soon before this luck wears off.

Just took a break and went out back to walk a few laps around the pool. Strange thing just happened--while walking I noticed Tess was laying on the grass with her head buried in her paws, which usually means she has caught something she shouldn't have. I go see what she's got and it is a little lizard, about six inches long. It is moving slower than normal as it was quite cold yesterday. Anyway, I pick up this little guy and start looking at him with Tess watching eagerly hoping I will drop it. I am wearing a hoodie (the new one I got to replace the STOLEN one) and low and behold, the lizard leaves my hand and escapes up the cuff of my sleeve of my immobile arm! I look at Tess and think, "this cannot be happening when nobody is home to help me." I had to just wait there for it to work its way toward my armpit so I could hopefully reach it. All I can say is I'm so glad it was not a spider or I'd have lost it. Probably wouldn't have picked it up in the first place though. Needless to say, I finally caught him without tearing out stitches and he is safe from Tess and out the front door. Thought of keeping him for Sara but don't need her losing it in the house. We already lost Tulip the hamster last month and had to cut a hole in the drywall to find him. No need to go down that path again.

Where was I...probably pain. Still taking painkillers, muscle relaxers, antibiotics and who knows what else. Seriously have little logical brain activity (HOPEFULLY) due to all the narcotics and things going in, mixed with chemo still in my body. I take a pill then about 20 minutes later ask Tom if he knows if I took a pill or not. Probably doubling up when I shouldn't be.

Poor Tom. He has endured so, so much with all this. I honestly could not ask for a better partner. He handles all this unbelievably well. He may go out and scream when I am not in earshot but one would never know. I think Ross has learned SO MUCH about what it means to be a real man and to stick by someone's side just by watching his dad. He and Ross hung Christmas lights outside the other night, got the tree out and strung it with lights (Sara and I will do most of the ornaments as I get stronger). He carries this family in so many ways. I am honored to be his wife. His heart is huge and his temper so controlled. He and Ross are at the Texans/Titans game with Barry and Mitch this afternoon. I miss him when he is gone but Lord knows, he needs to get out! Sara is with Laura and Tess is by my side (now that she has forgotten about the lizard thing) and Bear...who knows where he is? He is a cat after all.

Reading Psalms today. I enjoy it while doing it, even though I won't remember a thing I read.

Psalm 31:1-5

In His grip,

Amy

Guestbook Note

I was just reading your most recent post. I so appreciate your honesty and vulnerability. Our prayers continue to be with you and your family. I thank God with you for Tom's faithful partnership. I look forward to a big turnaround that I'm sure is out there for you ... and I hope it comes soon.

Guestbook Note
"I think Ross has learned SO MUCH about what it means to be a real man and to stick by someone's side just by watching his dad." I don't know how you're able to mix pain and profundity so often, Amy. I think the kids have a learned a thing or two by observing Mom, as well. Blessings.

Day 208, MONDAY, NOVEMBER 29, 2010 5:41 PM, CST

Amy: Sitting out back after taking 2 laps around the backyard. Looks as if a storm is slowly moving in. Very warm and humid. Feels kinda nice with the breeze. Christmas lights around the yard remind me how seasons have passed yet mine still remains. At least the warm weather remains too.

I got out today for the first time since Thursday. Tom and I went to IHOP. We were planning on running to the store for a look around but once our food arrived I decided the one stop was enough for the day. Sad thing is I was REALLY, REALLY wanting to go to a farewell gathering that is set for tonight at 7 p.m. but I keep getting sharp pains in the left side of my chest/breast, whatever you want to call it and I really don't think I should go out again.

Some new yet good friends of ours, Andra and Ferdi Mostert are leaving this week as Ferdi has new responsibilities with Shell, South Africa, and will be leaving the Houston group for the chance to return to their home country. Both of them have become special friends for both Tom and I and we hate to say goodbye (but I really wanted the chance to say goodbye). Tom will have to do it for the both of us. Andra and Ferdi...you have blessed us and many, many others in Texas and knowing you has been a true gift! We will certainly visit as Barry and Karin say they will show us a wonderful time in South Africa as well as a top-notch camera safari one day! I know where you live so I hope you want guests--Ross wants to see those breaching Great Whites out your back door! Safe travels and may blessings follow you all of your days.

My heart aches and I am becoming an emotional wimp lately. I cry like a baby so easily. The lyrics to one of my favorite songs keep coming to mind - Aerosmith's *Dream On*. The lines about looking in the mirror, the past is gone, like dusk to dawn…You know the rest, same with Boston's, *More Than a Feeling*. Two great songs with so much emotion. I feel like I am living those songs so much lately with life just going forward faster than I can keep up with. When you are not on the go as you normally would be, the reflective side comes to the surface much easier. Good and bad in that I suppose. You just want to grasp it and slow it for a measly second but you can't.

Sara is practicing her Christmas songs on the piano now. Time to go in when she is done and hang a box or two of ornaments on the tree. At my pace, the empty boxes will just get to the garage and it will be time to drag them out again!

Tom and I decided today that we will be flying to Phoenix rather than tackling the long drive – thanks to an extremely generous gift from the Kidd's. So much for the Griswold's Vacation road trip! Maybe next time. Deb and Tim have their flight plans and now we do too. Look out Goodyear retirees…they won't even know what hit them with the eight of us in town!

Trying to keep positive…sometimes I feel like a grump. Attitude, I have found is a huge part of my recovery. No more poor me. ARRGGHHHHHH!!!

Still in His grip, as I need that reminder every day since I don't always feel it, just know it as truth,

Amy

Day 210, WEDNESDAY, DECEMBER 1, 2010 2:13 PM, CST

Amy: Sitting out back soaking up some nice warm rays. Feels so good to put my feet up and rest a bit. If anyone calls my cell, I am so not answering for at least 30 minutes. How can I be so completely wiped out from just a shower and going to Ladies of the Loft, having a bagel then looking at emails? (Don't answer that, Lee!) It puts me in a not-so-happy-place.

It was so worth it though. I had not been to LOL for weeks and seeing so many cool women and talking about this Sheila Walsh book was just what I needed. We finished the book and the timing is perfect as Sheila is the speaker tomorrow night at the "main" building at church, for the women's event, *Let Your Heart Find Christmas!* Yippie and I mean that in a not-sarcastic way.

Stopped the pain meds last night and letting Tylenol do the pain killing. Helps my system and that is a HUGE relief. Neck and shoulders real stiff still but that will hopefully be improving daily. Much less chest pain, pretty much just stiffness now. Still scatter-brained as I struggle to remember what I was even writing about here in the first place...

Tom just got home and had to turn around and leave to fetch the carpool gang. It is a blessing that he is around now...who would have thought? God works in mysterious ways.

Have had a bit of a struggle with trusting God's plan these past few days. When pain is at a high level, it is harder for me to grasp the FAITH and TRUST part of His plan. On my knees yesterday about that very thing and asking for help with my uncertainty. I have hated feeling that way this week. I have found that knowing He is in control and having a peace with that is a much more comfortable place to be, so I've pleaded with Him to help me regain it. Seems He is doing that as later on in the evening I opened my book (<u>When a Woman Trusts God</u>) and the next chapter addressed that very thing...it was like He said: "Girl, just know you have to do the work sometimes or really, all the time. I have the book right in front of you but YOU need to open it...and your heart."

I am happy to say I think I am on my way back to a good place but in our God-given HUMANNESS (is that spelled right???) we keep taking back the reins of control. Trust me from all this experience, it feels SO MUCH better in His hands. My struggle is; why do we have to keep resorting back to our own ways and needs to be in charge?? I am starting to believe He also designed it that way. He loves to welcome us back, teach us about ourselves and our intricately designed weaknesses/ flaws, call them what you'd like, and open the door as many times as we will allow. A far better--yet along the same lines--kind of parent we hope to always be. It's fascinating really.

I think I will go lay my neck flat until the troops all arrive home shortly.

In His grip, even during my emotional highs and not-so-highs--
Healing. Comfort. Patience.
Amy

~ 52 ~

...And That's What It's All About.

DAY 211, THURSDAY, DECEMBER 2, 2010 10:32 AM, CST

Amy: I decided to read what was posted yesterday and to me, it does not even come close to what I was trying to convey. This is why sometimes I really wish I had just done a private journal. If I were to ever go back and read what was written BEFORE I was on muscle relaxers and painkillers, I am quite sure I would be able to see a drastic difference in my thought process...

I have not taken any today thus far. I wonder if the brain damage is permanent? Heading to a quick lung check. Making sure there is no pneumonia. Lungs are feeling strange. I feel STRANGE!

Oh joy. Falala la la, la la la la.

Maybe I'll wrap a gift today.

> **Guestbook Note**
>
> Amy, do not worry about what you are writing. I look forward to your posts. They are raw, real, sensitive, funny, heartfelt and scary. I am quite sure you are reaching a deep down spot in every person who reads them. You have done that for me. You have faced, are facing and

will leave behind a life altering situation. I thank you for sharing your journey.

Day 212, FRIDAY, DECEMBER 3, 2010 9:33 AM, CST

Amy: Sitting at Starbucks in Market Street. Free wifi at Starbucks now. I used to boycott the joint because they made you buy a gift card in order to get service on your laptop. That was so lame. I am hanging out while the house gets cleaned and Tom gets here from his Doc appointment and then we are going to HEB to get groceries together. He has been running ragged the past several days and we will finally have some time together before he leaves in the early morning for a flight to Des Moines. The kids and I really wish we could just all go together to visit all our very special friends while he is there for business matters but it just isn't realistic. They understand but would really, really like to see people. Hopefully that will happen sooner than later.

Last night was the *Let Your Heart Find Christmas!* event I had mentioned here before. Wow. It was so worth the neck and back discomfort to attend. I got to visit with Sheila Walsh for a few minutes and that was great. She seemed so interested in talking to all of us LOL gals before the event and she was even interested in talking about my hair and cancer. I really cannot wait until the conversation does not automatically go there as the conversations always revolve around me and that bugs me a bit, but it seems it is always the easier thing to discuss. Since I have pretty much stopped wearing a hat...my hairstyle is a conversation piece.

As I was saying, the event was top notch. Decorated beautifully, chocolate fondue on each table and music before the talk in the main sanctuary. I think I heard there were 700 women there. Coffee, chocolate and my inability to sleep sound as it is, was not a good combination for me though. Sheila talked about her testimony, which is a compelling story of how she struggled with depression and fears of "never being good enough for God," even as a Christian Talk show co-host with Pat Robertson on the 700 Club. She shared about her time in a mental hospital and her childhood struggles. She ended with singing 3 show stopping carols!

At the end of her pretty long talk, I snuck out to leave as my neck was really getting sore. As I was walking out the long side isle, the music started for her final hymn and her angelic voice started the lyrics to "It Is Well With My Soul!" As much as my physical body needed to get home, I just stopped in my tracks at the back of the sanctuary and had to sit and soak up all the passion in the song. It brought tears immediately (surprise, surprise) as I reveled in the words, as well as recalling the memories of the song being played at both my father's and my grandfather's funerals. It is such a bittersweet emotion for me when I hear that song - but mostly sweet. What a great way to end the night.

Tom is here and we are among the "beautiful people" everywhere. Not sure what I think about this area sometimes. If I could take a picture of some of the plastic surgery work in here, you would die. This woman in front of where Tom and I are sitting might melt right in front of my eyes if she gets too close to the espresso steamer. She wouldn't be the only one here that would happen to either. She "looks" 35ish but I am certain she is over 70. Sorry, but it's just odd.

The Woodlands isn't ALL like this but it seems to be more concentrated in Market Street and this is where we are most often since it is so close to our house. Doesn't usually bug me but at times it just makes me wonder just what IT'S all about. I think we know, yet at times it is so easy to get caught up in what the world thinks IT'S ALL ABOUT. You know (we all know) - the accumulation of stuff, the desire to have the perfect-LOOKING/outward APPEARING family and/ or spouse, the perfect bag, outfit.... It is a tug of war game, isn't it? You get it for a while, then you fall prey to the world's standard, then back again. Maybe it's just me. It's always been on my radar anyway. Baldness makes me just try and put on a somewhat cute outfit and a smile. Seems at this Starbucks, people turn away faster - but not everyone.

Once I saw a wall plaque that said, "What if the Hokey Pokey IS WHAT IT'S ALL ABOUT?" I never did buy that, but I LOVE that saying!! Unfortunately, some people might truly wonder. Not me.

Time to get groceries. Hope this doesn't offend the Woodlanders that read it. I really love it here and you know what I'm talking about. It's referred to as "the bubble" of Houston for a reason. Takes all types to make the world go round.

In His grip,
Amy

Guestbook Note

Hey, I'm pretty sure it's all about the "hokey pokey." There has to be some good theology in there somewhere! Pastor Tony

Guestbook Note

You are amazing and it is so evident in your writing how you are really in God's Grip! He is working through you and blessing all of us who are privileged to read your journal. I'm praying that God will continue to heal you and renew your strength and grow in some more of that pretty red hair!! Hang in there-your Dad would have been so proud of his little girl! We are proud of you too!

Guestbook Note

I'm sitting here at Heathrow safely and soundly. Final leg to getting back to Cape Town. I just loved your assessment on the plastic in Houston, and your further assessment of accessories etc.! Andy Nixon once wore a profound t-shirt while preaching at the Loft that said, "the thing about life is that it is not about things" (always wanted one - although it is a thing in and of itself) this stayed with me ever since, since I firmly believe in it. It also helped me through walking away from our Woodlands property and our invested equity. The thing about life is that it is not about things, it is about meeting people like you and Tom that makes life what it is! You GO girl!

Day 215, MONDAY, DECEMBER 6, 2010 8:25 AM, CST

Amy: After a few steps back from the surgery complications 10 days ago I can say for the first time in what feels like a long time, I feel GOOD this morning! Slept pretty well without too much back stiffness and just more overall energy than in weeks past. My blood levels must be getting back to a good level. Funny how you just know your body.

Plan to head back to the pool for the first time since my final surgery. That should feel good. One step forward.

For those that have been asking about my lungs...no more unusual stuff or feelings and I've been making conscious breathing efforts for several days to expand lung capacity so there should be no reason for the lung x-ray. Yeah. Another step forward.

Talked to Tom several times yesterday. He is preparing for this court hearing in Des Moines this morning. Prayers for justice to be served today on a stupid investment matter. He has enjoyed his first visit back home with many good friends. Staying with Pat and has been with Steve a bunch as well. Steve's father has a medical update site as well these past several weeks as he has undergone brain cancer surgery and is healing and going through chemo now.

Yesterday Tom went to the Bridge, our home church in Iowa. It was wonderful seeing so many friends and talking with so many that have been in our lives for years and years. As Tom agrees, we want to schedule a trip back, hopefully this summer, and plan in advance for get togethers and meals with so many of you. We will get that on the calendar and let you all know just when that will be. While the kids, Tom, and I agree that Houston is where we feel called to be now, we dearly love our friends in Iowa and always, always will.

I think our family must have gypsy blood somewhere in it as the four of us seem to thrive on change. Each of us are used to it to some degree or another. The comfort is in knowing that we have each other and knowing that we are the sheep and our Shepherd is always in front of us leading to still waters...not that we've always known or followed, but we know we are now. Don't always know just where He is leading but we continue to try and have the trust and faith in the knowledge.

Time to pack up the gym bag and head to the pool. Need a sweater today. High only of 60. Back in high 70's by Friday though. Sara and Laura plan to pitch a tent out back for a campout. I'll sleep in our bed. Maybe next time.

Remember Iowans...our door is always open if you need to escape the cold as the winter gets long. I will always miss people BUT I WILL NEVER MISS THE WEATHER. EVER. Ross and Sara would love a white Christmas. Tom and I prefer shorts. Speaking of Christmas, I am thinking I will forgo the Christmas card this year for the first time ever. I am thinking I have a good excuse. I am taking it. Maybe a Christmas in July update or something or maybe just plain-old skip it for a year. Trouble is there are lots of people on our "mailing list" that likely never see this site. Their loss. They will just have to sit and wonder if they have been removed from the Hauser 'list' for a whole year until 2011. Hopefully I won't be removed from theirs by skipping a year.

Happy day.
In His grip,
Amy

— 53 —

A Bigger Hurdle

D AY 218, THURSDAY, DECEMBER 9, 2010 12:58 PM, CST

Amy: In order to be true to this process...I want to make note that the choice of my highly knowledgeable cancer team to treat a stage 2, triple negative, Invasive Ductal Carcinoma with 6 rounds of TAC chemo, bilateral mastectomy with sentinel node dissection (3) then reconstruction and no radiation needed (CPR...complete pathological response) was right on.

I do have to say that I am only disappointed with my lack of understanding (which I am responsible for) of just how one should not minimize the difficulty of the last step and recovery from it all. You see, in my mind I thought that getting through the chemotherapy would be the biggest hurdle of all. I thought wrong. The body is an amazing thing as it reacts all on its own when it senses trouble. It makes you slow down when your conscious brain says go. The signals have been coming in loud and clear the past several days. I am on the mend but I have finally realized that the Christmas hoo-ha has to just wait a year. Parties, baking, cards and tons of shopping is just not as important as healing completely. Luckily my family agrees!

Lower expectations and a focus on the true gift of our Lord and Savior's birth this year has really been a gift in and of itself. I have a focus on healing and resting and slowing down, even on my walks I have realized I must stop trying to get back in shape as much as just healing my body and not pushing it too hard. That will come later. I've never been a patient person and this has been another humbling experience. So many lessons to learn that I never quite got before. Sad that it has taken me over 40 years to learn some of this stuff.

Felt like journaling today as in the past 24 hours I have learned of 3 people who have left this world and in turn have left so many people that love them behind. While they are in a much better place it still is so hard knowing that much pain, sadness and grieving has to happen going forward. Two of these losses were in Des Moines and happened suddenly and took gentlemen that were at the peaks of their lives.

One happened here in Texas. I think I had mentioned Danielle here before. She was a 12 year old from Covenant Christian School where Ross and Sara attend. Danielle was diagnosed last December with Medullablastoma - a rare form of brain cancer. Danielle and her parents have been a true witness for what a family can look like even while fighting the nightmare they had to handle. Why God allowed her cancer to return so quickly and to take her home at such a young age is something we will not know or understand on this side of Glory. She so touched and changed lives. Her death was certainly not in vain. While I had only met Danielle on one occasion, I know she will be missed by so, so many. Her services are this weekend. It will be a celebration of a life lived, although way too short a one.

Ross and Sara have learned much about life in the past several months in ways I wish they never had to learn, at least not at such young ages. However they are now so much stronger than I ever was at those ages.

Last week I met an angel. Her name is Audrey. She is a massage therapist. She has done 3 massages on me over the past week and a half. I go back next week again. She used to be an ENT and she has hands that KNOW were to find the pain and how to get to it. Once again, you don't have to look far in Houston to find a person of faith. I knew Audrey had one on some level by the decor hanging on her walls but we never really talked about it until after my last massage. She was saying how I am so tight in my neck and shoulders and that I am likely carrying all the stress from the whole cancer ordeal (and other difficult matters in life) and it is all in my back/neck, etc. Audrey began to explain how the mental and heart issues manifest themselves into physical and can intensify as a trauma or multiple traumas occur.

Long talk between her and I aside...she began to tell me her story. She opened her heart and shared how she had given birth to twins back in 1989 and she was all alone as a mother. Both were put on life support immediately. One died that day and the other was on breathing tubes and a machine in the hospital. After 18 months of staying with her newborn daughter day and night she was told she was well enough to go home. The following day her daughter got an infection and died. After she buried her second daughter, she quit her job, moved her other children and bought a dump of a home in Dallas. For 10 months she physically tore the house apart wall by wall with her own hands. She tore out the plumbing, sledge hammered the walls and even tore up the flooring after finding out how to level the cracked foundation. She says she must have been completely mad, literally. Audrey still doesn't know how she did all that physical destruction by herself without any help but she said she just did it.

Once she completely removed the flooring and saw the foundation, as sweat was pouring off her brow, God clearly said to her, "Now you are finished, you are not angry any longer. It's time to go home." She sold the land (as there really was no house remaining) and moved back to Houston. She said it was over and she was ready to move forward with her life and make the changes that needed to happen (other things that we did not get into) as she had lead a very "hard" life. As Audrey and I sat teary eyed, she said that our anger, stress and frustrations can bind us up if we let them and it's best not to run from them as they are likely to resurface at some point. Mine is in my back right now.

As I reflect on all that she and I discussed, I'm not so sure she was "mad" after all. So many of us take out our issues, hurts, disappointments, and so on, in much more destructive ways; like on our kids, spouses, friends and family, and those hurts can last for a lifetime.

Maybe I ought to get a hammer (when I'm strong enough). Audrey has taught me some good relaxation techniques and breathing exercises that are already beginning to help. Blessings come when you least expect them sometimes, no...usually. {Audrey graciously allowed us to use her story – thank you for sharing Audrey.}

In His Grip,

Amy

285

Illness is a loss. Not the same as a loss of a loved one but a loss of how and who we once defined ourselves. A sense of weakness and vulnerability enters the picture of your life and changes it up a bit. In Audrey's situation, she was unknowingly manifesting an internal need to get the pain and frustration out. To get to the foundation of the problem and find strength in what her foundation is. She knows it is Christ alone.

After personally battling cancer, the re-stabilization of my known foundation has been ongoing. The walls had been crumbling for years and the foundation I had thought was in good order clearly was not. The stress of the illness and wanting life to fit into a neat little box was starting to take its toll.

Was I trying TOO hard to be positive? Was there more I was not handling than I realized? More that I was just averting by my busyness, rather than being still and relying on the true strength of the God of my foundation – not just with words but deep in my soul? While I still don't know all the answers to these questions, I have learned to allow myself time to rest, to be sad and then to get over it and move on. The gift of understanding that both our body and soul must process pain and loss, and it WILL process, one way or another (internally or externally), was a turning point for me in working through the tension and the pain.

— 54 —

Final Sign Off

DAY 223, TUESDAY, DECEMBER 14, 2010 8:17 AM, CST

Amy: This is Tuesday, December 14, 2010. It is the first day since my mastectomy on October 20 that I can say I have very little pain of any sort. My back feels 95% better now. A stiff upper back and stiff neck are present but HARDLY a bother. My perspective of "without pain" has changed a bit. I am THRILLED with my state and thank God for seeing me through all this. I suppose the pain could return but I will take what I can get for now!! Went to the pool the past two days and did light elementary back and side stroking for about 15 minutes each day and some hot tub soaks afterwards. Think this has helped a great deal as well. Using my relaxation techniques and deep breathing which has retaught my body to try and relax the stress away. Very helpful indeed.

Just a few more days before the kids are out for the school semester and we are off to a Christmas celebration in Phoenix. Time has blurred one event into the next for me. I cannot believe a school semester has come and gone in the blink of an eye, while at the same time a cancer diagnosis and healing has waged war on my body in a play by play saga that seemed like it would never end. All that said...it has ended and thus so must this public journal.

I want to take this moment to try and convey my true and deepest thanks to all who played a part in getting my family and me through this season in our lives. The outpouring of love and support has blown our socks off (BTW, Myth Busters says that is not actually possible to do...saw the episode myself). We could not have come out still actually speaking to one another if it wasn't for each and every one of you and your willingness to be there for us. The sacrifice was huge on the parts of many and not a one has gone unnoticed or unappreciated. Just the offerings to help even though they might not have been utilized means the world to me. I just hope we can one day pay it all forward. I am speaking for all four of us when I say we clearly have experienced the hand of God's love through serving the needs of others in this difficult time and we are honored to have seen it in action. Thank you, thank you and thank you from the bottom of our hearts.

I know that this journey is not completely over as I have been told it will take months for me to regain my full level of energy. And get this, a website on "chemo brain" said the mental effects can take up to 10 years to fully leave the body! That was a serious downer in my day when I saw that one! I wonder if that one will become self-fulfilling now?

As my hair is growing in (even in places I never had it before...can you say FUZZ FACE!!) and my mental fog slowly starts to lift, I can begin to ponder what is next. Tom and I pray for guidance on what the Lord has in store for us. Anyone who wants to send up a prayer for that one as well is certainly welcome to do so! Although taking things slow is what I primarily need to do for the next few months, I hope to get the Made4MoreMinistries.com going soon. We will see where that ends up!

I have to say that having a journaling site has been a beacon of a resource that I am so grateful for. Having a link to friends and family when you are in the loneliest time of your life (for me thus far anyway) has been a way for me to do what is so essential for my sanity...staying connected. Thanks for so many notes throughout the past several months. They lifted me up when I needed it most. I will cherish them all forever.

In a week or so I will have this entire journal printed and will re-read it when the experience starts to slip away. Right now I cannot imagine that I will ever forget this chapter in our lives, but I know from the past that eventually the next big thing will come into focus and this too will seem but a distant memory. Not a one of you will be released from my heart though. Thank you for the gift of your friendship and loving care. There are no words to express how much you have lifted me up and helped carry my burdens and lighten my load.

"This is My commandment, that you love one another as I have loved you. Greater love has no one than this, than to lay down one's life for his friends." John 15:12-13 (NKJV)

"Therefore if there is any encouragement in Christ, if there is any consolation of love, if there is any fellowship of the Spirit, if any affection and compassion, make my joy complete by being of the same mind, maintaining the same love, united in spirit, intent on one purpose. Do nothing from selfishness or empty conceit, but with humility of mind regard one another as more important than yourselves; do not merely look out for your own personal interests, but also for the interests of others." Philippians 2:1-4 (NASB)

May your Christmas be all that you hope for and your New Year of 2011 be the best yet.

In His grip, right next to you!

Amy

Guestbook Note

Such a beautiful sign off. God has truly been glorified in your walk through this. We have all been changed. All thanks be unto Him.

Guestbook Note

I have benefitted so much from the journaling you have done and all the responses sent to you. It has truly been amazing to watch God in action as people loved on you and your family over the last several months. Those who question Christian's hearts and call us hypocrites need only witness the Christian love shown to you and evidenced by those of us around you. I continue to be amazed at the grace you have shown while walking through such a valley of pain and suffering. God has truly blessed my life with your friendship and I am so grateful. Glad to hear the pain is easing and hope that continues. I am looking forward to seeing how God will continue to use you in His ministries.

Guestbook Note

Many thanks to you for letting us share your battle and journey with you. May the Dear Lord keep you and your family ever in his glorious grip. You are a super brave and extraordinary woman who taught us all some very important lessons along the way... and through all your sufferings you did a fantastic job of ministering to all of us. God Bless You. "Merry Christmas" will have a deeper meaning this year because of you. May 2011 bring you continued good health, an abundance of happiness and countless blessings. I love you. Love to your fabulous husband, Tom, and to your special angels, Ross and Sara.

Guestbook Note

As Amy's mom, I am writing not so much to her but to all of you faithful friends and prayer warriors. This has been a journey that no one would ever plan, but it has been amazing with so much learned and felt. I must testify to the Lord's grace and love that has been shown so abundantly. He does indeed supply strength when you feel there is none left in your spirit.

Being so far from Amy while she was doing battle was very difficult but made bearable by being assured through this web site that so many of you were loving her, encouraging her... caring in more ways than I can list.

My words read so empty to me...I so want to express my gratitude and love to all of you!! You truly have stood in the gap for our family...blessing upon blessing.

Guestbook Note

Thanks for sharing your journey. One we all hope we never have to travel! I know God has used your communications to help others cope if and when they face a crisis. Amy, you and your family will remain in our prayers. Thank you for giving us a glimpse of how the Lord can carry you when you can't walk on your own!!

Guestbook Note

Only God knows if your challenges of this year will be more of an outward witness in the future, or an inner strength for you and those who have been in your life this year. I am quite certain, however, that you will continue to share the light of God and hope of Jesus with others in many ways. Mosaics, starfish, the love of LOL, and the strength of that great husband of yours will tell the story of God's grace in so many ways. Next year, infinity and beyond will be cool.

$\sim$ Epilogue $\sim$

The two year anniversary of the discovery of the "lump" will mark the near completion of <u>In His Grip</u>. I initially thought the discovery would change my whole world. In a way it did. While I was concerned that it might rock me off my foundation, it actually did quite the opposite. It cleared the foundation of clutter and allowed me to firmly anchor to that solid rock that was so readily available and intended for just that purpose. I just had to be willing to look and allow the clean up to take place. Storms do come and will continue to come. I don't welcome them but know they are inevitable. Storms in life, like rain on a parched land, can be opportunities for new life to emerge. Boy, do I wish I had seen prior challenges and roadblocks in life as a chance to see God at work. No regrets, just going forward one step at time.

Learning to do things at HIS pace and not our own has not been easy but has been infinitely more rewarding than anything else we have done in our personal or professional lives. Our learning, and His teaching, never cease to amaze me.

He has provided many opportunities to share *Beauty In Brokenness* and *Designed to Shine* programs, speaking engagements and birthing and growing small groups. M4M's desire is to offer relevant programs in such a way that they speak to each generation, showing them God DOES have a better plan for their lives.

For the men's ministry, it means reaching out to guys one-on-one and in small groups. As Tom says, "Stirring the men around me to boldly go after that 'something missing' in our lives. To step out of the comfortable, to face the giants. To finally live lives full of meaning, peace, fulfillment and eternal perspective."

So many men have been placed across his path. Our past struggles make more sense now as he is able to better relate, encourage and share hope.

He will continue to start ripples that will improve marriages, families, communities and our world - from the "least of these" to the "most of these." We will keep reaching one man, one group, one family, and one organization at a time.

From a consulting aspect, we have come alongside several growing ministries and not-for-profits needing guidance. We have been blessed even as we seek to bless others. There is no shortage of need, with so many worthy ministries desperate for Christian business expertise with forming; growing and developing boards; setting up or updating accounting, operating policies and procedures; and simply surviving in a difficult environment. Tom could donate 80 hours per week on this portion of the ministry alone, but hopes to selectively spend his time where it will do the most good, is most needed and will have the greatest impact for the Kingdom. Always balancing the arms of M4M and the challenge of supporting the family.

For cancer outreach, M4M plans to use In His Grip as an inspiration and a resource for others dealing with breast cancer or other struggles. I have created a program entitled HORSES-HEALING-HOPE (HHH) that offers a unique approach for survivors to face and embrace the various emotional phases during and after treatment. HHH helps survivors navigate these inevitable changes, both external and internal. Using horses, nature and a relaxed, peaceful environment, women are offered a brief respite from hospitals, clinics and the often chaotic new world of cancer. Horses have the unique gift of mirroring our own emotional state. They get to the heart of the matter.

HHH pilot programs are underway for women entering their "new normal" phase. These women have already completed treatment and are sorting through the baggage that accompanies the life changes thrust upon them. A second program, for women newly diagnosed with breast cancer, connects women with others who have already walked the same path, while providing a brief escape to regroup and grow in their walk with Christ. A unique program for caregivers is also on the drawing board.

Working with horses and sharing with women who have experienced struggles that have gotten in the way of their relationship with Christ moves me. I am starting to understand that we are *made for more* than the sum of our own efforts. Without our plans meshing with God's, it is impossible to be who we were designed to be. I can't explain how wonderful it feels to uncover a bit of who I am and Whose I truly am.

As we continue to discover what MADE FOR MORE really means, I dream of sharing it at a place we will call Healing Ranch. What that means or looks like exactly, well, we are not privy to those details just yet. I suppose I am okay with that for now.

Every day, God reveals to us a bit more of what HE wants M4M to be. Through our various ministry activities, we are increasingly encountering opportunities (needs?) to share our story. Of how putting Christ in the middle of our lives and our marriage has impacted both. Of how when we sought His will and let go of our need to control image, status, being right and looking the way the world says we should, we began the journey of being who we were made to be. We began to realize and accept that there is more to life than what we could make of it ourselves. As we work to trust God, admit our faults and failures and seek to improve upon what needs tended to, our lives and our marriage thrive. Our kids thrive and our purpose grows in clarity.

Please consider visiting us at www.made4moreministries.com and see what God is currently doing through the ministry. Our signature verse is 1 Peter 4:10 which reminds us, *"Each of us has been blessed with one of God's many wonderful gifts to be used in the service of others, so use your gift well."* (Underline mine.) I hope you will be encouraged to seek Him in all that you do. As you do, He will open doors and shine His light upon you. He has a plan for each of His children and is eagerly waiting to show the way. He knows, and I hope you know, we were all MADE FOR MORE! If you have to walk through a dark place in order to find out just what is on the other side, fear not...for God is hemming you in on all sides. And He has a far bigger plan. He never said it would be easy, instant or without heartache, but it will be worth the effort, I promise.

━ UPDATES ━

APRIL 2011 - Months Pass

I was wide awake once again around 4:40 a.m. as I still so often am, but this time I decided to listen to that voice that said to get up and do some more writing. Here I am on the couch sitting by the glow of my laptop. It is warm and cozy and Tess is the only one up with me while the rest of the house still slumbers. Even Bear the cat did not stir to see what we were doing up.

Unfortunately, I still sleep very little and so often feel the nudge to get up and do a bit of writing but I rarely heed the call and trying to get a bit more sleep wins out. Today I felt I should give an update on what has been happening since December, so here it goes. As I see my last post was just before Christmas, I will say the past four months have been BUSY! Getting back from a great trip to Arizona for Christmas, 2010 and starting off a new year in more ways than one has been time consuming, to say the least!

Just reflecting back to early January now, I see how much progress I have made in regaining strength and it is amazing to me. Today I can say that I feel almost 100% back to normal. Okay, maybe 90%. Regaining full strength takes time. As a few friends have told me, one year out you feel about back to normal. My year will be toward the end of May, so I am getting close. Wow...it has almost been one year. What an experience this all has been.

I can honestly say that I don't think I would give it back if I could. I have learned so much, seen so much and experienced so much of life. There has been pain, loss, and such an array of emotions experienced in it all, yet I have seen and experienced so much perspective that I know I would be lacking for most of a lifetime had I not walked in this particular valley. I am certain they were things I needed to have in my life. Things I was lacking and now I see just a little more clearly. Do not get me wrong...I pray that I never have to experience ANY of it again.

I will not live in fear of a recurrence though. Life is to be lived as fully as one can, and that is my intention.

So here is a brief update to the happenings thus far at the Hauser household since my last entry (which was intended to be the last but I have not yet officially shut this site down).

- After much prayer and nudging of the spirit, Tom and I have decided to start putting all our time and talents into ministry. For the time being, we are working together with the founder of Forever Faithful Horse Ranch and we have been piecing together business plans for helping her take that ministry to the next level, God willing.
- We are also launching *Made For More ministries* as a couple. This will be a ministry that serves men, women and children and be tied in with various service based ministries through-out Houston - really, it will be whatever God says it should be. Between trying to launch these ministries and all that is involved with such an undertaking, trying to heal my body and regain strength...I have not found a ton of free time to write. Sorry to those that have been asking for an update!
- (Bear cat is up now. About time he joins Tess and me!)
- I am off my Ambien completely and while I am not sleeping fabulously yet, I am drug free and resting more than I was months ago! I will take what I can get and if I am supposed to write, I will write!
- The chemo brain fog is lifting slowly, yet better each passing day. There are days that I feel I am clueless and I think my family would agree. Those days are fewer and fewer all the time though. Or maybe, now that I think about it, the family and friends around me might just be used to it and I could likely still be a total wreck. Not sure. It doesn't really matter, I suppose.
- After dealing with so much back pain that started after my surgeries, I finally decided to check into a chiropractor that came highly recommended by some friends, Dr. Chris Zaino. He is a Maximized Living doctor who incorporates fitness plans, faith, and optimized, healthy eating strategies into a total health program. He has been an answer to prayer. The whole family

goes to the practice and we are 'rocking and rollin' now. My pain is gone for the most part and so many other parts of my internal body are functioning better than they have in a long time. We look forward to the long term affects of proper, ongoing spinal health. These guys are all over the country and I think they are on to something really good.

- Attending yoga classes a few times per week (even Tom is doing this once a week with me, too!) and walking several times per week to get back strength and trying to find time to do weight training. This is not happening as much as I would like but hopefully the discipline will come sooner than later.

- Have thoroughly enjoyed being a part of the kids' activities this second half of the school year! Covenant Christian School has warmly welcomed our family and the kids have had a hugely successful year. Ross is playing baseball for the varsity team and has actually had some pretty decent playing time. Much more than we thought he would as a freshman and we are grateful for that! Tom has been one of a couple of dads that help the head coach and that has been fun for him, to say the least! I think Ross has been good with it, too!

- Sara has been able to play this last bit of the soccer season for Rush Club after being in a boot for 6 weeks due to a lingering recurrence of a previous soccer injury. She is playing in her final game tomorrow. Much time is spent at Forever Faithful ranch, riding and doing lessons and trail rides when time allows. She also performs in a school talent show playing the piano in a few weeks.

Life seems to be quite full for the kids. Time with friends, family and extra-curricular activities seems pretty well balanced somehow. For this, Tom and I are so grateful. We still manage to have some time to spend together. That is what I think matters most. I'm pretty sure neither child will become a career athlete, but I am certain one day they will be career leaders in raising a family and trying to balance a life outside of our home. I think they will be well equipped for that. Life has tossed them around a bit with moves, losses, joys and pain. But through it all, faith in God and a relationship with a Father that does love them like no other, has taught not just them but all of us that; while in this life there will be heartaches, there is a promise for a TOMORROW that far outweighs even the best TODAY.

What else has been happening here...Oh my, I have hair! Lots of thick hair. Why, I even had it cut a few weeks back. I need to update the profile picture on my Facebook so you can see. If I took a shot from my Mac right now, it would look rather wild and sleepy, so I had better not do it now. The short look is in now, so I just might keep it this way for a while. At least through the hottest part of the year, anyway.

I am so very tired now. I must try and rest for a short while before the family wakes. Lastly, my mom just left yesterday after a visit for a few days. It was great to get out and do things this time rather than being a patient. I love feeling well once again. It is such a huge gift.

A friend of ours in Des Moines now has leukemia and is waiting for news about a bone marrow transplant. She is in for a very long recovery and completion of treatment before she is at the same point I am. A journaling site has been a real blessing for her as well. Another friend of ours just found out her liver cancer has returned and endured surgery last week to remove it.

The interesting thing in all of this is that the three of us were in Alpha together about 5 years ago. Mikki was wrapping up her liver cancer journey at that time. Another friend in our group had knit a prayer shawl without realizing it had gone to Mikki at the time. Linda and Mikki mailed me the prayer shawl last year. In February this year, I mailed it back to Linda in her need. Now it needs to go back to Mikki.

As I mentioned on Linda's site, the shawl is a wonderful, tangible expression of God's loving arms around us in time of need, but His omnipotent presence through the Holy Spirit is with each and every one of us fully at all times, unlike that shawl. He is there when we call. His arms can be more tightly around us than we might ever imagine. He just waits for us to ask.

My prayers are with my friends, even if I cannot be there with you both today. We plan to see so many great friends once again soon though! Planning a visit to Des Moines over July 4th.

Make it a super day.

In His grip,

Amy

Several months have passed since this entry and today both Linda and Mikki keep in touch with others through their blogs. Mikki posts more often as she is currently undergoing treatments and fighting a daily battle with a cancer that won't quit. The cancer didn't realize what it was up against though – A woman that won't quit either!

Linda is growing stronger each day yet still has many post cancer effects. Both women are walking with what God has allowed in their lives. Allowed in a fallen world, not a punishment. It is time the world began to understand that. We all have obstacles to either overcome or stumble on. Some are more outward and others less evident. No two are the same. No two serve the same purpose or test us the same. In the end, we must decide if we are willing to bring glory to God in our encounters or push the experiences down deep inside and make them our own. Mikki, Linda and I have walked similar beginnings of runs with cancer yet each will discover our own levels of peace, pain, loss and growth. Similar yet distinctly personal.

AUGUST 2011 - Little Did We Know

It has been awhile, but I said I would one day give a link to the ministry I had been praying would eventually come to fruition, and would give you all an update once I started to post again. Well, guess what...that day is here. While the ministry gig is still in the conceptual state and likely will be for sometime, I wanted to share just where things are at this point in time. Together, Tom and I have started a website... far from a finished product, mind you, but a start nonetheless.

We would love for you to check it out periodically (www.made4moreministries.com) to gain an understanding of where we feel God is leading us and how we hope to be used. It is our goal to share how our lives have been impacted over the years in our walk with Christ and how we hope to help others along the way, especially those facing struggles of one form or another, as we all seem to be. We are committed to serving and we look forward to the journey.

If you would like to keep up with the new journal entries in this next portion of our walk through breast cancer and more, you will find blogs/journals listed on the main menu of our site. There will be periodic updates from both Tom and me. Nothing fancy or professional...just our perspective and from the heart.

Once again, I thank each and every one of you as you took the time to read, write, pray, serve, and encourage our family over the past 15 months. I think of you all so often and cherish the blessings that have been poured out to our family. The healing continues and takes time. Lots of time. Don't think I would trade it, though. Life is crazy. God is good...all the time.

In His grip, right with ALL of you!

Amy

Guestbook Note

Thanks for sharing your endeavor. We seldom realize God's plan for our lives and what He will use to grow us and use us for His purpose! As you may know my husband is now battling cancer. We have started the long hard journey to recovery. You have been an inspiration. Little did we know while we were reading your journal that we would have one in the near future! We will pray that your ministry will grow and be used to comfort many.

Also in His Grip.

For Shaun (author of the previous guestbook entry) and Duane, the cancer was persistent and eventually brought Duane home to the Lord. Duane was a shining star throughout the tough battle. He shared so much about life and a loving relationship in and through Christ right up through his final days. He certainly was resting IN HIS GRIP.

MAY 2012 - Long Walks and Old Habits

It is the spring of 2012 now, and today once again I took our Golden Retriever, Tess, for a walk on the trails near our home. We both look forward to and enjoy these times together, and so does my body. These walks remind me of how far I have come along this journey, and I love the regaining of strength that I sense, both physically and spiritually. As we got to the trailhead, I removed Tess's leash so that she was free to run and to chase squirrels, as she loves to do.

As she ran and I reflected, I couldn't help but notice several things that so beautifully symbolized where I have come from and where I am going during this time in my life. While cancer represents the worst news for many, little had I known just how God had been preparing me for years to face it head on. There are many things that refine us as individuals, even as a couple; things that can either leave us better than it found us, or knock us off balance. Cancer has been only one of the many and maybe not even the most difficult.

When I am on walks, I like to take in all that I can of the incredible variety that surrounds me. I love nature and cannot help but notice all the little ecosystems that exist within larger ones. Whether in the forest, the desert or the sea: life carries on in the most amazing ways. It is a beautiful reminder of God's creation and His attention to the intricacies of life in all its detail.

As I breathed in the hot, humid Houston air, I first noticed the variety of flowers in bloom. It is May 1 and many wild flowers have already blossomed, many more will follow all the way through late November. Each week I see something new and different. Last week it was the powerful scent of jasmine that stopped me in my tracks as I looked high and low for the source of the fragrance. I found it and tried to bottle the sweetness into my senses. This week it was the striking beauty of at least six different boldly colored flowering "weeds" that lined the underbrush; deep, dark purples, reds, yellows and blues. "Weed" is a funny label. Something growing unintentionally that will bloom if allowed to fulfill its God-given potential. Some of the most unique and beautiful blooms come from these weeds. Blooms with little chance of flowering for a variety of reasons - unintended location, unattractive foliage, unidentifiable traits, or simply not part of a planned garden. Of course, some do have the potential to choke out things around them. Maybe they are just in the wrong place at the wrong time!

The trail almost seems to be a different place from week to week. Before dark times hit our lives, I did not spend much time taking in the abundant goodness around me. I certainly didn't take the time to stop and search for the source of good things, whether in others or in the way God was moving in the world around me. Now, through the struggles and God patiently waiting and working on me, I have learned a great deal. And it has changed me dramatically.

As Tess and I continued our walk, we saw a variety of lizards and turtles, a heron, two gar in the creek, a copperhead snake, and a butterfly that seemed to follow us. In this area, you frequently see things that make you think you just might be in a zoo. My favorites are the owls and the giant turtles. Tess's personal favorite would probably be the opossums, skunks or occasional armadillo that cross our path. Needless to say, I usually lose her for a few frightening minutes on these encounters!

There was a scary moment as I was running along side of Tess. In mid stride, I happened to glance down to see that I was directly on top of a two-foot copperhead snake that had slithered off the golf course into the shaded forest! It was still as could be with its head fully erect. I surprised myself with a loud scream as I cleared it with my stride. I continued ahead and calmly called Tess to me so I could attach her leash. Knowing copperheads are not typically aggressive, I was compelled to walk back to take a closer look at the serpent. Keeping Tess close to my side, I approached until it started to move off of the path and into the woods. Both of us closely followed it until it disappeared into the camouflaged covering of pine needles and twigs that lay on the wooded earth. Tess and I just looked at each other as if to say, "Wow, that was a thrill!" Dangerous and intense, but a thrill just the same!

It occurred to me that this particular episode was a bit like how I had lived my life: enthralled with close encounters with danger and mystery. It certainly wasn't the first time we had encountered venomous snakes in Houston, I am sure it won't be the last. At least I didn't test its limits. I wish I could say the same about my past.

Well, maybe I did test them a little by going back and taking a closer look. Old habits die hard and evil will rear its head in the world on a regular basis. Now, with God's help, I am learning not to follow it into its hiding places, at least not most of the time!

At a small waterfall near the bridge, the sunlight was just right so as to illuminate two beautifully spotted gar resting next to the rocky shoreline. Attractive fish on the outside, yet a load of tiny sharp teeth on the inside. They seemed large for this part of the creek. We usually see only small fish, tadpoles swimming with turtles, and frogs and the occasional water snake (probably moccasins in these parts).

I stood and pondered the visual of these images, thus reminding me of what I had been striving to be for so many years: (yes, even as a couple, like the two gar) beautiful on the outside with little regard to what lay on the inside. All the time, wanting Tom to fit the image I had in my head of what we ought to be and what we ought to look like, and leaving him guessing as to whether he was on target or missing the mark; with the only gauge being the acceptance or rejection displayed through my actions. Not a good way to live, and not who I want to be. By chasing such false yet powerful gods, those razor sharp teeth become more powerful each day. Like the gar, I carefully disguised them; but nevertheless they were there. Just ask those closest to me.

As Tess and I journeyed along on the last half of our walk, a brilliantly colored butterfly seemed to be following us, and then leading the way toward the end of the trail. She would flutter around and I would almost run into her as I picked up my pace. Then suddenly, she was no longer in sight. This reminded me of when, during the cancer treatments, as I felt strong enough I would walk as long as my body would cooperate; and when the tiniest and most amazing things would come into view, I would know these were very special times for me to listen to God. I talked to Him plenty, but listening was not so easy. Not only would I hear Him clearly out here, through thoughts, ideas and feelings, but also I would sense His presence through the experiences I encountered. I know angels had surrounded my family and me so often, and today was such a reminder that winged blessings will guide and follow us all, as we encounter both the joyful and the dangerous moments of our lives.

Today's walk began with an overcast sky and hot, humid air and ended just as an unexpected and much needed gentle rain shower began. Like the sudden rain, the challenges of life are a given. Some we bring on ourselves, some are cast upon us, and others just happen, regardless. What we do with them is what really matters in the end.

Our family has faced numerous trials; many of which we did not learn from, at least not as we now believe God had likely intended. The good news is that our Father in heaven gives second, and beyond, chances. Today God spoke to me. He is always willing to meet us where we are, and thus He spoke in my language when He chose to share His love and promises through nature. He knows me better than I know myself. He knows you better than you know yourself. Today the plans Tom and I have for ministry are now becoming more *His* plans. The refining is still going on; nonetheless the movement has begun.

Enjoying His Grip,
Amy

MAY 2012 – New Roads

Before my diagnosis of breast cancer and even more so *during* the cancer, I've had a yearning to find my purpose in serving and sharing my life experiences with others in hope of letting the light of Christ shine though the ups and downs of my walk. A bit of a longing to redeem my past too, I suppose.

Relentlessly, God has been working out my selfish desires and pursuits and working His plan to the forefront. The waiting and arm wrestling of just what He wants from both Tom and me, as a couple and as individuals, is slowly working itself out. While the grooming process has been painful at times, the joy that has come from the refining has been well worth the efforts, gains and losses. These life changes have been long overdue. Changes I wish I had had the foresight to have made years ago.

I must also share just how this "Phase II" is a continuation of God's teachings in my life. While much of the cancer walk was unexpected, I have to say that, for me, even more of the next phase has been. For each of us, healing is multi-faceted. The external or physical is what the world sees and tends to measure, yet the various forms of healing are much more complex. When the physicians release you and mark you as "cured," a new set of fears and doubts enter in. Many internal wounds still need tended to, as they are revealed much further down the road – at least this has been my experience. It can be a lonely place to travel. Without the proper tools for navigation, the experiences can isolate and immobilize. For me, the best tools I have found are: the Word of God, prayer, and more than anything else a heart to know, surrender to and serve our Lord.

As I travel this new road, I will continue to write when I feel the need to put order to my emotions. The keyboard has become a sort of companion. Like an old friend with whom you long to sit down and have uninterrupted time to catch up. What an unlikely gift this has been, one that connects and adds order to a mix of thoughts and ideas floating aimlessly in my mind. After getting things "out," I leave refocused and life makes a little more sense than it did before. For me, I experience God as that companion when I think, ask, and listen to my Best Friend.

I must admit that through this journey I have found my writings to be a personal sort of therapy. Any overflow of blessings to come from them has been God at work. Should I continue to post, I encourage you to comment as well. Through our sharing and experiencing of this earthly life together, as one body, the Holy Spirit will move in mighty ways! In the sharing of our struggles, He will help us all work fear and worry right out of the picture. Join me in living life to the fullest. God intends for there to be a bit of heaven here on earth when we seek Him with all of our hearts, minds and souls.

It has been a blessing to be able to share HIS story with you. I hope you will continue the gift giving and do the same with your own experience of God's hand in your life one day. Thank you for sharing in our…no, HIS story.

IN HIS GRIP, RIGHT WITH YOU!

Amy

"Seek the Kingdom of God above all else, and he will give you everything you need." Luke 12:31 (NLT)

July 2012 – Gemma's Legacy

When HORSES-HEALING-HOPE went from a nudging to reach out to breast cancer survivors in a unique way through the use of horses and nature while sharing Christ's love at the same time, to an actual full fledged program, I felt God smiling. I know He felt me smiling too. It was a process of a life changing that was, in turn, changing lives. Just the kind that the Bible talks about. It is about taking one wounded soul turned over to Christ, and in the midst of THAT healing process, stepping out to help others that are hurting in similar ways. The cycle works wonderfully when God is smack in the middle of it all. I loved stepping out and allowing beautiful things to happen that I had always been too afraid to try on my own. Now with God in charge, I was becoming more confident in my steps as He directed them.

HORSES-HEALING-HOPE has felt as though God himself had been orchestrating our every move right from the beginning and beautiful things were happening each week. One of the ranch horses seemed perfect for the program. Gemma, a 20 year old Gypsy Vanner mare, had previously been quite sick with persistent recurring infections. Linda Darnall, PCI Ranch founder, had received word from the Texas A&M Equine Veterinary School that a bilateral mastectomy was necessary for Gemma to recover from her illness. This is a procedure that is rare in the equine world. How fitting for the breast cancer program though!

Throughout our program, women were touched in ways we never thought possible as they helped nurse Gemma back to health each week as part of the session. What began as a challenge for Gemma, ended up being a blessing for women that had gone through the same experience. It was evident that Gemma felt the love and had more attention during her time of need than probably any horse ever had! The coming together of others in our struggles and a chance to serve and care for another of God's creatures, even in the midst of our own pain, allowed God into places where we were not even expecting. As program facilitators, we were in awe of God's unique ways of shining through darkness. We thought we understood just how He was going to work in all of this.

As I write this part of the story, today is my 45th birthday. The rain has been steady for almost a week with short periods of sunshine scattered throughout the daytime. Today the rain started just before a little birthday lunch party was to begin. The phone rang as the rain pounded and it was Linda from the ranch. Gemma had died this morning. Only two months after her surgery. The ranch had flooded this week and waters had ravaged the grounds, barns and paddocks. All the horses had to be moved in shoulder-high waters and then moved again as the water receded. It was stressful on everyone, especially the horses. Gemma was still in a fragile state and the additional stress did not help. The vet says it was likely a heart attack.

The celebration will have to wait. I changed from my church clothes and grabbed my mud boots and went to see her lifeless body. I didn't want an umbrella--just the healing touch of the rain as I walked to the ranch and entered the pasture where she lay. Tears flowed as I approached her in the falling rain, mud puddles forming around her frame. I pulled back the tarp and knew she was not there, just a shell of a wonderful working horse that had a purpose to serve so many. She is at rest now. As Shirley, Linda, and I cried together and stroked her peace-filled face, we didn't have any answers.

We felt the heaviness of all the happenings of the week, yet counted the blessings of the group of new women going through the HHH program. This Thursday morning will be our final week with this group of survivors and they have gotten to know Gemma well. There is a bit of dread in telling them about her passing.

As I took a few moments alone with Gemma and with God before returning home, I talked to God about a few things. I cried about my current anxiety with the fact that I have my six-month cancer checkup Wednesday. About how this weekend had been filled with fear as I prepared for the pending appointment with all my blood tests this past Friday. About the wondering if a recurrence is in my future looms whether I verbalize it or not. The fear of my own fate looms. As I look at Gemma's lifeless body lying in the mud and rain, it is hard not to think of myself. It's hard not to do, when you have stared your own mortality in the face. It's a weight that can be heavy if you allow it to be. I was holding it for a few days and became determined in that moment it was not going to grab hold of me any longer. I allowed the sadness to form for a few moments, then purged them on my walk home with verses of truth and promises from God's Word. Thank you for this gift, Jesus.

Then, it occurred to me that maybe this is the next conversation that needs to happen with the women of HHH. Maybe it is a reality that needs to be addressed with the women as we close the program in sessions to come. While I don't have this completely worked out yet and trust God will show me just how it should look, we need to realize it is actually inevitable. None of us gets out of here alive. It may be breast cancer, but likely will not, yet it is a fear that needs to be faced head on. God will have the final word, not evil. He will soothe the fear of death and the unknown. Rest in His grip, Gemma. We love you and thank you for the blessings you have brought to so many.

LINKS TO ORGANIZATIONS MENTIONED IN THE BOOK

Each of these organizations holds a special place in our hearts. We have been blessed by having each in our lives and we would like to share them with you:

Abundant Life Chiropractic & Dr. Chris Zaino – abundantlifechiro.com

Caring Bridge – www.caringbridge.org

Covenant Christian School – www.covenantonline.com

Creative Consulting & Andrew Brockenbush – andrewbrockenbush.com

Forever Faithful Ministries – www.foreverfaithfulministries.com

Freedom Place - www.freedomplaceus.org

Loft Church / The Woodlands United Methodist Church – www.LoftChurch.com

Made For More ministries – Made4MoreMinistries.com

Meredith Drive Reformed Church / The Bridge – www.MeredithDrive.org

Ocean Star & Christina DiMari:
     www.designedtoshine.org/_Christina_DiMari.html
     www.mountainfountaincreations.com/Mountain_Fountain_Creations/HOME.html

Panther Creek Inspiration Ranch – www.pciranch.org

Texas Surf Camps – www.texassurfcamps.com

Voice of Wilderness – www.VoiceofWilderness.org. A Christian outdoor adventures organization we are currently working with.

CPSIA information can be obtained at www.ICGtesting.com
Printed in the USA
LVOW101815201112

308200LV00008B/26/P